Taylor Swift and the Philosophy of Re-recording

Also available from Bloomsbury:

*Introducing Aesthetics and the Philosophy of
Art* by Darren Hudson Hick
New Philosophies of Film by Robert Sinnerbrink
Aesthetics and Music by Andy Hamilton
Philosophy of Comics by Sam Cowling and Wesley Cray

Taylor Swift and the Philosophy of Re-recording

The Art of Taylor's Versions

Edited by Brandon Polite

BLOOMSBURY ACADEMIC
LONDON • NEW YORK • OXFORD • NEW DELHI • SYDNEY

BLOOMSBURY ACADEMIC
Bloomsbury Publishing Plc
50 Bedford Square, London, WC1B 3DP, UK
1385 Broadway, New York, NY 10018, USA
29 Earlsfort Terrace, Dublin 2, Ireland

BLOOMSBURY, BLOOMSBURY ACADEMIC and the Diana logo are
trademarks of Bloomsbury Publishing Plc

First published in Great Britain, 2025

Cover design: Louise Dugdale
Cover image: Photo by Kevin Mazur/Getty Images

A catalogue record for this book is available from the British Library.

A catalog record for this book is available from the Library of Congress.

ISBN: HB: 978-1-3504-2155-4
         PB: 978-1-3504-2156-1
       ePDF: 978-1-3504-2158-5
      eBook: 978-1-3504-2157-8

Typeset by Integra Software Services Pvt. Ltd.
Printed and bound in Great Britain

To find out more about our authors and books visit www.bloomsbury.com
and sign up for our newsletters.

For Katie, Max, and Beckett.
—Brandon

Contents

Notes on Contributors

Elizabeth Cantalamessa (she/they) is Assistant Professor in Philosophy at St. Bonaventure University. Her research lies at the intersection of social philosophy, philosophy of language, and aesthetics. She has published on topics including democratic deliberation, conceptual engineering, aesthetic disagreement, and copyright law.

Michael Thomas Connolly (he/him) is an audio engineer, producer, and musician with over twenty-five years of experience in the field. The owner of Empty Sea Studios in Ferndale, WA, he has recorded and mixed more than 130 albums across a variety of genres. His playing as a multi-instrumentalist spans a list of more than fifteen instruments and has been captured on more than sixty commercially released albums. As a touring musician, he has shared the stage with the Indigo Girls and Brandi Carlile. His writing on recording theory and practice has appeared on the philosophy website *Aesthetics for Birds*.

Ley David Elliette Cray (she/they) teaches in the Philosophy department at New Mexico State University. Her research interests include philosophical aesthetics, philosophy of music, philosophy of comics, and philosophy of gender. She is the co-author of *Philosophy of Comics: An Introduction* (2022).

Darren Hudson Hick (he/him) teaches at Furman University in Greenville, SC. He works centrally on philosophical problems in intellectual property and related issues, including authorship, plagiarism, and forgery. He is the author of *Artistic License* (2017) and *Introducing Aesthetics and the Philosophy of Art* (2023), and General Editor of the Bloomsbury Contemporary Aesthetics collection.

Sherri Irvin (she/her) is Presidential Research Professor of Philosophy at the University of Oklahoma. She has written about many topics in aesthetics and philosophy of art, with occasional forays into art criticism and curating. She is the editor of *Body Aesthetics* (2016) and the author of *Immaterial: Rules in Contemporary Art* (2022).

Alex King (she/her) is Associate Professor of Philosophy at Simon Fraser University in Vancouver, Canada. Her research interests concern issues in ethics, aesthetics, and the philosophy of art. She has written about the nature of moral obligations, as well as high and low art, subtlety, emoji, and cosplay. She is editor-in-chief of the philosophy of art website *Aesthetics for Birds* (www.aestheticsforbirds.com) and the author of *What We Ought and What We Can* (2019).

Cristyn Magnus (she/her) is an independent scholar and artist living in upstate New York.

P.D. Magnus (he/him) is Professor of Philosophy at the University at Albany, State University of New York. His research is in the philosophies of science, art, and technology. He is the author of *A Philosophy of Cover Songs* (2022).

Christy Mag Uidhir (he/him) is Associate Professor of Philosophy at the University of Houston. His primary research is in the philosophy of art, where he has written on issues such as the nature of artistic intentions, pictorial depiction, film authorship, imagination and film fictions, suspense, character acting, film and race, and cinematic evil. He is the author of the award-winning *Art and Art-Attempts* (2013).

Irene Martínez Marín (she/her) is a postdoctoral researcher in philosophy at Uppsala University. Her main areas of interest are aesthetics, moral psychology, and issues to do with reasons and rationality. She has published on the nature of taste, aesthetic akrasia, aesthetic understanding, and the role of emotions in aesthetic appreciation. Her contributions have earned recognition from organizations such as the European Society of Aesthetics (Fabian Dorsch Essay Prize, 2019) and the American Society for Aesthetics (Irene H. Chayes New Voices Award, 2021).

Ron McClamrock (he/him) is Associate Professor of Philosophy at the University at Albany, State University of New York. His primary research is in the philosophy of mind and psychology, with interests in perception and phenomenology. He has also played in several cover bands over the years.

Brandon Polite (he/him) is Professor of Philosophy at Knox College in Galesburg, IL. His research interests focus on aesthetics, especially issues related to the philosophy of music. He has written on listening to music with others, watching others play video games, and arguing about art on the internet. He is also host of the YouTube series (and soon to be podcast) *Polite Conversations: Philosophers Discussing Art* (https://www.youtube.com/c/PhilosophersDiscussingArt), where this book was conceived.

Preface

What you're about to read is the first book-length examination of Taylor Swift's project of re-recording her first six studio albums. That there's a book on this topic likely won't surprise you. Taylor Swift is arguably the most famous person on the planet right now and her re-recordings (called "Taylor's Versions") have been the subject of intense public scrutiny ever since she announced them. What may surprise you is that this is a philosophy book.

Philosophers aren't exactly known for dealing with timely issues, especially those from popular culture. We're thought of as dealing with the Big Questions, a set of timeless issues that transcend culture: What is the nature of reality? What is the meaning of life? Does God exist? What are good and evil? Can we ever really know anything? Philosophers definitely still grapple with these issues. But in recent decades, there has been a major shift in the field toward using the resources developed to deal with the Big Questions to help us think through smaller questions, ones that are more relevant to our daily lives. While questions about Taylor Swift maybe less lofty than those about, say, the meaning of life, they are by no means less important or less worthy of philosophical investigation—especially since she and her music contribute so much meaning to so many people's lives.

The philosophical investigation into Swift's re-recording project that this book undertakes is specifically pursued within the subfield of *aesthetics*. From the eighteenth century through the early twentieth century, aesthetics was dominated by one of the Big Questions: What is beauty? A lot of time and effort was spent examining beauty in the natural environment and in human-made artifacts, especially works of art.

The emphasis on beauty eventually led aestheticians (the philosophers, not our friends in the skin care and cosmetics business) to focus almost exclusively on what the French call the *beaux arts* ("*beaux*" being French for "beautiful"). In English, this is what we call "fine art," which includes what one typically sees in museums, hears in symphony halls and opera houses, reads in literature classes, and so on. As a result, aesthetics was primarily concerned up until very recently with what is also called "high art," and thus with art reserved for high-class people, over and above popular and commercial art, the art most people engage with most of the time. In short, aesthetics was rife with snobbery, reflecting the ivory tower elitism that plagued philosophy as a whole for much of its history. Aestheticians were also likely afraid that the field's reputation would suffer within the wider intellectual community if we started taking such "lowly" artistic endeavors seriously. For similar reasons, aestheticians also largely ignored the work of women artists until relatively recently. This neglect reflected the broader historical failure within philosophy—and, let's face it, the world as a whole—to take the ideas, interests, and concerns of women and girls seriously. The same is true, it is worth noting, for people of color, indigenous people, LGBTQiA+ people, and members of other historically oppressed groups or those outside the broadly European tradition, whom the larger philosophical community similarly began to take seriously only recently.

As little as thirty years ago, a collection of philosophical essays on Taylor Swift (or, rather, since she would've only been in preschool, let's say Madonna) could have never been published. It took some bold innovators in the 1990s, many of whom were women, to help free aesthetics from its snobbery and transform it into the exciting field it is today—a field where you're just as likely to find discussions of comic books, horror films, video games, internet memes, street art, fan fiction, perfume, and fashion as you are to find discussions of Kierkegaard, Camus, and classical music. I've had discussions on all of these topics (both the "low" and the "high" ones) and many, many more on my YouTube series, *Polite Conversations: Philosophers Discussing Art* (https://www.youtube.com/c/PhilosophersDiscussingArt). In the series, as its name indicates, I talk to other philosophers about their work in aesthetics. And, as my name indicates, I do so politely.

The seeds for every chapter in this book were first planted there. I had written a short essay on Taylor Swift's first re-recorded album, *Fearless (Taylor's Version)*, for the Bloomsbury Contemporary Aesthetics library, a collection of case studies in aesthetics edited by Darren Hudson Hick, who has contributed this volume's first chapter. In writing the essay, I realized just how much more there was to say about Swift's re-recording project. But rather than say it all myself, I felt it would be more worthwhile to talk about Taylor's Versions with some of the philosophers whose work I referenced in the essay. I also brought several others into the conversation whose philosophical or, in one case, musical expertise illuminates important aspects of Swift's project. These conversations became a miniseries of episodes that I called "Nothing New? Taylor Swift and the Philosophy of Re-recording." Now, after nearly two years of thinking through our ideas more deeply and carefully, my contributors and I present you with this collection of essays.

The chapters that follow will help you think through the complicated legal, economic, social, political, ethical, and metaphysical implications of Taylor Swift's re-recording project, all filtered through the lens of aesthetic theory. Our goal isn't just to illuminate what's interesting and worthwhile about Swift's project. It's also to showcase, by taking Taylor Swift, her work, and also her fans seriously, just how worthwhile philosophy can be to our daily lives as well as how cool and vibrant the field of aesthetics has become since we shook off the snobbery and entered into our very own fearless era.

Brandon Polite
February 15, 2024

Acknowledgments

This book would not exist without the support of many people. I would first like to thank Colleen Coalter at Bloomsbury for first having been so receptive to my initial pitch for the book and for her guidance from that point forward. I would also like to thank Suzie Nash and Aimee Brown at Bloomsbury for editorial insights that helped make this book the best version it could be.

I am indebted to all of the contributors for writing such insightful and engaging essays on the various aspects of Taylor Swift's re-recording project. Without them there literally would be no book—only a lonely essay of my own that may have never found a home. I would especially like to thank Darren Hudson Hick for guiding me through the processes of pitching a volume of this sort and the ins and outs of editing one (and for all the gifs).

This book was born out of a series of discussions with many of the contributors on my YouTube series, *Polite Conversations: Philosophers Discussing Art*. Thanks to Knox College for supporting the series and for the two students who have helped me with it: Charlie Ericksen and Athko Ehrnstein. I'd also like to thank my friends and colleagues within the wider aesthetics community for supporting the series and encouraging me to keep it going.

Thanks also to the many, many Swiftie students I've taught in recent years for fruitful discussions of Swift, her work, and her fandom. And special thanks to the students in my 2024 Aesthetics Today course, who helped me beta test every chapter in this book. The book was very much improved as a result of our conversations.

I'd also like to thank Mary and her terrific crew at the Beanhive in Galesburg, IL for providing the perfect atmosphere for me to put this book together and for the caffeine to sustain my authorial and editorial efforts.

Finally, I owe perhaps the greatest thanks to my wife, Katie Koca Polite, and my two children, Max and Beckett, for their love and patience. You belong with me, forever and always.

Glossary

album sale royalties The money from album sales that is paid to the recording artist. Rates are determined by negotiation between the recording artist and their record label.

back catalog A collection of earlier works by a specific artist or group, which are typically owned by a particular record label.

Big Machine Records Taylor Swift's record label from 2005 until 2018. It was owned by Scott Borchetta until 2019, when it was purchased by Ithaca Holdings. Borchetta stayed on as the label's CEO after the sale.

Borchetta, Scott The founder, president, and CEO of Big Machine Label Group, including the imprint Big Machine Records. Taylor Swift was the first artist he signed to the label in 2005.

Braun, Scott "Scooter" An entrepreneur, executive, and entertainment manager who once managed Kanye West. He also founded Ithaca Holdings, which purchased Big Machine Records in 2019. As a result, Braun acquired the rights to the master recordings of Taylor Swift's back catalog—the first six studio albums she recorded with the label.

copyright A set of exclusive legal rights, including the right to make or authorize reproductions (copies, adaptations, performances, etc.) of a creative work, such as a song, recorded track, or album.

holding company A company whose sole purpose is to buy and control other companies.

Ithaca Holdings A holding company founded by Scooter Braun in 2013 that focuses on buying entertainment and media companies. It purchased Big Machine Records from Scott Borchetta in 2019 for $330 million, acquiring the rights to Swift's back catalog in the process. The company subsequently sold the rights just to Swift's catalog for $300 million in 2020.

master recording The original sound recording, specifically, the finalized studio mix, which serves as the authoritative source used to produce genuine copies of a track or album.

mechanical royalties The set amount of money that goes to the copyright holder or holders every time a copy of a track or album is sold, whether as a physical product (vinyl record, CD, etc.) or as a digital download. Rates are determined by legal statute.

performance royalties Money paid to songwriter and publisher based on the broadcast (radio, television, streaming) or live performance of protected songs. Rates are determined by performing rights organizations.

re-recording The act, or the product of the act, of producing an audio duplicate or near-duplicate of a previously recorded song or album.

Swifties The most passionate and loyal of Taylor Swift's fans.

Timeline of Taylor Swift's Career

1989   Taylor Alison Swift is born—December 13

2004   Swift signs a publishing contract with Sony/ATV Music Publishing

2005   Swift signs a six-album recording contract with Big Machine Records

2006   *Taylor Swift* is released (Swift's debut album)—October 24

        Billboard 200 chart debut: number 19

        US first-week sales: 40,000 units

2008   *Fearless* is released—November 11

        Billboard 200 chart debut: number 1

        US first-week sales: 592,300 units

2010   *Speak Now* is released—October 25

        Billboard 200 chart debut: number 1

        US first-week sales: 1,047,000 units

2012   *Red* is released—October 22

        Billboard 200 chart debut: number 1

        US first-week sales: 1,208,000 units

2014   *1989* is released—October 27

        Billboard 200 chart debut: number 1

        US first-week sales: 1,287,000 units

2017   *Reputation* is released—November 10

Billboard 200 chart debut: number 1

US first-week sales: 1,238,000 units

2018   Swift leaves Big Machine Records, signs with Universal Music Group

2019   Big Machine records is sold to Ithaca Holdings—June 30

Lover is released—August 23

Billboard 200 chart debut: number 1

US first-week sales: 867,000 units

Swift announces her intention to re-record her first six studio albums—August 25

2020   Swift leaves Sony/ATV, signs with Universal Music Group

Folklore is released—July 24

Billboard 200 chart debut: number 1

US first-week sales: 500,000 copies

Evermore is released—December 11

Billboard 200 chart debut: number 1

US first-week sales: 329,000 units

2021   *Fearless (Taylor's Version)* is released—April 19

Billboard 200 chart debut: number 1

US first-week sales: 179,000 units

Red (Taylor's Version) is released—November 12

Billboard 200 chart debut: number 1

US first-week sales: 369,000 units

2022   *Midnights* is released—October 21

Billboard 200 chart debut: number 1

US first-week sales: 1,578,000 units

2023   Swift takes the Eras Tour on the road—March 17

Speak Now (Taylor's Version) is released—July 7

Billboard 200 chart debut: number 1

US first-week sales: 507,000 units

1989 (Taylor's Version) is released—October 27

Billboard 200 chart debut: number 1

US first-week sales: 1,359,000 units

2024   *The Tortured Poets Department* is released—April 19

Billboard 200 chart debut: number 1

US first-week sales: 2,610,000 units

Introduction

The Story of Taylor's Versions

Brandon Polite

A Strange Night at the Club[1]

Imagine you're at a club where a DJ is spinning records using the classic two-turntable setup. Unbeknownst to you, she's spinning two separate copies of the same recording: the 7-inch single of Taylor Swift's "Shake It Off" from her 2014 album, *1989*. The DJ starts spinning the two copies at the exact same moment, and, as they play, she seamlessly cuts back and forth between them. As a result, you're hearing the recording distributed across the two copies. But it seems to you as though nothing peculiar is going on: you're just listening and dancing to "Shake It Off" as you normally would.

This situation is unusual. Normally, we listen to a recording (a single track or entire album) by means of just one of its copies in one of any number formats: on vinyl, cassette tape, CD, MP3, etc. However, the DJ hasn't done anything especially impressive. Anyone with the right equipment and desire could sync up two copies of the same recording in just the way she did and produce the same sort of distributed playback that she has produced. She also hasn't done anything aesthetically dubious. We all know that many copies of any given recording exist (sometimes millions of them) and that playing any one will afford us a genuine experience of it. So, even though the DJ is cutting back and forth between multiple copies, she's still giving you a genuine experience of one and the same track: the original recording of Taylor Swift's smash hit "Shake It Off."

Now imagine that you're listening to "Shake It Off" at the club as before. But this time the DJ is cutting between a copy of the 2014 recording and a copy of Swift's 2023 re-recording of the track, called "Shake It Off (Taylor's Version)." As before, it seems as if you're enjoying a single copy of Swift's original recording of "Shake It Off." And just like before, the DJ isn't doing anything technically impressive. But this time she *is* doing something aesthetically dubious. She's leading you to believe that you're experiencing a single recording when, in fact, you're listening to alternating snippets of two recordings that were created nine years apart.

This second made-up scenario is quite strange. But its hypothetical strangeness owes entirely to the real-world strangeness of Taylor Swift producing new recordings of "Shake It Off" and every other song off of her first six studio albums that very closely duplicate the original recordings. Our interest in this book is to examine and evaluate Swift's real-world project of re-recording her back catalog and explore its philosophical implications—that is, what it can tell us about the nature of re-recorded music, about how we should appreciate, evaluate, and assess the meaning of re-recorded music, about the music industry's ethically dubious practices, and issues related to these. Before we can proceed to the philosophy, though, we first need to do something philosophers rarely do—at least, not in their published work anyway. We need to sift through what in some corners might be dismissed as mere celebrity gossip.

Look What They Made Her Do

Since 2019, Taylor Swift has been engaged in a years-long project of producing near-duplicates, which she's calling "Taylor's Versions," of her first six studio albums. The first of these was *Fearless (Taylor's Version)*, a re-recording of her 2008 album *Fearless*, which she released in April 2021. This was followed by Taylor's Versions of *Red* (2012/2021), *Speak Now* (2010/2023), and *1989* (2014/2023). By the time you're reading this, Swift may have released re-recorded versions of the other two albums: *Taylor Swift* (2006) and *Reputation* (2017).

What prompted Swift to undertake this project was the sale of her former record label, Big Machine Records, which she signed to in 2005 when she was just fifteen years old and stayed with until 2018, for $330 million to the securities holding company Ithaca Holdings in June 2019.[2] As a result of the sale, Ithaca Holdings gained control of the master recordings of the six studio albums Swift recorded for Big Machine, which by 2018 accounted for 80 percent of the company's revenues.[3] "Masters" are the recordings from which all copies of a track or album are made. The copies of Swift's albums that anyone owns, streams, hears on the radio, etc., were copied from the masters. Whoever owns the masters has exclusive rights to how they're reproduced. Because of this, Ithaca Holdings could prevent anyone from using Swift's recordings for any purpose—including Swift herself, as she claims they in fact did.[4] This is how recording contracts typically work: artists own the rights to their songs, but record labels own the rights to the recordings. Although artists earn royalties from record sales and licensing fees, it's usually a pittance (12–20 percent of net sales) compared to what the labels earn.[5]

One important reason for Swift to re-record her albums, then, is financial. By producing new masters that sound just like the original recordings, Swift is able to license them in place of the originals. Why would an advertising agency or movie studio pay to use the original tracks when there are perfectly good sound-alikes produced by Swift herself available? This is especially true since any company that chooses to license the originals runs the major risk of upsetting Swift's large and fiercely loyal (and, as Ticketmaster found out in 2023, quick-to-mobilize[6]) fanbase: the Swifties. The upshot is that all of the money the re-recordings earn from licensing—as well as from album sales, radio airplay, etc.—will go directly to Swift herself (or, rather, her company), instead of a small percentage to her and the rest to an external entity. In light of this, she stands to earn significantly more from the re-recordings than the royalties she'd receive from the originals being licensed.[7]

Perhaps more importantly, however, if Swift can convince her fans to buy and stream her versions of her tracks and albums instead of the originals, she might be able to significantly deflate her back catalog's economic value. This could make its owner want to offload it before it loses even more value, which would give her the opportunity to acquire it and thereby finally own her work. Whether this is Swift's actual end game is unclear. It seems plausible; yet, I'm merely speculating. What is clear, however, is that by getting her fans to stay away from the original tracks and albums, which they have taken to calling "stolen versions," Swift was aiming to hurt Ithaca Holdings. If her gambit were successful, she would deprive the company of potentially hundreds of millions of dollars.

Swift isn't the only artist to re-record her music for financial reasons. Re-recording was a common practice in the 1950s and 60s. An artist or group would sign to a new label, which would have them record knockoff versions of their greatest hits to cash in on their past success. The practice largely went out of fashion in the 1970s, but started to come back in the 2000s. In 2008, for instance, American rock band Journey released a double-album called *Revelation*, the second disc of which contains re-recordings of the band's greatest hits with their new lead singer faithfully reproducing their original singer's vocal performances. In 2010, British new wave band Squeeze released an album called *Spot the Difference*, composed entirely of re-recordings of their greatest hits. In 2012, British glam metal band Def Leppard released re-recordings of two of their biggest hits, "Rock of Ages" (1983) and "Pour Some Sugar on Me" (1987), followed a year later by a re-recording of "Hysteria" (1987).[8] All of these artists (and there are a few others) re-recorded their tracks in order to earn more money from sales and licensing than they were getting from their original releases, since, like Swift, they didn't (and presumably still don't) own the master rights to those recordings.

While Swift may not be the first artist to re-record her music, her project is pioneering nonetheless. She's the first major artist who has re-recorded an entire studio album; and she's done it four times so far—with two more on the way. She's also the first artist to aim at re-recording her entire catalog from a previous label. Moreover, while all of the artists I just mentioned are (with apologies to them and their fans) legacy acts whose careers peaked decades before they set out to re-record their tracks, Swift was still a viable artist when she began re-recording her albums. More than that, she was one of the top-selling and most beloved recording artists in the world. Her two most recent albums before 2021's *Fearless (Taylor's Version)*, *Folklore* and *Evermore*, both debuted at number one on the US *Billboard* 200 chart the year before, with each selling over a million copies worldwide in their first week.[9] And while re-recordings by other artists have met with little fanfare or financial success, Swift's re-recordings have helped her reach new critical and commercial heights. The four Taylor's Versions released so far have sold millions of copies, have been streamed billions of times, and all debuted at number one in the United States and multiple other countries. Indeed, *1989 (Taylor's Version)* and *Speak Now (Taylor's Version)* were, respectively, the first and third best-selling albums of 2023.[10]

But Swift's reasons for re-recording her albums are more than merely financial. As she laid out in a Tumblr post after the sale of Big Machine in June 2019, her most important reason was that, at the time of the sale, Ithaca Holdings was owned by Scooter Braun, whom Swift charges with years of "incessant, manipulative bullying" and with attempting to dismantle her musical legacy.[11] Prior to becoming a big-time music investor, Braun managed a number of musical acts, including Justin Bieber, Ariana Grande, Carly Rae Jepsen, and Kanye West. Braun's relationship with West is the source of Swift's problem with him.[12]

In his 2016 track "Famous," West takes credit for making Swift, whom he calls a bitch, famous by interrupting her acceptance speech at 2009 MTV Video Music Awards, suggesting she should repay him with sexual favors. Swift called out West for the song's misogyny and for impugning her reputation soon after its release. In response, West's then-wife Kim Kardashian leaked a snippet of a secretly recorded phone call in which Swift appears to give West her blessing to say those things about her on the track. The full recording of the phone call was eventually leaked, revealing that the snippet Kardashian posted had been misleadingly edited. Although this vindicated Swift, her reputation did suffer a major hit in the meantime. Swift claims that Braun orchestrated both the leak and the subsequent social media campaign against her.[13] She also believes that he bears some responsibility for the music video for "Famous," which Swift calls "revenge porn" in the Tumblr post. In the video, West lies in a cartoonishly wide bed with a number of hyper-realistic mannequins of several naked celebrities, suggesting the calm after an orgy. The ones that lie immediately next to West are of Kim Kardashian on his left and Taylor Swift on his right.

It makes sense why Swift wouldn't want Braun to have control over her first six albums. These are the works that she poured her heart and soul into starting from when she was just teenager and that, contrary to West's assertion, are the actual source of her fame. And even though Ithaca Holdings sold the rights to Swift's albums (for $300 million) shortly after acquiring them,[14] and Braun has since sold the company,[15] her decision to re-record duplicate versions of her albums doesn't seem so drastic. While doing so may have been (and continues to be) a massive technical and financial undertaking, Swift clearly has the resources and level of fame and acclaim to make it the overwhelming success that it's been.

But a question remains. Why have fans actually gone out and bought albums that sound just like albums they already own and love? One reason is that Swift has given them a compelling story in which they themselves can play an active role. She has presented herself as the victim of a bully and suggested that by supporting her they're helping her stand up to him. And her fans have definitely listened, having bought the re-recordings by the millions and streamed them by the billions. They have also supported her project in other ways—for instance, by posting detailed instructions for how to avoid ever encountering the "stolen versions" of her albums, as they've taken to calling them, on Spotify and elsewhere online and thereby deprive Braun of a lucrative income stream.[16]

Swift is a savvy enough businesswoman not to rely on sympathy alone to generate interest in her re-recordings. A second reason for fans to buy the re-recordings is that, in addition to including the duplicate album, each Taylor's Version includes "From the Vault" tracks. These bonus tracks are new recordings of songs that didn't make it onto the original albums, many of which fans have been eagerly waiting to hear for years. Unlike the re-recorded album tracks, the ones from the vault don't aim to faithfully reproduce previously released versions of the songs, that is, when such versions exist—as bonus tracks on deluxe editions, etc. Instead, Swift has updated many of the songs to reflect her current style and brought in guest artists like Phoebe Bridgers, Chris Stapleton, and Paramore's Hayley Williams to help her do so. The arguably most significant of these tracks so far has been the extended ten-minute version of "All Too Well," a fan-favorite deep cut from 2012's *Red*. It was released as a lead single from *Red (Taylor's Version)* with an accompanying fifteen-minute short film which marked Swift's filmmaking debut. The short film was screened at the Tribeca[17] and Toronto film festivals in 2022,[18] had a limited theatrical run,[19] won numerous awards, including multiple MTV Video Music Awards[20] and a Grammy,[21] and was projected behind Swift during a show-stopping *Saturday Night Live* performance.[22]

A third reason for fans to buy the re-recorded albums is the fact that they aren't perfect duplicates of the original albums. Each re-recorded song deviates from the original album version in subtle ways. But some also diverge in more substantial ways, including different lyrics ("Better Than Revenge"), vocal choices ("Long Live"), and instrumentation ("Girl at Home"). The most pervasive deviation, though, is that the mixes are updated to sound more contemporary, as is especially noticeable on the Taylor's Versions of the older albums, *Fearless* and *Red*, lending them the feel of being remastered editions in addition to re-recorded versions. These departures from the original recordings offer longtime fans a way to engage with Swift's music not available to mere casual listeners: they get to pore over the tracks note by note and breath by breath to spot the differences between the new tracks and the old ones that they know so well.

But that the re-recordings don't sound exactly like the originals poses an obstacle to enjoyment for some fans. They know the original recordings so well (all too well, in fact) that the re-recordings can fail to trigger the positive nostalgic feelings that the originals do. This presents fans with a moral dilemma: continue listening to albums they grew up loving but which Swift has disowned or else abandon the old ones for "new and improved" versions that just don't scratch the same emotional and aesthetic itches that the originals do. The first option wrongs Swift, to whom they wish to remain loyal. But if they take the second option, they may fail to be true to themselves, to their own aesthetic preferences. What is a Swiftie in this situation to do?

Welcome to This Book

Philosophers aren't typically in the business of telling people what to do. What philosophers do, instead, is critically analyze the situation we all find ourselves in—our shared natural, social, political, economic, etc., reality—from every imaginable angle to gain a better understanding of the way things are and the way they could be. By thinking through these issues *together*—with other philosophers, with the students in our classes, and with the general public—we aim to help each other think through *for ourselves* how best to live our lives. The book you're about to read is offered in this spirit.

In the nine chapters that follow, a group of ten professional philosophers and two philosophically inclined non-philosophers explore the situation we find ourselves in as listeners and fans of popular music. Our goal isn't to tell you what to think about Swift, her re-recordings, or the music industry. Instead, we aim to provide you with the factual, critical, and theoretical resources to think about these issues in a more informed and refined way than is common in public debates (whether in the popular media, on social media, or elsewhere) about them.

In Chapter 1, Darren Hudson Hick dives into the tangled world of recording contracts and copyright law to get to the heart of why Taylor Swift and other artists rarely own the music they make. In doing so, he reveals that Swift's project can be understood, in part, as an attempt to strike back at the music industry's exploitation of its creative class. Hick then argues for a radical change to copyright law—a change that would make the music industry a more equitable and just institution for those who actually make the music it profits from.

In Chapter 2, Cristyn Magnus, P.D. Magnus, Christy Mag Uidhir, and Ron McClamrock consider whether Taylor's Versions are covers of Swift's original recordings. Concluding that our notion of a cover is too ill-defined to provide a definitive answer, they draw on lessons from their exploration of covers to help us better understand what Swift's re-recordings are and how to evaluate them. In particular, they reveal that whether Taylor's Versions are mere faithful reproductions of her earlier recordings or new interpretations of them affects how we determine their meanings and artistic merits.

In Chapter 3, Sherri Irvin considers Swift's re-recording project in relation to conceptual art. In doing so, she sheds light on aspects of Swift's project that are especially innovative and successful: specifically, how Swift appropriates her earlier work to create new experiences for her fans and how she has gotten them to participate in her attempt to economically harm her back catalog. But connecting the project to conceptual art also reveals where it has thus far come up short: namely, in how Swift appears to conceive of victory over the music industry's exploitative practices primarily in terms of her own commercial success rather than in terms of the more widespread change she may have the power to influence.

In Chapter 4, Michael Thomas Connolly, who is a recording engineer, music producer, and musician, sheds light on what goes into producing re-recordings like Taylor's Versions. He describes the process of taking a song from a mere idea to the track we hear, showing how the features that define a song emerge from the countless creative decisions made by the recording artist and their production team in the studio. By deciding which features to maintain and which to discard when re-recording a track, Connolly argues, an artist and their team reveal their collective beliefs about what constitutes a song's identity.

In Chapter 5, Brandon Polite considers whether re-recording can provide Swift with a legitimate means to reclaim her original tracks and albums by producing genuine instances of them. He concludes that it does not, arguing that Swift's re-recordings are distinct works of art from the original versions. Because of this, the only way for Swift to reclaim the originals in a literal sense would be to acquire their masters. Yet, this doesn't mean that her project is a failure—if Polite is right, it's an even greater success because of it.

In Chapter 6, Alex King considers whether a song's meaning can change as a result of being re-recorded. She argues that it can because an artwork's meaning is partly determined by the artist's intentions as well as the broader social, political, or historical context in which it was created. According to King, Swift's songs take on new meanings in the re-recordings due to Swift's act of trying to reclaim her music from its current owners—a moral and political act aimed at getting Swift's fans to perform a moral and political act of their own: to abandon albums they love to support the artist they love.

In Chapter 7, Irene Martínez Marín considers the central challenge that longtime fans must confront in giving up Swift's original albums: namely, the loss of an important source of value in their lives, one that connects them in a profound way to their younger selves. Trying to appreciate Swift's re-recordings as much as the originals, she argues, gives fans the opportunity to navigate the complex evolutions of taste and self that accompany growing up together with—or, really, alongside—an artist you love. In particular, they have the chance to reshape their attitudes toward who they used to be, mirroring Swift's own process of interrogating and revising her past selves in re-recording her earlier work.

In Chapter 8, Ley David Elliette Cray further examines Swift's exploration of her past selves through her re-recordings. Showing that the particular version of themself, or "persona," that an artist adopts on a recording affects how we assess its meaning and value, Cray considers which version of Taylor we're hearing on Taylor's Versions. She argues that Swift neither maintains the personas from the original albums nor adopts the persona from the most recent album (whether *Evermore* or *Midnights*) on the re-recordings. Instead, Cray contends that Swift assumes a new persona on the re-recordings, one that critically engages with her earlier work and past selves while also challenging the music industry's exploitative practices.

In Chapter 9, Elizabeth Cantalamessa examines a version of Swift that exists largely outside her control. Unlike her personas, which she can tailor to her own artistic and commercial ends, this other version of Swift—which Cantalamessa calls a "zombie"—advances others' commercial interests. Swift's zombie emerged when the real Swift signed away the rights to her works to become a professional songwriter and recording artist as a teenager. Cantalamessa reveals how Swift's re-recording project, wherein she zombifies the original recordings in making the new ones, is best understood as a political battle with her zombie counterpart—or, rather, with those who own and control it and the exploitative music industry practices that enable them to do so.

We invite you to think through the fascinating legal, economic, social, political, ethical, metaphysical, and most especially aesthetic implications of Swift's re-recording project together with us over the course of these chapters. If you accept this invitation, you may find everything has changed about your views on Swift, on her re-recordings, and on popular music as an art form and an industry.

Notes

1   Appropriately enough, given that this is a book about new versions
     of preexisting works, the first two sections of this introduction are
     new versions of the first two sections of Brandon Polite, "Taylor Swift,

Fearless (Taylor's Version)," *Bloomsbury Contemporary Aesthetics*, ed., Darren Hudson Hick (London: Bloomsbury, 2023), http://dx.doi. org/10.5040/9781350895737.0014.

2   A security holdings firm, or holding company, is a company whose sole purpose is to buy and control other companies. For more on the nature of holding companies, see Amy Fontinelle, "Holding Company: What It Is, Advantages and Disadvantages," *Investopedia*, July 9, 2023, https://www. investopedia.com/terms/h/holdingcompany.asp (accessed January 18, 2024).

3   Chris Willman, "Taylor Swift Stands to Make Music Business History as a Free Agent," *Variety*, August 27, 2018, https://variety.com/2018/music/ news/taylor-swift-stands-to-make-music-business-history-as-a-free-agent-1202918336/ (accessed January 18, 2024).

4   Specifically, Swift claims that Braun and former Big Machine Records label head Scott Borchetta refused to let her play a medley of her songs on the 2019 American Music Awards because they would count as re-recordings before she was legally allowed to re-record her music. (See Taylor Swift, "For years I asked, pleaded for a chance to own my work," *Tumblr*, June 30, 2019, https://taylorswift.tumblr.com/ post/185958366550/for-years-i-asked-pleaded-for-a-chance-to-own-my [accessed January 18, 2024].) Artists typically have to wait two years from when their previous contract expired, and between five and seven years from when the earlier recording was released, before they can legally release a re-recorded version of a song; however, record companies want to change this in light of the success of Swift's re-recording project. Some are aiming to prevent artists from ever being able to re-record their music. (See Monica Mercuri, "Why Record Labels Are Upset with Taylor Swift's Success," *Forbes*, November 3, 2023, https://www.forbes.com/sites/ monicamercuri/2023/11/03/why-record-labels-are-upset-with-taylor-swifts-success/ [accessed January 18, 2024].)

5   See Mark Tavern, "An Artist's Guide to Royalties, Recoupment and Cross-Collateralization," *DJBooth*, July 30, 2020, https://djbooth.net/ features/2020-07-30-kreayshawn-contracts-recoupments-record-labels (accessed January 18, 2024). See also David Byrne, *How Music Works* (San Francisco, CA: McSweeney's, 2012), chap. 8, for a helpful discussion

of the variety of contractual relationships that artists can enter into with record labels.

6   Jennifer Korn, Ramishah Maruf and Camila Bernal, "Taylor Swift Fans Take Ticketmaster to Court over Eras Tour Ticketing Chaos," *CNN*, March 27, 2023, https://www.cnn.com/2023/03/27/media/taylor-swift-ticketmaster-court/index.html (accessed January 18, 2024).

7   Anne Steele, "As Taylor Swift Rerecorded Her 'Red' Album, Universal Reworked Contracts," *Wall Street Journal*, November 12, 2021, https://www.wsj.com/articles/as-taylor-swift-rerecorded-her-red-album-universal-reworked-contracts-11636741201 (accessed January 18, 2024).

8   Def Leppard's re-recordings are striking in their fidelity to the original recordings. They're about as perfect as re-recordings can get. For evidence in support of this claim, see Scott Haskitt, "Rock of Ages 1983 vs 2012!! (Def Leppard A/B comparison)," July 19, 2012, video, https://www.youtube.com/watch?v=I7QkpXNm76M (accessed January 18, 2024).

9   Chris Willman, "Taylor Swift's 'Evermore' Sells a Million Worldwide in First Week," *Variety*, December 20, 2020, https://variety.com/2020/music/news/taylor-swift-evermore-sells-million-first-week-1234867490/ (accessed January 18, 2024).

10   And which album occupies the number two spot? Swift's own *Midnights* (2022). (See Hugh McIntyre, "Taylor Swift Claims the Three Bestselling Albums in American in 2023," *Forbes*, November 5, 2023, https://www.forbes.com/sites/hughmcintyre/2023/11/05/taylor-swift-claims-the-three-bestselling-albums-in-america-in-2023/ [accessed January 18, 2024].)

11   Swift, "For years I asked."

12   For more on the bad blood between Swift and Braun, see Constance Grady, "The Taylor Swift/Scooter Braun Controversy, Explained," *Vox*, July 1, 2019, https://www.vox.com/culture/2019/7/1/20677241/taylor-swift-scooter-braun-controversy-explained (accessed January 18, 2024).

13   Swift, "For years I asked."

14   Shirley Halperin, "Scooter Braun Sells Taylor Swift's Big Machine Masters for Big Payday," *Variety*, November 16, 2020, https://variety.com/2020/music/news/scooter-braun-sells-taylor-swift-big-machine-masters-1234832080/ (accessed January 18, 2024).

15 Jon Blistein, "Entertainment Giant HYBE, Home of BTS, Purchases Scooter Braun's Ithaca Holdings," *Rolling Stone*, April 2, 2021, https://www.rollingstone.com/pro/news/scooter-braun-ithaca-holdings-hybe-purchase-merger-1150462/ (accessed January 18, 2024).

16 Hannah Marder, "A Twitter User Showed How to Hide the Old Version of Taylor Swift's 'Fearless' and It's So Important to Do," *Buzzfeed*, April 9, 2021, https://www.buzzfeed.com/hannahmarder/how-to-hide-the-older-versions-of-taylor-swifts-fearless (accessed January 18, 2024).

17 Rob Sheffield, "Taylor Swift, Film Nerd: 'All Too Well' Singer Gives Rare Solo Performance at Tribeca," *Rolling Stone*, June 11, 2022, https://www.rollingstone.com/music/music-news/taylor-swift-tribeca-film-festival-all-too-well-1366715/ (accessed January 18, 2024).

18 Michael Ordoña, "Taylor Swift, in the Race for an Oscar, Brings 'All Too Well' to TIFF," *Los Angeles Times*, September 9, 2022, https://www.latimes.com/entertainment-arts/music/story/2022-09-09/taylor-swift-tiff-oscar-all-too-well-toronto-2022 (accessed January 18, 2024).

19 Shania Russell, "Taylor Swift's All Too Well Short Film Has Higher Letterboxd Ratings Than Parasite," *Slashfilm*, November 15, 2021, https://www.slashfilm.com/662048/taylor-swifts-all-too-well-short-film-has-higher-letterboxd-ratings-than-parasite/ (accessed January 18, 2024).

20 Keith Langston, "2022 MTV VMAs Winners: See the Full List," *Entertainment Weekly*, August 29, 2022, https://ew.com/mtv-video-music-awards/mtv-vmas-2022-winners-list/ (accessed January 18, 2024).

21 Taylor Weatherby, "Taylor Swift Makes Grammy History (Again) with Best Music Video Win for 'All Too Well: The Short Film,'" *Grammy.com*, February 5, 2023, https://www.grammy.com/news/taylor-swift-all-too-well-the-short-film-best-music-video-winner-2023-grammys (accessed January 18, 2024).

22 You can watch the full performance on Taylor Swift's YouTube channel here: https://www.youtube.com/watch?v=nJr_8l0AEWE

1

Taylor Swift, Justice, and the Fundamentals of Copyright

Darren Hudson Hick

Introduction

In 2019, Taylor Swift announced a curious and unprecedented project: she was going to re-record and re-release her first six albums: *Taylor Swift, Fearless, Speak Now, Red, 1989,* and *Reputation.* The new albums, dubbed "Taylor's Versions," would be near sonic duplicates of the albums that the public already knew so well and had already bought millions of times over. This was no small project, and was no mere publicity stunt. She wasn't doing this for the public; she was doing it for herself. This was Taylor Swift finally getting to embody the agency and autonomy that had been denied her since she first entered the music industry.

Swift's "Taylor Versions" project was famously prompted by the sale of Big Machine Records—the label she had signed to when she was fifteen years old—to Ithaca Holdings, a company owned by Scooter Braun. There was already a lot of bad blood between Swift and Braun—blood that began to boil when Big Machine released without her approval (indeed, apparently without even the courtesy of letting her know) a live album of performances by Swift dating back to 2008.[1] Swift publicly passed the move off as a money grab, but one can't help but see it as a flex by Scooter Braun, who Swift once called out in an awards speech as "the definition of toxic male privilege in our industry."[2] Big Machine owns what are called Swift's master recordings—the authoritative source used to produce her albums—allowing them (and now, Scooter Braun) to make a lot of money from Swift's work. And, so far as it goes, there was nothing that Swift could do about that. Even after Scooter Braun sold Swift's masters to another firm, Shamrock Holdings, in 2020, it was under the arrangement that Braun would continue to profit from her work.[3] With Big Machine and Braun refusing to sell her masters to her, Swift's only remaining move was to create *new* masters, which *she* would own, and which (if all went according to plan) could act as substitutes, undercutting the originals.

It's hard to look at the details of the Taylor Swift case without a sense that Swift is fighting to get out of an unhealthy relationship. But even if her re-recording gambit succeeds, Scooter Braun may forever be taking from her. Swift's audacious project is something new, but the position that she found herself in is anything but. Creators and the music industry have long existed in a symbiotic but asymmetric relationship. Creators—especially those first starting out—need publishers and need labels. At the same time, those publishers and labels wouldn't exist without the creative output of artists. But creators tend to have extremely limited bargaining power compared with the publishers and record labels of the music industry.

The heart of the problem is found in the details of copyright law, and it's here that I suggest the solution might be found—a solution not just for megastars like Taylor Swift, but for every young, creative hopeful entering the music industry.

The Nitty-gritty of Copyright

There is a fair bit of confusion out there about who owns what, exactly, when it comes to Taylor Swift's creative output. So far as her first six albums go, Swift effectively owns very little. In 2004, when she was fourteen years old, Swift signed a publishing contract with Sony/ATV (hereafter "Sony"[4]) assigning a 90 percent interest in the copyright to all musical works created in whole or in part by Swift for the duration of the term of the contract, along with worldwide, exclusive, perpetual rights to license those works.[5] Copyright, among other things, includes the exclusive right to make or authorize reproductions of one's work—say, on a vinyl record or digital download—and the exclusive right to publicly perform that work, whether live or via broadcast. Swift stayed with Sony until 2020, when she moved to Universal. The copyrights that she assigned to Sony, however, stay with Sony.

Because she has assigned exclusive rights to license the works, the little percentage of the copyright that Swift retains to her own songs is effectively meaningless—she has effectively no control over the songs. Her contract with Sony does, however, allow for what is called a "controlled composition" clause, authorizing her to work with another company to produce recordings of her songs. That's where Big Machine comes in. In 2005, when Swift signed a six-album recording contract with Big Machine Records, she would have assigned copyright in the master recordings to Big Machine in exchange for a percentage of the album's gross sales, which then would have been shared with Sony.[6] The master recording is what's copied onto every physical album and every digital copy. So, Sony owns the copyrights in Swift's songs, and Big Machine owns the copyright to the master recordings of those songs. Owning the copyrights in the songs means Sony gets to decide how they can be used, generally, including whether Swift herself can record or publicly perform them. When Swift adapted her own song "All Too Well" into a short film in 2021, she would have needed Sony's permission. Owning the copyrights in the master recordings of Swift's songs means Big Machine gets to make and authorize copies of those particular recordings—whether as physical albums or digital downloads, on streaming services, or in movies or advertisements.

When an aspiring musician signs all these copyrights away, it is in exchange for the publisher and label's promotion of their work, and for royalties—and there are several kinds of royalties at play.[7] The publishing contract (in this case, with Sony) specifies a breakdown of what are called "mechanical royalties," a set amount that goes to the copyright holder(s) every time a copy of the work is sold, whether as a physical product (a vinyl record or CD) or as a digital download. In the United States, there is a set rate for mechanical royalties generated by physical copies or downloaded songs: currently $0.091 for songs under 5 minutes, or $0.0175 per minute for songs longer than 5 minutes. Swift's original contract with Sony gives Swift 75 percent of the mechanical royalties and gives Sony 25 percent, the industry standard.[8] Mechanical royalties are collected and distributed by the publisher or by a mechanical licensing administrator like the Harry Fox Agency.

"Performance royalties" are paid based on the broadcast (radio, television, streaming) or live performance of protected works, and are split between the songwriter and the publisher. How they are split depends upon negotiation between parties. The songwriter's portion of performance royalties may itself be split between multiple creators, including songwriters and producers.[9] Performance royalty rates are determined by performing rights organizations (PROs), who license recording artists' works with businesses looking to perform them, including radio stations, restaurants, and streaming services, among others.[10] Rates vary by PRO, but a commercial AM or FM radio station that plays a song at a peak time might pay up to $5 for each "spin." A spin on satellite radio might bring in $35 in performance royalties. Performance on government radio like Canada's CBC or Britain's BBC might bring up to $79 per spin.[11] Performance royalties are normally collected by a PRO or a collective management organization (CMO), and sent directly to the songwriter and publisher, minus any administrative fees. ASCAP says that "[a]bout 90 cents of every dollar we collect is distributed back to our members as royalties."[12]

Finally, there are album sale royalties. Where mechanical royalties and performance royalties go to the songwriter and publisher, album sale royalties go to the recording artist. In Swift's case, she's both songwriter and recording artist, which makes things a little easier for us.[13] When Swift signed with Big Machine Records in 2005, she was a relative unknown, and Big Machine was (despite its name) a small start-up label. As an industry standard, as an untested talent, Swift was probably offered between 10 and 15 percent royalties on the wholesale price of her albums.[14] The typical recording contract will often also include what is called a recoupment clause, specifying that before royalties are paid to the artist, those royalties will first be used to pay back the label for all of the costs that the label fronted for producing and promoting the album. Swift's contract with Big Machine also included a standard re-recording clause, which prevented Swift from re-recording any of the songs from her first six records until November 2020.[15]

All of these royalties work slightly differently when we look at streaming services like Spotify. First, a streaming service pays the owner of the master (typically, the recording label) a negotiated licensing fee to use a given song or album. Each recording artist will have negotiated a percentage of that licensing fee as a royalty—usually between 15 and 20 percent.[16] Beyond that, streaming also generates mechanical and publishing royalties. Calculation for these royalties starts with the gross income of the streaming service. Subtract the cost of public performance (including what is paid out in licensing fees), and 10.5 percent of what's left makes up the "all-in" royalty pool, which includes both performance and mechanical royalties, and are then distributed to rights holders. Rates, as such, will vary year over year, but one recent estimate has Spotify paying $0.00318 per stream, strikingly less than a digital download or physical album sale.[17]

All of that might seem like Swift's publisher and her label are unjustly exploiting her. Yes, Taylor Swift is undoubtedly a billionaire, but Sony and Big Machine haven't simply been along for the ride. If Taylor Swift is taking 15 percent of the wholesale price of every copy sold of *Fearless* (after she has paid back the costs of production and promotion), Big Machine takes 85 percent, with a similar breakdown for streaming licenses. Indeed, by 2018, 80 percent of Big Machine's income came from Taylor Swift.[18] One might generously think of Sony and Big Machine as savvy investors, wisely hitching their collective wagons to Swift's rising star. But Swift's publisher and her label are not mere backers: between them, they *own* every song, every recording, that Swift made between 2005 and 2018. And all of this might well seem outrageous, but it's also the industry standard. This is normal.

Swift broke with Big Machine in 2018 and signed a new recording contract with Universal Music Group. Two years later, she left Sony and signed a new publishing contract with Universal, consolidating her creative output under the Universal umbrella. After the move from Sony to Universal, the copyright notices in her new albums changed from "©[Year] Sony/ATV Tree Publishing/Taylor Swift Music (BMI)" to "©[year] TASRM Publishing, administered by Songs Of Universal, Inc. (BMI)," suggesting that Swift's superstardom has finally allowed her to retain copyright in her own works ("TASRM" is likely an acronym for "Taylor Alison Swift Rights Management"). Her move to Universal likely also included a substantially higher royalty rate on album sales—50 percent or better.[19] She almost certainly owns all of the new master recording she generates with Universal. By 2020, Swift had sold in excess of 100 million albums, suggesting a rather high bar for those creators hoping to retain the copyright in their creations. The average (even the average successful) recording artist doesn't have that kind of bargaining power.

Swift is *very* interested in her autonomy, both as a creator and as a businesswoman. In 2014, Swift published an op-ed in the *Wall Street Journal*, pushing back against streaming services giving away free content, in effect reducing the royalties going to artists:

> In my opinion, the value of an album is, and will continue to be, based on the amount of heart and soul an artist has bled into a body of work, and the financial value that artists (and their labels) place on their music when it goes out into the marketplace. Piracy, file sharing and streaming have shrunk the numbers of paid album sales drastically, and every artist has handled this blow differently …. Music is art, and art is important and rare. Important, rare things are valuable. Valuable things should be paid for. It's my opinion that music should not be free, and my prediction is that individual artists and their labels will someday decide what an album's price point is.[20]

Swift pulled her work from Spotify, returning only three years later after changes were made to Spotify's promotional policies.[21] In 2021, with the release of the first of her re-recorded songs, "Love Story (Taylor's Version)," Swift posted on Instagram: "artists should own their own work for so many reasons, but the most screamingly obvious one is that the artist is the only one who really *knows* that body of work."[22]

Sony owns 90 percent of "The Outside," a song that Taylor Swift wrote when she was twelve years old:

> This is one of the first songs I ever wrote, and it talks about the very reason I ever started to write songs. It was when I was twelve years old, and a complete outcast at school. I was a lot different than all the other kids, and I never really knew why. I was taller, and sang country music at karaoke bars and festivals on weekends while other girls went to sleepovers. Some days I woke up not knowing if anyone was going to talk to me that day.[23]

Sony owns that. Sony *still* owns that. It's Swift's creation, but it's not *her* song anymore. Sony owns 90 percent of "Tim McGraw," a song that Taylor Swift came up with in math class when she was fifteen years old, and thinking about the fact that her boyfriend was about to graduate, and they would have to break up.[24] A Taylor Swift album is like a diary. Swift's songs are deeply personal, but *they're not hers anymore*. I don't think I'm alone in thinking that's really weird.

Artistic License

In 2017, I published *Artistic License*, a philosophical examination of copyright and artistic appropriation. In the book, I develop an account meant to capture our intuitions about why a creator should gain ownership over what she creates. My view is that, by selecting things that nobody owns (individual words, sounds, colors, shapes), and arranging them into something original (i.e., something that comes from *you*), you have created something that owes its existence solely to you—an authored work. And, as such, you lay a claim to that thing—a claim against all others. You don't own those individual words or sounds or colors; you own their *arrangement*—that's what came from you. That's what conveys your meaning to the world.

Ownership, generally speaking, is the right to exploit a thing for the sort of thing that it is. I centrally exploit my house or my land by occupying it. I exploit my coffee mug or my computer by using it, and using it in a way that may exclude others from doing so. But an authored work—an arrangement of words or sounds or shapes and colors—isn't centrally exploited like a material object is, excluding others from using or occupying it. Indeed, multiple people can "use" a song or a story or a movie, and all at the same time. Rather, an authored work is exploited by *reproducing* it—by making *copies*. So, insofar as someone *can* claim ownership over something like a song, I argue, the exclusive right to that authored work will consist centrally in the creator's right to reproduce that thing. Whether writing out a song on paper, capturing it on a recording, or performing it live, you are (in one form or another) reproducing that song, and *that's* what copyright is centrally about.[25]

Formally, my argument modifies a view developed by John Locke in the seventeenth century. Locke's argument is, like mine, a sort of "natural rights" argument. His view is that one comes to own a thing by taking what is unowned and acting on it in a way that brings about new value:

> Though the Earth, and all inferior Creatures be common to all Men, yet every Man has a *Property* in his own *Person*. This no Body has any Right to but himself. The *Labour* of his Body, and the *Work* of his Hands, we may say, are properly his. Whatsoever then he removes out of the State that Nature hath provided, and left it in, he hath mixed his *Labour* with, and joined to it something that is his own, and thereby makes it his *Property*.[26]

Although Locke's view is about physical property, several philosophers have worked to straightforwardly map the view onto intellectual property. The problem has always been that doing so requires some notion of creative or artistic labor that has never really been worked out. In the end, we tend to value artistic *inspiration*—genius—as much as we value the intellectual or physical labor that an artist puts into her work, and the Lockean view has no easy way to account for that element.

The *heart* of my view runs closer to the "personality rights" views offered by Immanuel Kant and G.W.F. Hegel in the late eighteenth and early nineteenth centuries. On this view, an artist comes to own what she creates because she puts something of herself into it. As such, in doing so, she has claimed some part of the external world as a part of her—an embodiment of her personality. This is the view that tends to underlie the approaches to copyright taken in continental Europe, where courts ask whether some given object carries the mark of the author's personality—whether it embodies the creator's personal and individual choices. Actual tests for finding the mark of the author, however, focus on evidence of choices *as* evidence of personality. And the creator's choices are nowhere more apparent than in how she has selected and arranged the elements (the words, the sounds) that make up a work—what my view suggests the creator gains rights to.

All of this is in contrast to the official party line in the United States, where copyright is grounded constitutionally in the goal of "promot[ing] the progress of science and the useful arts."[27] As a matter of law, the creator of a copyrightable work gains copyright in that thing the moment it is created.[28] And it's Taylor Swift's ownership of her songs that allows her to make a living off them. And certainly, all of this will be inspiring to young artists of all stripes to create *more* works, thus seeming to satisfy the constitutional goal. However, the music industry has ensured that this will only happen if you *sell* the copyrights to your work. And it's at least strange that satisfying the justification for copyright would depend on your giving it away.

Toward the end of the book, tying up some loose ends, I raise the issue of copyright duration. Under current US law, a creator's copyright normally lasts for the duration of their life plus seventy years. When that term is up, the work goes into the public domain, and anyone can use the work without permission or restriction. Other countries set different lengths. In China, typical works are protected for life plus fifty years. In Mexico, life plus 100. That American copyright cuts off seventy years after the creator's death is an arbitrary line, but the US Constitution, in specifying that rights to intellectual property shall be secured "for limited times," requires that *some* line be drawn.[29] America is the only country that has made the limited duration of copyright a constitutional matter, though I am unaware of any country that recognizes perpetual copyright. But if copyright is a property right, it is strange that—unlike ordinary property—it vanishes some two generations after the creator expires. I don't, after all, have to worry about the government coming for the silverware or jewelry that has been handed down in my family over the years. On the other hand, if (as I contend) copyright is a sort of natural right grounded in the creative act, then it is strange that it outlasts the creator at all. Why would *your* rights to *your* creation outlast *you*? Indeed, it is equally as strange that copyright might be sold or given away while the creator is still alive.

"So," I noted in the book: "our central question is, does our natural right give rise to ownership that may be *transferred* at or before the author's death? Answering this question would require more argument than I can devote to it here, but I am in principle open to either possibility."[30] This was a total dodge, but nobody called me on it. There is indeed a dilemma at the heart of this issue: is the notion of copyright as a natural right commensurable with the notion of copyright as a property right? How can it be that a right that you earn *as a creator* is something you can then *give to someone else*? I had happily buried the issue in my own mind until Taylor Swift's case dragged it back into the light. And here, I found it wrapped up in an issue of justice.

As it currently exists, the recording industry depends on the ability of creators to transfer their copyrights. As long as it's possible for creators to sell the ownership in what they create, publishers and record labels will demand that they do so. With extraordinarily rare exceptions, up-and-coming musicians simply lack the bargaining power to demand anything else. They can walk away from what they're being offered, but the next publisher, the next label, will offer more or less the same deal: *we'll front the money for you to produce your work, but we own what you make (and you have to pay us back all that money we fronted you).*

A Two-part Approach to Copyright

We have two problems on the table—one, a conceptual conundrum; the other, a matter of justice. I suggest that a solution to the first might offer some hope for the second.

The first step takes it for granted that copyright is a natural right to one's intellectual property, a right arising from and grounded in the author's creative act. The *reason* that you have such a right is that you're the sort of being who has, and who has exercised, the power to select and arrange elements (words, sounds, colors, shapes) as constitutive of a new thing: an authored work.[31] You made that thing; it owes its existence entirely to you; that's why it's yours.[32]

The second step comes in recognizing the incoherence of transferring (selling, giving away, bequeathing) a natural right—a right one gains through one's creative act—to someone else. What, after all, would justify *their* right? A natural right is not a reward, like a trophy granted by others for a job well done. It may be *recognized* by others (or not), and it may be protected by the state (or not), but it arises and subsists in the agent. As commonly understood, a natural right is inalienable: it cannot be *taken* away, and it cannot be *given* away.[33]

Transferring property ownership under John Locke's view required building an additional layer on the natural right to property: money. Locke introduces money as a good that, by a "tacit and voluntary consent" among people, might be exchanged for any commodity whatsoever, apparently including such property as one owns as a matter of natural right.[34] Now, as there seems nothing wrong with taking money for one's labor—getting paid for a job—there would seem nothing wrong with taking money for the *products* of one's labor. But this is a strange thing. Does one give up one's exclusive right to one's labor when one is paid to do a job? Quite the opposite—it is only *because* one owns one's labor that one can *choose* to use that labor in pursuit of another's ends. The converse seems to simply clash with what Locke has said about the acquisition of property.[35] As Locke notes, one gains property by mixing one's labor with what is unowned, and "this labour being the unquestionable property of the labourer, no man but he can have a right to what that is once joined to."[36] There is a long debate about whether Locke himself espoused a view of natural rights as inalienable.[37] But it simply seems a conceptual non-starter that one might transfer a natural right without first transforming it into something else—after all, if the recipient had naturally what the right arose from, they would already have the right. And it is unclear how such a right *might be transformed*.[38]

Rather, then, than thinking of copyright as a thing which is gained as a natural right, and can be transferred thereafter (as a natural or nonnatural right), I would suggest that we think of two kinds of copyright: one that vests in the creator as a natural right, and one that may be licensed to a publisher. For the sake of reference, let's call these "copyright" and "copylicense," respectively.

As a natural right—inalienable and nontransferable—copyright should most reasonably expire with the creator. I simply cannot conceive of a good argument that a creator's family (or, indeed, anyone else) should have any natural right to what that artist creates, and it is difficult to think of any reason that a natural right should be extinguished before the rightsholder herself expires.

Copylicense, by contrast, would be a nonnatural right, and as such subject to an array of competing rights and interests as arise between individuals and groups.[39] Where the government has a duty to protect such natural rights that may exist (the Declaration of Independence lists "Life, Liberty and the pursuit of Happiness" as "unalienable" and to be "secured" by the government), it also has a duty to legislate and enforce such accessory rights and duties as are required for the best functioning of society, but which may not rise to the level of natural rights. This is where a nonnatural right like copylicense would come in.

In order to pursue one's own happiness, it might well be best to enter into a contract with a music publisher or record label. Copylicense, as I imagine it, would allow for the licensing of worldwide, exclusive rights to copy and distribute a creator's work. At the same time, in order to protect a natural right like copyright, the law should not allow such a license to be perpetual. When I publish an article or a book, I typically have to sign one of two contracts. The first grants the copyright in my work to the publisher. The second doesn't grant copyright, but does grant a worldwide, exclusive, perpetual right to reproduce and license reproduction of that work. The difference between these contracts is largely semantic: granting a worldwide, exclusive, perpetual right to reproduce and license reproduction of a work in effect hands over copyright in all but name.[40] Anything less than a perpetual license, then, requires drawing a line in the sand. Asking where we should draw that line means asking what is best for all parties involved. Here, we might look to the model of patent, another form of intellectual property.

Where copyright protects creative output, patent protects useful inventions.[41] Patent expiration is based on balancing what is best for society with what is best for the patent holder. Typically, US patents expire twenty years from the date of filing the patent.[42] Thereafter, the protected invention goes into the public domain for anyone to use. The twenty-year period is meant to give the developers ample opportunity to recoup the costs of development and earn profits on their invention.[43] As the thinking goes, it is in all our interests that inventors work to bring us better machines, better pharmaceuticals, and generally more comfortable lives. Patents are also in the best interest of inventors, allowing them opportunity to make a decent living with their creations. But, after a time, the public's wider interests (including improving upon those inventions and in accessing those inventions at lower costs) begin to press, and that's where Congress has drawn the expiration line. James O. Young has suggested a similar model for the duration of copyrights to fictional characters, and for similar reasons.[44]

In the case of the proposed copylicense, I would suggest that the interest that weighs against the music publisher or record label's interest in recouping their costs and earning profits is the creator's own interest in not being exploited unjustly. Taylor Swift is an extraordinary case. Swift's first, self-titled album was a sleeper hit. It sold a modest 40,000 copies during its first week in October 2006. Little more than a year later, however, it had sold more than 1 million copies. By the start of 2008, it was selling 187,000 copies a week. After three and a half years, it had sold 5.5 million copies. As of this writing, it has sold in excess of 11.2 million copies worldwide. Each of Swift's studio albums with Big Machine has outsold the first album, and this in an era where album sales have given way to streaming. As of this writing, Swift's songs have been streamed over 68 billion times on Spotify. At what point is it unreasonable that a publisher should be profiting at the same rate that the artist signed on as an unknown? At a rough guess, I would say that three years is ample time in most cases to realize the value of a work—to see how the work has been both critically and commercially received—and to have made ample profit where profit is to be had. It is exceedingly rare for a song to peak more than three years after its initial release.

If a song or an album is a flop, a publisher or record label may not be interested in relicensing it from the copyright holder. If the artists involved still believe in the work, and think the original label or publisher has not properly marketed the work to bring it to its full potential, they could try again elsewhere. If, on the other hand, the song is a hit in its initial release, statutory expiration limits on a copylicense would allow the creators the opportunity to shop the work around with a revised estimate of its value, rather than watching the original label fill its coffers at the rate offered to an up-and-coming artist. The sort of renegotiation that Taylor Swift was able to achieve only after becoming a megastar should be available to every creator.

Conclusion

On her initial signing with Big Machine Records, Swift opined: "Getting a record deal means being able to do what I want to do …. The best part about getting a record deal was that it wasn't just *a* record deal; it was the right deal for me."[45] Hindsight is 20/20. But the deck was stacked against fourteen-year-old Taylor Swift, and had been for so long that it had become "just the way it is."

At the heart of the music industry is a system built on the unjust exploitation of creators. On my understanding of copyright as a natural right, it is simply incoherent to demand that a creator sign over the copyrights to her creations. And a system that requires—is, indeed, built on—creators relinquishing such rights in their works is always going to be unjust. Certainly, music publishers and record labels offer valuable resources to creators, and a songwriter or recording artist (or, in Swift's case, both) should be free to enter into business arrangements so as to make a living from her talent and efforts. But the music industry has turned a partnership into a Faustian deal with the devil. As the musician Prince once put it, "If you don't own your masters, your master owns you."[46] Taylor Swift has managed, through sheer talent, grit, and determination, to reclaim her agency so that she can chart her own path forward. But she lost a part of herself along the way—the part that she put into "The Outside," the part that she put into "Tim McGraw," the part that she put into each song and recording that now belongs to Sony or Shamrock Holdings—and she isn't likely to get that part back.

Notes

1   Tim Ingham, "Taylor Swift: Scooter Braun Paying \$330M for Big Machine 'Wasn't Exactly a Wise Choice,'" *Music Business Worldwide*, April 23, 2020, https://www.musicbusinessworldwide.com/taylor-swift-scooter-braun-paying-330m-for-big-machine-wasnt-exactly-a-wise-choice/ (accessed July 20, 2023).

2   Mark Savage, "Taylor Swift Blasts 'Toxic Male Privilege' during Woman of the Decade Speech," *BBC News*, November 13, 2019, https://www.bbc.com/news/entertainment-arts-50763774 (accessed July 20, 2023).

3   Ben Sisario, Joe Coscarelli and Kate Kelly, "Taylor Swift Denounces Scooter Braun as Her Catalog Is Sold Again," *New York Times*, November 16, 2020, https://www.nytimes.com/2020/11/16/arts/music/taylor-swift-scooter-braun-masters.html (accessed July 20, 2023).

4   Sony/ATV was a joint venture of Sony and Michael Jackson's ATV Music, established in 1995. In 2016, Sony/ATV acquired the Jackson estate's portion of the venture, making Sony/ATV a wholly owned subsidiary of Sony. (https://www.sonymusicpub.com/en/about)

5   This is according to a leaked copy of the "Exclusive Songwriter Agreement," dated November 1, 2004. The provisions laid out in the contract are fairly standard for a publishing contract. The original contract period lasts one year, and specifies two optional extensions, each a year apiece. As Swift maintained a publishing agreement with Sony/ATV until 2020, later contracts or extensions may have changed some of the details, but liner notes for the "Taylor's Version" re-recordings continue to list "Sony/ATV" as a copyright holder on Swift's songs.

6   By one estimate, a typical base royalty for album sales would be between 12 and 20 percent of the gross sales. (Mark Tavern, "An Artist's Guide to Royalties, Recoupment & Cross-Collateralization," *DJ Booth*, July 30, 2020, https://djbooth.net/features/2020-07-30-kreayshawn-contracts-recoupments-record-labels [accessed July 20, 2023].)

7   Typically, a songwriter will also receive an advance on royalties. In the case of Swift's leaked contract with Sony/ATV, the initial advance was $50,000, increased each year the contract was extended. For the sake of space, I have not included discussion of synchronization (or "sync") royalties—royalties earned when a song is used alongside video—in a commercial, movie, TV show, or video game.

8   Dale Kawashima, "The History of Music Publishing—An Overview," *SongwriterUniverse*, December 20, 2022, https://www.songwriteruniverse.com/historyofpublishing.htm (accessed July 20, 2023).

9   Outside the United States, many countries also recognize "neighboring rights," and neighboring rights royalties are paid to the owner of the master.

10 Typically, a business will gain a general license, allowing it to play any music in that PRO's catalog. A PRO like ASCAP, BMI, or SESAC will calculate royalty payments from the data it collects about what music is being played, and allocate payments based on a credit system that accounts for type of use, venue, song popularity, and even time of day of that performance. (https://www.ascap.com/help/royalties-and-payment/payment/royalties)

11 Liam Duncan, "How Much Do Songwriters Make Per Song, Per Stream & in Other Situations," *Music Industry How To*, December 29, 2022, https://www.musicindustryhowto.com/how-much-do-songwriters-make-per-song-per-stream-in-other-situations/ (accessed July 20, 2023).

12 https://www.ascap.com/help/royalties-and-payment/payment

13 When Detroit metal band I Prevail released a hardcore cover of Swift's "Blank Space" as a single in 2014, it was with (appropriately enough) Fearless Records. Both mechanical and performance royalties for sales and plays of I Prevail's recording would go to Taylor Swift and Sony. Album sales royalties, however, would go to the members of I Prevail.

14 Abigail Freeman, "Taylor Swift Is 'Free' Again, But Just How Much Is Her 'Fearless' Strategy Worth?," *Forbes*, April 9, 2021, https://www.forbes.com/sites/abigailfreeman/2021/04/09/taylor-swift-is-free-again-but-just-how-much-is-her-fearless-strategy-worth/ (accessed July 20, 2023).

15 Jeffrey H. Brown, "The Legal Take on the Taylor Swift Recording Dispute," *Best Lawyers*, December 5, 2019, https://www.bestlawyers.com/article/taylor-swift-recording-contract-controversy/2747 (accessed July 20, 2023).

16 Juan C. Sarassa, "How Spotify Royalties Actually Work," *Hypebot*, November 4, 2021, https://www.hypebot.com/hypebot/2021/11/how-spotify-royalties-actually-work.html (accessed July 20, 2023).

17 Sean Fitzjohn, "Streaming Payouts Per Platform & Royalties Calculator," *Producer Hive*, June 21, 2023, https://producerhive.com/music-marketing-tips/streaming-royalties-breakdown/ (accessed July 20, 2023).

18 Chris Willman, "Taylor Swift Stands to Make Music Business History as a Free Agent," *Variety*, August 27, 2018, https://variety.com/2018/music/news/taylor-swift-stands-to-make-music-business-history-as-a-free-agent-1202918336/ (accessed July 20, 2023).

19 Freeman, "Taylor Swift Is 'Free' Again."

20 Taylor Swift, "For Taylor Swift, the Future of Music Is a Love Story," *Wall Street Journal*, July 7, 2014, https://www.wsj.com/articles/for-taylor-swift-the-future-of-music-is-a-love-story-1404763219 (accessed July 20, 2023).

21 Andrew Flanagan, "Taylor Swift Returns to Spotify, Amends Her Relationship to Streaming," *NPR*, June 9, 2017, https://www.npr.org/sections/therecord/2017/06/09/532238490/taylor-swift-returns-to-spotify-amends-her-relationship-to-streaming (accessed July 20, 2023).

22 Taylor Swift (@taylorswift13), "I'm thrilled to tell you that my new version of Fearless (Taylor's Version) is done and will be with you soon," *Twitter*, February 11, 2021, https://twitter.com/taylorswift13/status/1359854050544615425/photo/2 (accessed July 20, 2023).

23 Taylor Swift, liner notes for *Taylor Swift*, Big Machine Records, 2006, compact disc.

24 Swift's collaborator, Liz Rose, shares writing credit on "Tim McGraw" and sixteen other Swift songs, though Rose admits, "Basically, I was just her editor …. She had such a clear vision of what she was trying to say." (Liv Spencer, *Taylor Swift: Every Day Is a Fairytale—The Unofficial Story* [Toronto: ECW Press, 2010], 32.) Swift says, "I love writing with Liz …. When we write, I usually come in with a melody and some lyric content, and then we'll work on creating the rest of the song. She's a really good song editor." (Dale Kawashima, "Taylor Swift Interview," *SongwriterUniverse*, February 16, 2007, https://www.songwriteruniverse.com/taylorswift123.htm [accessed July 20, 2023].)

25 This is a much-condensed version of the view I present in chapter 6 of Darren Hudson Hick, *Artistic License: The Philosophical Problems of Copyright and Appropriation* (Chicago: University of Chicago Press, 2017). Copyright actually consists in a *bundle* of rights—but the right of reproduction is at the heart of it all.

26 John Locke, *Two Treatises of Government*, ed., Peter Laslett (1689; repr., Cambridge: Cambridge University Press, 1988), II.27.

27 US Constitution, Art. 1, sec. 8, cl. 8.

28 Under US law, the work must be "fixed in a tangible medium of expression"—written down or recorded, for example.

29 US Constitution, Art. 1, sec. 8, cl. 8.

30 Hick, *Artistic License*, 167.

31 This is my definition of authorship. See Hick, *Artistic License*, chap. 4.

32 My view is far from universally accepted, but arguing more fully for its preferability over competing views would take a good deal more room than I can give it here. Happily, again, I already did so in Hick, *Artistic License*.

33 See A. I. Melden, "Introduction," in *Human Rights*, ed. A. I. Melden (Belmont, CA: Wadsworth, 1970), 3.

34 Locke, *Two Treatises*, II.50.

35 And yet, Locke says that "a freeman makes himself a servant to another, by selling him, for a certain time, the service he undertakes to do, in exchange for wages he is to receive" (Locke, *Two Treatises*: II.85). Perhaps, like me, Locke simply found himself with a dilemma, and chose to simply leap between horns.

36 Locke, *Two Treatises*, II.27.

37 See A. John Simmons, "Inalienable Rights and Locke's Treatises," *Philosophy & Public Affairs* 12, no. 3 (1983): 175–204.

38 Under the sort of natural right proposed by Hegel and Kant, ownership would persist in an item so long as that item continued to embody one's personality. When it ceases to do so, one's natural right to that thing dissipates, and someone else may claim it as their own. On a view like this, the angsty poetry I wrote as a teenager ceased to be mine when it ceased to be the sort of thing I would write.

39 Natural rights, too, may come into conflict with the rights and interests of others: that a right is inalienable does not mean that it is absolute. See John Finnis, *Natural Law and Natural Rights* (Oxford: Oxford University Press, 2011), chap. 8.

40 As such, my arguments in this chapter would apply as much to book and article publishing as it does to music publishing.

41 The line between the two is subject of some debate.

42 Design patents, which protect ornamental design, last fifteen years. Due to international harmonization, most patents worldwide operate according to similar term limits. In the United States, the expiration of patent is based on the same line about "limited times" in the Constitution as copyright.

43 The history of term limits to both copyright and patent in the United States is fascinating. For an overview, see Tyler T. Ochoa, "Patent and Copyright Term Extension and the Constitution: A Historical

Perspective," *Journal of the Copyright Society of the USA* 49 (2001): 19–125.

44   James O. Young, "Appropriating Fictional Characters," in *The Aesthetics and Ethics of Copying*, ed. Darren Hudson Hick and Reinold Schmücker (London: Bloomsbury, 2016), 153–72.

45   "Taylor Swift: A Place in This World," directed James M. Rink (Nashville, TN: Rink Entertainment, 2006). You can view the entire documentary here: https://www.youtube.com/watch?v=4q2gNvaDtyA.

46   Anthony DeCurtis, "O(+> Free at Last," *Rolling Stone* 748 (November 28, 1996): 61–3.

2

Tell Me Why This Isn't a Cover

Cristyn Magnus, P. D. Magnus, Christy Mag Uidhir, and
Ron McClamrock

Introduction

In 2021, Taylor Swift released *Fearless (Taylor's Version)* and *Red
(Taylor's Version)*. In 2023, she followed these up with *Speak Now
(Taylor's Version)* and *1989 (Taylor's Version)*. Re-releases of her
eponymous debut album and *Reputation* are, we are told, forthcoming.
She does not own the masters to her earlier albums, and the new
releases give her versions of the songs from those albums which she
does own. Each of the new tracks is titled with the name of the earlier
track plus the suffix "(Taylor's Version)," an addition which seems
mostly to be about establishing brand identity. Adding to the title
makes it easy to tell the new versions from the old ones on streaming
services. When referring to the first re-release, she has called it
"Fearless (My Version)."[1]

In addition to Taylor's Versions of all the original tracks, there are
also tracks which were written at the time of the earlier album but
which were—for one reason or another—not previously published.
These are labeled as "(From the Vault)." In addition, *Red (Taylor's
Version)* features a ten-minute version of "All Too Well," resulting in the
mouthful of a title "All Too Well (10 Minute Version) (Taylor's Version)
(From the Vault)." The new tracks mean that the albums as a whole are
not just remakes, but our focus here is on Taylor's Versions rather than
the From the Vault tracks.

Are These Covers?

If some random musicians were to record Taylor Swift's back catalog with painstaking sonic fidelity to the originals, the products would be cover versions. So, should we say the same about Taylor's Versions?

One strategy is just to apply the definition of "cover," which would work fine if the word had a formal or legal definition. It does not.

The term "cover" began to be used in the music industry in the 1940s. It was not a term that people outside the industry used. In 1952, quoting a band leader who described covering a track, a reporter in Chicago felt like he had to add that "cover" is "trade jargon meaning to record a tune that looks like a potential hit on someone else's label."[2] This has the primary sense of *coverage*. Just as a band might learn contemporary hits to play live when audiences requested them, they might record their own versions of contemporary hits. Yet, it also often meant an attempt to steal sales that might have gone to the original recording, possibly displacing it entirely. Covers were sometimes intended to *cover up* or *cover over* the original on record store shelves.

By the late 1960s, the word "cover" had become a term of everyday English. Even though providing precise definitions of everyday terms is usually a mess, one might insist that a version is a cover when there is already a recording by someone else. A typical dictionary definition specifies this. Other random musicians would be making covers because they are not Taylor Swift; so, perhaps Taylor Swift cannot cover her own work precisely because she is the one who made the originals. One might exclaim, "*A musician cannot cover themselves!*"

Why yell in italics about this? The suggestion is that it is not just an incidental fact that musicians don't cover themselves, but instead that it is true by definition. Some philosophers have objected to the thought that any claims are true by definition, but we can allow that precise domains like mathematics allow for truths of that kind. What is not at all obvious is that the concept of cover is precise enough to yield such a conclusion. In common usage, ordinary people do use the word "cover" to describe works by the same artist as the original. For example, one online database allows the tag *self-cover*, which is more specific than the general tag *cover*, explaining it as "a special case of cover song where the artist covered their own song."[3]

Moreover, the 1950s definition does not mention different musicians but different labels, and Taylor's Versions have a different owner and are distributed by a different label than the originals. Considering the original use of the term, Taylor's Versions do seem to qualify as covers. They are intended for *coverage*, because Swift would like to own the master recordings for some version of those songs. And they are intended to *cover up* the originals, because Swift would like her versions to displace the originals in the market. So, they function as covers in both of those senses.

To try and sort this out, let's consider two thought experiments. The first, we think, is a plausible conjecture: In twenty years, the existence of the earlier versions will just be a bit of trivia. Taylor's Versions will be the default versions of these songs. This seems to be how Swift intends for it to go. Before the release of *Red (Taylor's Version)*, she commented, "I think that the version that we're putting out tonight is gonna be … the new … standard version … of what this song is, because it is the original form."[4] And this seems to be how it is going. In November 2021, iHeartMedia announced that all of their radio stations would replace the original tracks with Taylor's Versions as the latter became available. An executive at iHeart commented, "Whenever Taylor re-records a new track, we immediately replace the old versions."[5] In the end, we suspect that the originals will just be odd variants—like tracks by an American band that have alternate versions on the Japanese release or a movie that has a different cut on the laser disc.

These analogies suggest, perhaps, that Taylor's Versions are not covers but default versions. A cover, after all, counts as a cover because of its relation to a canonical earlier version. In the plausible conjecture, Taylor's Versions will be canonical in twenty years. However, there are covers—versions that everybody agrees count as covers—which have eclipsed their originals. Aretha Franklin's "Respect" (1967), for example, was a cover of Otis Redding's song (1965) by the same name. Yet, many listeners today do not know about Redding's original. R.E.M.'s "Superman" (1986) was a cover of an obscure original (1969) by a forgotten band called the Clique. The ability to overshadow an earlier recording might even be taken to be a defining feature of covers, because they can *cover up* the original. So, the plausible conjecture suggests that Taylor's Versions are covers without decisively establishing that they are.

The second thought experiment is this: Suppose Taylor Swift were able to acquire ownership of her early albums, the ones she has not re-recorded yet. Suppose that the cost was not too high and that none of the money would go to people she finds especially objectionable. She probably would not go on to re-record those other two albums. She might re-release them in new editions with the addition of some From the Vault tracks, but she would simply include the original recordings rather than making Taylor's Versions of the original tracks. If that is right, then Taylor's Versions are not merely new versions recorded in the usual way. Their function is precisely the commercial function that early covers had: publishing coverage and covering over the originals.

One might reply that these commercial functions are no longer typical of covers. In recent decades, covers have often been tributes that called attention to the original. Listeners might go back and listen to old recordings when they hear a new cover. Nevertheless, there still are some covers which compete with and displace originals. So, this second scenario also suggests that maybe Taylor's Versions are covers after all.

Nevertheless, the various functions of "cover" talk pull in different directions. We do not see any way to decisively settle whether Taylor's Versions are covers or not.[6] The word "cover" will not bear this much weight. So, let's take a step back and consider some lessons from the philosophy of cover songs. There are insights and distinctions which we can apply to Taylor's Versions regardless of whether they count as covers in a strict sense or not.

Among covers, it is important to distinguish *mimic covers* (which are intended to sound the same as the original) from *rendition covers* (which are not intended to sound the same). Note that the difference is not whether the cover actually does sound the same or not. A poor mimic cover might sound different because the musicians who played it simply lacked the skill to do better, and a straight rendition cover might sound fairly similar to the original. The difference instead lies in the intention with which they are made and the relevant appreciative standards.

In addition to sounding different than the original, a cover can *mean* something different than what the original means. Some covers not only mean something different but also have a meaning that is *about* the canonical original. (A much-discussed example is Sid Vicious's cover of "My Way" [1978]. The canonical version of the song is by Frank Sinatra [1969], and Vicious's version mocks both the original version and Sinatra himself.[7])

With that framework in mind, we can ask: Are Taylor's Versions mimics or renditions? Do Taylor's Versions mean something different than the tracks that they remake? Are Taylor's Versions about the original tracks?

Mimics and Renditions

Of course, Taylor's Versions do not sound *exactly* the same as the original tracks. Some differences are inevitable. Calling them new versions would be untenable if the digital masters were bit-for-bit identical. Even allowing that there must be some difference, though, they might sound so similar as to make no aesthetic difference. Some of Taylor's Versions, it seems to us, are that similar to the originals. When they are put together with the originals, cross-fading back and forth, the product sounds like one unified track rather than two tracks stitched together.[8]

Some other tracks have different decisions in production and mix. Some have different stylistic choices and sound noticeably different. For example, "Girl at Home" (from *Red*) has guitar in the original replaced with synthesizers in Taylor's Version. This shifts it to being clearly a pop track, rather than something that can be heard as country.

Unsurprisingly, different listeners disagree on the details. Diehard fans, who are more familiar with the original versions, are more likely to notice differences between the originals and Taylor's Versions. For example, Taylor's Version of "All Too Well" (the one with just the original verses, not the 10 Minute Version) sounds rather like the original to us. The differences are subtle, and we do not prefer one over the other. But a fan comments online, "When it comes to 'All Too Well' i cant choose between old or new. The old one sounds so pure, raw and it felt many stories about a woman who's heart just got brokened yesterday."[9]

Regardless, a great deal of effort was spent on the recording and production to make sure all the parts were there and the timing was the same. Professional musicians who would not play those tunes in precisely the same way under ordinary circumstances nevertheless did so for Taylor's Versions. The overwhelming work here was to duplicate. If a tribute band had versions that sounded this much like the originals, they would be highly successful mimics.

Moreover, as we noted above, the difference between a mimic and a rendition is not whether a version *actually* sounds the same as the original or not. Rather, what matters is the intention. After the release of *Red (Taylor's Version)*, Swift contrasted her approach with Taylor's Versions with her approach to the From the Vault tracks. She said:

I think recording it … was going back and trying to create as authentic a replica of the originals as I possibly could. With songs on the original album, I wanted them to sound exactly alike. Then with the Vault tracks, I wanted to be as creative as I possibly could. These are songs that no one's heard before, so I wanted them to be the best version.[10]

Swift's word choice here is telling. To think of Taylor's Versions as *replicas* is to think of them as mimics. A replica of a sculpture is best if it is indistinguishable from the original. Every difference is a demerit. It may have the word "replica" embossed on the bottom, of course, but that is a concession to practicality rather than an aesthetic addition. A mimic cover is like a replica in this respect.

Furthermore, recall the second thought experiment from the previous section: If Swift were able to acquire ownership of her remaining albums on terms she found agreeable, would she give up the project of re-recording them? We think she would. What she wants, ultimately, is to own her music. She has taken the unusual step of making faithful copies precisely because she does not own the earlier versions. If she did own them, then she would have no need for Taylor's Versions. This function makes them seem like mimics rather than renditions.

How do Taylor's Versions fare, if we take them to be mimics? Although a mimic cover need not—and typically will not—sound exactly like the original, more resemblance to the original is always better than less resemblance. So, if we take Taylor's Versions to be mimics, they are good but not perfect. Moreover, a mimic cover usually has no artistic significance beyond that of the original. Instead, it is an exercise of skill and craft. Taylor's Versions are impressive, but only in the way an excellent replica of an awesome statue would be impressive.

Because of the great care taken with Taylor's Versions, the small differences from the originals are likely to have been deliberate—for example, the synths in "Girl at Home." The clearest and most consistent difference is in Swift's singing. She has made little attempt to emulate her earlier vocal quality. She sounds like the same person, yes, but older. On Taylor's Versions, she sings like a fully mature woman who is looking back at a painful, heart-broken time from years ago. So, perhaps these self-conscious differences are enough to make it not count as a mimic after all.

In an interview promoting *Fearless (Taylor's Version)*, Swift said, "I really did want this to be very true to what I initially thought of and what I'd initially written. But better. Obviously."[11] In describing it this way, she suggests that the aim was not to make Taylor's Versions match the original tracks but instead to make them match her original conceptions of the songs. Perhaps the original records fell short of her original vision, and the new versions better realize what she had intended all along. Understanding them in this way treats Taylor's Versions as renditions.

Unlike a mimic, a rendition cover can be appreciated in two different modes. First, it can be appreciated in relation to the original. A rendition can be good or bad both because of the ways it differs from the original and also because of the ways it does not differ. The changes that are made reflect artistic choices, but there are also artistic choices in not changing other features. Second, a rendition cover can be appreciated on its own, without consideration of the original. One can listen to it and respond to how it sounds, considered just as an instance of the song in question.

If we were to understand Taylor's Versions as renditions, then, we would need to consider them in both modes.

First: Considering them in relation to the originals, they fail to live up to the potential of new versions. They seem boring and pointless as additional artifacts, alongside the originals. Even a straight rendition requires small touches and twists in order to be anything more than uninspired repetition. If we do not take them to be mimics, then it is a bad thing that they sound like sonic replicas. There is something suspect about a rendition that is too easy to mistake for a mimic. (Recall again the second thought experiment, which suggests that she would stop making Taylor's Versions if there were not the issue of ownership at stake.)

Although the new versions match the originals remarkably well, Taylor's Versions *could* have sounded even more like the originals if that is what she had wanted. Perhaps she intended for there to be just enough difference that a discerning listener could tell the difference between the two, so that a fan could tell whether they were hearing the objectionable old version or the commendable new version. If that were so, then the differences would not serve any artistic purpose at all. Instead, they would serve as a kind of musical watermark—differences that would slip below the attention of a casual listener, but provide a mark of authenticity for anyone who knew to listen for it.

Second: Considered on their own, Taylor's Versions seem fine. However, this is only because they sound more-or-less the same as the originals. The charms one would find listening to Taylor's Versions without considering the originals are basically the same charms one would find listening to the originals without considering Taylor's Versions. This is not usually the case with renditions—at least, not with good ones.

Contrast the tracks from Ryan Adams's *1989*, a song-for-song remake of Swift's *1989*. Ian Crouch of the *New Yorker* writes that "Adams took songs that, due to their popularity, belong to the world, and made them his own."[12] It is certainly an album of renditions. Adams transmogrifies bouncy pop into his particular flavor of alt-Americana. He intends his tracks to sound very different from Swift's originals, and nobody would mistake one for the other. Crouch, an avowed fan of Adams, suggests that Adams's album is "more earnest and, in its way, sincere and sentimental than the original."[13] Most critics discuss the tracks on Adams's album in explicit contrast with Swift's, sticking to the first mode of evaluation. Yet, critics also draw other contrasts; a common point is to consider "Welcome to New York" (from *1989*) and Adams's earlier song "New York, New York" as rival anthems for New York City. And critics—some of them at least—also listen to Adams's tracks for the features they have by themselves. Crouch, in a critical moment, writes of one track that Adams's singing is "flat and a bit rushed, as if he had memorized the words in a language he doesn't speak."[14] Kyle Coroneos makes the charge more sharply, suggesting that Adams's album "sounds like a dirge; like a low, monotone groan … or like the color grey interpreted into music by players purposely told to not put any life into the effort."[15] Here they consider Adams's covers in the second mode, for what they can offer musically apart from the comparison with Swift's original tracks. If Adams's tracks are good renditions, it would be because the alchemy of converting pop to indie is an interesting transformation or because the result is intrinsically gold. Conversely, if neither obtains, then they are bad renditions. Regardless, it is easier to know how to assess them than it is with Taylor's Versions.

A further dimension of covers is that they can mean something different than the original. We turn to this in the next section.

What It Means When She Sings

A common motivation in recording a rendition cover is to capture a particular feature or aspect of the original, discerned or selected by the artist recording the cover. As Bonnie Fraser of the band Stand Atlantic comments, "I think at the end of the day a cover is supposed to bring two worlds together."[16] This is precluded for Taylor's Versions in the obvious sense that both the original and the new version are recorded by Taylor Swift, but also in the deeper sense that she is not bringing a substantially different musical approach to the new versions. However, one might still ask whether there is a different approach or point-of-view in Taylor's Versions. Do they give us any new insight? Do they mean something different than the originals?

Taylor's Versions on the remake of *Red* feature a woman in her thirties telling about her life as a 21-year-old. However, that kind of perspective is often the case for older songwriters. Even as they develop new material, fans still want to hear the classics. So, years later the singer performs or even records lyrics that are written from the point of view of their younger self. The emotional content may be different in the remake, but it is still the same song and—typically, at least—has more or less the same meaning as the original track.

When Swift sings, she is performing in the persona of the woman in the song. The persona was closer to her actual self when the songs were newer and she was younger, but there has always been pretense involved. Just as she can sing in the persona of a woman who murders her friend's husband (in the song "No Body, No Crime," from *Evermore*), she can sing in the persona of a 21-year-old.[17]

Yet, perhaps it is more complicated than this. Recording Taylor's Versions is an act of defiance, rebuking her old label and the people who own the originals. If this is part of the artistic content of Taylor's

Version, rather than merely its commercial context, then she is not singing in the persona of a 21-year-old in Taylor's Version of *Red*—or, at least, she is not merely doing that. Instead, she is also expressing a defiance that is absent from the original. To appreciate the new versions, a listener ought to understand them as a protest against her treatment by her old production company. Understood in this way, Taylor's Versions would be *about* the originals in a way that the originals are not about themselves. In short, they would be *referential.*[18]

If Taylor's Versions are referential in this way, listeners would need to know about the originals in order to understand the new versions. It is plausible even to think that listeners would need to compare the new versions to the originals. The fullest appreciation would require listening to the two side by side. The discerning listener would still seek out the originals, for the sake of comparison, which would yield profits for the owners of the original. This would undermine Swift's plan that Taylor's Versions should displace the originals. So, taking Taylor's Versions to be referential in this way makes their artistic success incompatible with Swift's commercial goals. That would be a tragic Catch 22.[19]

Whether or not Taylor's Versions are referential depends, at least in part, on Swift's intentions. And certainly she does not intend to tragically frustrate her own intentions. So (we think) the best interpretation is that Taylor's Versions are not referential after all. The relation to the originals is a commercial and historical one, rather than one of artistic content. We would not lose anything aesthetically if her plan succeeds and the originals fall into obscurity. Knowing the original would become trivia, like knowing about foreign bootleg versions of those tracks.[20]

So, Should We Listen to Taylor's Versions?

We have not taken a definite stand on the question of whether Taylor's Versions are covers or not. The word "cover" is not precise enough to carry that kind of weight. What we have claimed is that they are *like* covers in important respects, more so than the usual case when an aging artist simply records or performs new versions of their earlier hits. Regardless of whether we call them covers or not, distinctions from the philosophy of covers help us think about what is going on here. Taylor's Versions (most of them, anyway) are best understood as mimics. In singing them, Swift is occupying the same persona that she occupied in the original. Even if she is singing in defiance of her old label, she is not singing *about* that defiance.

There is an adjacent question with more practical upshot: If you are going to listen to Swift's albums, should you listen to Taylor's Versions or the originals? The decision is a commercial and symbolic choice, regardless of aesthetic considerations or artistic taste. If you are listening to the radio, the choice will be made for you.

Notes

1   In a speech at the Nashville Songwriter Awards in September 2022. (See Jessica Nicholson, "Taylor Swift Accepts Songwriter-Artist of the Decade Honor at Nashville Songwriter Awards: Read Her Full Speech," *Billboard*, September 21, 2022, https://www.billboard.com/music/country/taylor-swift-nashville-songwriter-awards-full-speech-1235142144/ [accessed June 1, 2023].)

2   Will Leonard, "Tower Tracker," *Chicago Daily Tribune*, April 16, 1952, A4.

3   *VocaDB*, "Self-cover," last modified February 7, 2024, https://vocadb.net/T/391/self-cover (accessed February 13, 2024).

4   Taylor Swift, "Taylor Swift's 10-Minute Version of All Too Well Almost Wasn't Recorded (Extended) | Tonight Show," interview by Jimmy Fallon, *The Tonight Show*, November 11, 2021, https://www.youtube.com/watch?v=0Kr4JO9591c (accessed June 1, 2023).

5   Chris Willman, "iHeart Promises to Only Play Taylor Swift's New Versions of Her Songs, Once They're Out," *Variety*, November 17, 2021, https://variety.com/2021/music/news/iheart-taylor-swift-will-only-play-new-versions-1235114816/ (accessed June 1, 2023).

6   On the difficulties in defining "cover," see P. D. Magnus, *A Philosophy of Cover Songs* (Cambridge, UK: Open Book Publishers, 2022), chap. 1.

7   See Cristyn Magnus, P. D. Magnus and Christy Mag Uidhir, "Judging Covers," *Journal of Aesthetics and Art Criticism* 71, no. 4 (2013): 361–70; and Cristyn Magnus, P. D. Magnus, Christy Mag Uidhir and Ron McClamrock, "Appreciating Covers," *Nordic Journal of Aesthetics* 63 (2022): 106–25.

8   For example, see sara, "Taylor Swift Love Story 2008 vs 2021 Re-recording (Vocal Comparison)," February 12, 2021, video, https://www.youtube.com/watch?v=osLG1XnYkbQ (accessed June 1, 2023).

9   Grammar and spelling as given. Comment on Swift Leaks 2.0, "Taylor Swift—'Red' Album Comparison (2012 vs Taylor's Version)," April 14, 2022, video, https://www.youtube.com/watch?v=geK8WKHNMXo (accessed June 1, 2023).

10 Taylor Swift, "Taylor Swift Reacts to Princess Diana's Revenge Dress Fan Theory," interview by Scott Evans, *Access Hollywood*, November 12, 2021, https://www.youtube.com/watch?v=XQEvgkfu5Dk (accessed June 1, 2023).

11 Taylor Swift, "Taylor Swift Says She Went 'Line By Line' on Every 'Fearless' Song | PEOPLE," interview, *People*, April 9, 2021, https://www.youtube.com/watch?v=QAnbsUz1fOs (accessed June 1, 2023).

12 Ian Crouch, "Haters Gonna Hate: Listening to Ryan Adams's '1989'," *The New Yorker*, September 22, 2015, https://www.newyorker.com/culture/culture-desk/haters-gonna-hate-listening-to-ryan-adams-1989 (accessed June 1, 2023).

13 Ibid.

14 Ibid.

15 Kyle Coroneos, "Bullshit," *Saving Country Music*, September 21, 2015, https://www.savingcountrymusic.com/album-review-ryan-adams-1989/ (accessed June 1, 2023).

16 Bonnie Fraser and Miki Rich, "Behind Stand Atlantic's Like a Version 'Righteous' (Interview)," interview, Triple J, August 27, 2020, https://www.youtube.com/watch?v=6CrtLf-BC5k (accessed June 1, 2023).

17 For more on Swift's personas, see Ley David Elliette Cray's chapter in this volume.

18 The label here echoes our discussion of *referential covers*.

19 The editor points out that a longtime fan might already own the originals and that a new fan might illegally download them, so that the owners of the originals would make no money. However, this would mean that the true audience for Taylor's Versions is just old fans and pirates—a contortion that we find implausible.

20 Ley David Elliette Cray reaches a different conclusion in her contribution to this volume. While we agree that Swift's project of re-recording is an act of defiance, we do not see how that defiance becomes part of the artistic content of the tracks themselves.

3

Conceptual Art (Taylor's Version)

Sherri Irvin

Introduction

Let's say you signed your first record contract when you were a teenager. This was your dream, so of course you accepted the terms, which included signing away the rights to your master recordings. This gave the record label the power to license your songs for movies, TV shows, ads, and streaming services. You became a huge star with an incredible career, and you wanted to renegotiate, to buy back the masters and regain artistic control. But the negotiations failed, and you left the label. Then the label was bought by your nemesis, your bully, giving him the power to license your work—and the profits. But there was a loophole: the law allows you, as the songwriter, to produce new recordings. So that's what you did: you recorded new masters, replicating the sound of the originals, and encouraged your fans to abandon the originals and switch to the new versions. It worked: your huge and loyal fan base gravitated to the new records, sought them out on streaming platforms, and shared tips about how to hide the old versions. The new records were huge sellers, topping the charts. Anyone licensing the earlier versions for an ad or movie would risk alienating your fans and mobilizing a campaign of resistance. You won: you wrested back control over your early works and the associated profits.

This is the story of Taylor Swift's ongoing project of re-recording her first six studio albums. I'll use the name *Taylor's Versions* to refer to this project as a whole. At a glance, the project might seem more financial than artistic: it's a copying project designed to put control and profits back in the artist's hands. But I want to explore another way of understanding the project, one that positions it in the tradition of conceptual art. This might seem surprising: conceptual art is often thought of as an arcane and unapproachable art form involving weird or boring objects in museums. But over the decades conceptual art has broadened into a movement that encompasses explorations of institutional power, social hierarchy, and community participation. I'll argue that it is fruitful to think of *Taylor's Versions* as conceptual art, even if Swift herself doesn't see the project directly in those terms. Seen in this light, *Taylor's Versions* has both notable strengths and marked limitations.

Taylor's Versions as an Artistic Project

My primary focus will be less on specific albums, such as *Red (Taylor's Version)*, and more on the *project* of which they are a part: Swift's project of re-recording her early albums and securing the new versions' uptake as replacements for the originals. Understanding the project will require thinking about individual songs and albums and how they relate to the earlier recordings. But looking at *Taylor's Versions* as a unified project will help us identify features of Swift's artistic practice that connect to conceptual art.

As an artistic project, *Taylor's Versions* involves more than just making the recordings. Swift's goal was and is to motivate her fan base, and those who might license her music, to shift away from the earlier versions and toward the new versions. This is far from a given and requires a specific strategy. After all, there is nothing preventing anyone from continuing to license the originals, which have historical authenticity and popularity on their side. Previous re-recording projects by other artists have often stumbled badly at the uptake stage. After Swift announced her intention to re-record her albums, Tim Ingham of *Rolling Stone* interviewed music industry experts about re-recording, revealing general pessimism. English new wave band

Squeeze re-recorded several of their hits to make them available for licensing at lower cost, but songwriter and lead singer Glenn Tilbrook noted, "10 years later, we've not had a single uptake."[1]

Allen Kovac, who manages major acts including Blondie (who re-recorded several hits) and Mötley Crüe, suggests that re-recording projects are rarely successful due to what we might call a loss of flavor:

> When you re-record, do you ever capture that same atmosphere? Do you have the same band, the same studio? What is it you're trying to do—say to your fans, "Don't listen to the music you already love"? I don't know fans like that …. If you could show me [one artist for whom] it's worked out well, I'd say it's a great idea and everyone should do it; I just haven't seen any evidence of that.[2]

Kovac notes that proposals to license re-recordings rather than originals to reduce cost are usually rejected for this reason.

Securing uptake requires direct attention, over and above simply making re-recordings. As we will see, the stunning success of *Taylor's Versions* so far reveals Swift's creative attention to uptake as a key element.

What Is Conceptual Art?

To get a handle on my claim that *Taylor's Versions* can fruitfully be seen as a conceptual art project, we need to know what conceptual art is in the first place. Conceptual art has often been framed as art that foregrounds ideas as much as (or more than) sensory structures like pictures or melodies.[3] While conceptual art narrowly construed had its heyday in the 1960s and 1970s, its precursors date back to the early twentieth century, and the expression "conceptual art" is now used broadly to refer to works that have a key conceptual element even if they also involve an elaborate sensory experience.

A few examples will provide a sense of the flavor and development of conceptual art. In 1915, Marcel Duchamp took an ordinary snow shovel, painted the words "In advance of the broken arm" on its rim, and hung it from the ceiling of a gallery for display.[4] In 1952, John Cage composed *4'33"*, a work of music that musicians perform by remaining silent.[5] In 1953, Robert Rauschenberg acquired a drawing by painter Willem de Kooning and erased it, leaving behind only suggestive smudges, to produce Rauschenberg's work *Erased de Kooning Drawing*.[6]

In 1966, On Kawara began his series *Today*, for which he made thousands of paintings, each simply showing the current date on white against a monochrome background, using the date conventions of the region where he made the painting.[7] In 1969, Robert Barry created *All the Things I Know but of Which I Am Not at the Moment Thinking: 1:36 pm; June 15, 1969*. The work is displayed by inscribing the words of its title in pencil on the wall.[8] Many of these early conceptual works exhibited a stripped-down minimalism—it doesn't get much more minimal than silence, after all—along with resistance to the idea of the artist as a fabricator of elaborate objects or melodies.

In the 1970s and beyond, conceptual art reintegrated much more sensory richness. It continued to raise questions about the nature of art, the artist's role, and—increasingly—the institutions and power structures in which artists and their works are caught up. From 1973 to 1979, Mary Kelly created *Post-Partum Document*, a massive work that integrated babies' garments, soiled diaper linings, and crayon scribble drawings with tables, diagrams, and notes documenting the child's development and the mother's reflections, bringing into the art world a set of topics and concerns that had long been invisible due to women's exclusion from art creation.[9] Starting in the 1980s, Louise Lawler took photographs of artworks by other artists in various settings of preparation, sale, and display: at auction, during museum installation, and in private boardrooms and bedrooms, where they serve decorative or corporate purposes at odds with the ideals touted for high art.[10] In 1985, the Guerilla Girls started their campaign of posters highlighting the fact that women are present in museums primarily in nude depictions rather than as artists.[11]

Elements of interaction or participation have been increasingly prominent in conceptual art of the past few decades. From 1986 to 1990, Adrian Piper created *My Calling (Card) #1*, a series of interactive performances in everyday settings that involved Piper presenting a pre-printed calling card to people who made racist comments in her presence.[12] In her 2010 performance *The Artist Is Present*, Marina Abramović sat for almost three months in a chair at the Museum of Modern Art for all of its opening hours, allowing visitors to sit across from her and gaze into her eyes for as long as they chose.[13]

Art in the broadly conceptual vein, then, can take a wide variety of forms, involving either simple or complex objects and experiences. But a common thread is that it often consists in the artist challenging concepts of art or intervening in the roles, power structures, and social practices that govern the creation and circulation of art. In the following sections, we'll see how *Taylor's Versions* exhibits many of the same tendencies as works squarely in the lineage of conceptual art, including the appropriation of structures that already exist into a new work, critique of the institutions and power structures that govern the circulation of art, and an essential element of audience participation.

Appropriation

Conceptual art has often involved appropriation, the artistic practice of incorporating material from other artworks or cultural domains directly into a new work. Duchamp appropriated a snow shovel into *In Advance of the Broken Arm*, Rauschenberg appropriated a drawing by de Kooning into *Erased de Kooning Drawing*, Kelly appropriated diaper linings and babies' garments, and Lawler appropriated the works of other artists by photographing them. Other artists have gone even further with appropriation, making works that are close copies of earlier artworks. Starting in the 1960s, Sturtevant produced close copies of work by artists including Andy Warhol and Roy Lichtenstein, using similar techniques and materials. She even borrowed one of Warhol's screens to produce her appropriations of his Marilyn Monroe works.[14] For her 1981 project *After Walker Evans*, Sherrie Levine re-photographed a series of photographic works by famed Depression-era photographer Walker Evans and presented the results as her own works.[15]

Of course, any time you record a song that has been recorded before, you are appropriating a structure from another work into a new context. But since this is part of standard practice in pop music, that's not the act of appropriation that stands out. What stands out is that Swift has appropriated the precise sonic qualities of her earlier recordings, with results that are near simulacra.

Like her predecessors in appropriation art, Swift is not trying to deceive us: in adding "*(Taylor's Version)*" to the titles of her re-recorded albums, she openly acknowledges that these are new versions that she endorses and over which she has a proprietary right. Swift has also, like some appropriation artists before her, added marks that distinguish her new works from the originals, such as the inclusion of new songs and longer versions of original songs as bonus tracks on the *Taylor's Version* albums. Sturtevant, similarly, incorporated an element in each of her works of appropriation to distinguish it visually from the original.[16]

The fact that *Taylor's Versions* involves self-appropriation, rather than appropriation of work by others, distinguishes it from most conceptual artworks involving appropriation. But self-appropriation is not unprecedented: for her 1995 work *They Have Always Wanted Me to Do This*, Louise Lawler photographed one of her own earlier photographic works, itself depicting two other artists' works at auction, hanging in a gallery.[17] While Lawler's self-appropriation points wryly toward the prospect of indefinite regress in appropriation, self-appropriation can also be used for political purposes. Justo Serrano Zamora and Macarena Martín Martínez use the term "self-appropriation" to describe the intentional reclaiming, re-deployment, and recontextualization of one's cultural products, and even one's very body.[18] For instance, Martín Martínez describes an example of an Afro-Latina who writes and performs slam poetry to "re-appropriate the agency over her body by moving from a self-imposed invisibility and silence," developed in response to racist and misogynistic self-conceptions foisted upon her under white supremacy, "to a non-objectified visible position" that includes a "self-representative embodied narrative."[19] Through this act of self-appropriation, she reclaims the ability to define herself and her own experiences.

Swift's act of self-appropriation, somewhat like those Serrano Zamora and Martín Martínez describe, involves resistance to hierarchical power structures. As a woman artist in a male-dominated industry, Swift is caught up in and responding to relations of domination. The fact that Swift, as a teenager and emerging artist, had no leverage to resist signing away the rights to her master recordings is a symptom of systemic music industry exploitation. Swift has sometimes been dismissed as writing about trivialities, in line with the long-standing dismissal of the concerns of women and girls as merely private and not of broader intellectual or artistic interest—the same situation Kelly was responding to with *Post-Partum Document*. By reappropriating her own earlier cultural productions, Swift reasserts the value and importance of her teenage concerns and artistic production from her new position as an influential cultural figure who brings years of additional life experience to bear.

The fact that Swift is not simply replicating, but also evaluating and endorsing, her earlier work is indicated, somewhat ironically, by her decision to change a lyric in the song "Better than Revenge" on *Speak Now (Taylor's Version)* to remove a slut-shaming connotation. Not everyone approves of the change. Larisha Paul, for instance, argues that it would be better for the historical record of Swift's gradual path toward intersectional feminism, and missteps along the way, to remain intact.[20] But by making the change, Swift signals that the appropriation of original songs in *Taylor's Versions* is not simply a rote copying exercise: Swift is critically evaluating the original works along the way, and, where no changes are made, this signals her current endorsement.

Institutional Critique

Swift is using a loophole to do something few artists have previously done, and none with the same degree of comprehensiveness and success: re-record and release her earlier works in a way that undermines an entrenched system of corporate property rights, restoring the artist's ability to control and profit from their own artistic production. In this way, *Taylor's Versions* challenges power dynamics in the music industry. This positions the project in relation to another movement in conceptual art: institutional critique, which highlights the arbitrary and oppressive role of art institutions in restricting the production, distribution, and valuing of artworks.

Conceptual art has sometimes been very pointed in highlighting exploitative art world practices. In 1987, James Luna (who is Luiseño, Puyukitchum, Ipai, and Mexican) first presented *Artifact Piece*, a work involving two vitrines, one containing Luna's personal belongings such as photos and his college diploma and the other containing a bed of sand on which Luna would sometimes lie, wearing a loincloth.[21] *Artifact Piece* skewers museum practices of including Native Americans only as historical objects of study (which has often involved disrespectfully displaying human remains as artifacts for viewing) and not taking them seriously as artists and active members of living contemporary cultures.

For his groundbreaking 1992 work *Mining the Museum*, Fred Wilson appropriated and displayed works from the collection of the Maryland Historical Society in ways that revealed the violent underpinnings of the collection and the society it represented. In one room, Wilson juxtaposed honorific busts of Henry Clay, Andrew Jackson, and Napoleon Bonaparte, all on elaborate pedestals, with three empty pedestals labeled with the names of Benjamin Banneker, Frederick Douglass, and Harriet Tubman.[22] The former group are white men, none with a special connection to Maryland, two of whom owned slaves and the other of whom reversed the French abolition of slavery. The latter group are all prominent Black Marylanders who fought for Black liberation yet are not honored with a bust in the museum's collection. Elsewhere, in a display titled "Metalwork," Wilson juxtaposed elaborate silver serving pieces with slave shackles, underscoring the vicious economy that made it possible for whites to enjoy drinking from silver goblets.[23]

Sometimes conceptual artists intervene directly in institutional practices of acquiring and displaying art. Through his performative artworks, Tino Sehgal has interrupted museums' standard ways of doing business. His 2002 work *This Is Propaganda*, acquired by Tate, requires the museum to train a performer dressed as a museum guard to sing a certain song each time a visitor enters the gallery where the work is displayed.[24] Normally, on acquisition of such a work the museum would do extensive video, photographic, and written documentation to ensure continuity and accuracy of the performance standards over time. But Sehgal forbade the museum from creating an official record. He trained the museum staff directly on the performance requirements, and while staff members are allowed to make notes for their own use, these notes cannot be shared or integrated into an official file.[25] On acquiring the work, then, Tate committed itself to an ongoing practice of oral transmission if the work is not to be lost. Through these processes, Sehgal throws into question the standard museum processes of pinning a work down through an elaborate bureaucracy rather than treating artworks as dynamic, evolving entities within social practices.

With *Taylor's Versions*, Swift is deploying an available but rarely exercised artistic prerogative to disrupt standard music industry practices and economic structures. Normally, the label that owns the master recordings retains the ability to control and profit from the artist's work as presented on those recordings; an artist unable to negotiate for their masters simply moves on to produce new work, though they might occasionally record new (and clearly sonically different) versions of earlier songs. Re-recording that aims to reproduce the sonic qualities of earlier recordings has been uncommon. Decades ago, artists including Chuck Berry and the Everly Brothers re-recorded their hits when they changed labels, allowing the new labels to release greatest hits albums. But as David Browne describes in *Rolling Stone*, "those redos amounted to often bloodless collections that only satisfied their new bosses."[26] More recently, Def Leppard went to great lengths to produce faithful re-recordings of several hits in a dispute with their label, referring to the new recordings as "forgeries" of the originals. But their ability to profit from the new recordings was abetted by contractual terms different from those available to Swift: as Def Leppard's Joe Elliott put it, "Our contract is such that [the label] can't do anything with our music without our permission, not a thing …. So we just sent them a letter saying, 'No matter what you want, you are going to get "no" as an answer, so don't ask.'"[27]

Swift has gone against custom and beyond precedent by producing faithful re-recordings of multiple albums and working to deprive the label of the ability to exercise rights it still holds. As her statements about the project have made clear, she is doing so in response to the exploitative tendencies of the standard arrangements as well as to the gendered power structure that tends to leave men with creative control over—and an outsized share of profit from—women's artistic production.

In her discussion of the motivation for producing *Taylor's Versions*, Swift directly invokes concerns about power and domination. The initial impetus for *Taylor's Versions* was the fact that the label owning her masters was purchased by Scooter Braun, whom Swift has accused of years of "incessant, manipulative bullying," including involvement with client Kanye West during the production of a video that Swift characterizes as revenge porn, showing Swift nude in bed with West.[28] In the CBS interview with correspondent Tracy Smith where she first clearly announced her intention to re-record her albums, Swift gives a chilling account of the stakes of men's nonconsensual sexualization of a woman artist:

> Swift: Since all my addresses are on the internet, people tend to
> show up uninvited. Like, you know, dudes that think we have an
> imaginary marriage.
> Smith: And you mentioned that you keep wound dressing with you?
> Swift: Yeah. I've had a lot of stalkers show up to the house, armed. So,
> we have to think that way.[29]

Swift also notes a gendered double standard for evaluating artists' business choices: "There's a different vocabulary for men and women in the music industry …. A man does something, it's 'strategic'; a woman does the same thing, it's 'calculated.' A man is allowed to 'react'; a woman can only 'over-react.'"[30]

By painstakingly re-recording her early albums and (as we will see in the next section) creatively deploying her fan base, Swift has depleted much of the economic value of her early masters and regained creative control, thereby shifting the balance of power back to herself while also drawing attention to gendered power structures and the tendency of standard industry practices to exploit the vulnerability of early-career artists. In a social media post about her re-recording plans, Swift expresses her hope that "young artists or kids with musical dreams will read this and learn about how to better protect themselves in a negotiation. You deserve to own the art you make."[31]

Participation

While institutional critique had its heyday between the 1960s and 1980s, Swift updates her critique for the twenty-first century with a third hallmark of conceptual art: a participatory element, namely, the creative deployment of her large and dedicated fan base. Because the original albums were wildly popular and Swift had no power to quash them, mobilizing her fans to abandon the much-loved originals and shift to Taylor's Versions is essential to the project's success.

Over the past several decades, artists have increasingly provided opportunities for audiences to interact with or participate in art.[32] In the 1960s, Brazilian artist Lygia Clark created a variety of sculptural works that audience members could manipulate, play with, reshape, and even wear. This allowed for different kinds of experiences than are available simply through looking or listening, both by engaging more senses (including touch, hearing, and smell) and by giving the audience the opportunity to interact with objects that sometimes seemed to have a mind of their own. Of her *Bichos* (critters), hinged sheet metal sculptures that audiences were invited to reconfigure, she said:

> Each *Bicho* is an organic entity that fully reveals itself within its inner
>   time of expression. ...
> It is a living organism, a work essentially active. A full integration,
>   existential, is established between it and us.
> There is no room for passivity in the relationship that is established
>   between the *Bichos* and us, neither from them nor from us.
> What happens is a body-to-body between two living entities.[33]

Audience accounts confirm that interacting with the *Bichos* is an experience of one's own agency confronting another agency, rather than simply manipulating a passive object.[34]

Audience members have sometimes been invited to affirm commitments or engage in transactions. Adrian Piper's *The Probable Trust Registry: The Rules of the Game #1–3* (2013–17) gives viewers the opportunity to affirm three statements:

> I will always mean what I say.
> I will always do what I say I am going to do.
> I will always be too expensive to buy.[35]

Each statement has its own desk where the participant can commit to the statement by signing a contract. Those who sign are added to a registry that all other signatories have access to, making for a degree of joint accountability. Piper's work invites audiences to reflect on their own integrity and raises questions about the relationship of art contexts to real-life contexts: does signing the contract as part of an art experience actually mean anything, or is it more like reading lines in a play?

Other artistic projects have moved audience participation out of the primarily artistic context and explored new modes of social and economic organization. Fran Ilich's *Spacebank*, beginning in 2005, allowed participants to invest in a virtual currency to micro-finance art and community projects.[36] With his *Edible Estates*, also starting in 2005, Fritz Haeg has worked with families and communities to create community gardens that enrich outdoor space and provide edible produce.[37] The gardens shed light on what is lost when lawns are the prevailing landscape: opportunities for sensory richness, meaningful creative activity, engagement with nature and community, and nourishment. Mammalian Diving Reflex, with their work *Haircuts by Children* (2006–), organizes children to run a hair salon and invites brave passersby for haircuts.[38] While lighthearted, the work explores the tendency to see children as unfit for serious responsibilities—though they often embrace such responsibilities when offered—as well as the sense of risk and vulnerability inherent in giving up control over a prominent aspect of our bodily appearance, even when the change is temporary. With their 2004 work *Guaraná Power*, SUPERFLEX collaborated with Brazilian farmers who grow guaraná to create and market a new guaraná drink to compete with those marketed by a global monopoly that had undermined the farmers' livelihood by drastically driving down the price of the crop.[39] SUPERFLEX expanded their support for guaraná production with their 2007 work *Free Beer* by creating a free, open-source recipe for a beer with added guaraná and colorful branding materials, publishing these elements under a Creative Commons license so anyone can use them. *Free Beer* has been produced by brewers around the world.[40] SUPERFLEX "describe[s] their projects as tools for spectators to actively participate in the development of experimental models that alter the prevailing model of economic production."[41]

Participatory projects don't always bear clear hallmarks of art. While Haeg's *Edible Estates* are sometimes commissioned by art museums and are often accompanied by a more traditional art exhibition, the garden itself need not be understood as an artwork by everyone who participates in creating and maintaining it. Likewise for *Spacebank*, *Haircuts by Children*, *Guaraná Power*, and *Free Beer*. What marks these projects as art is the fact that an established artist or art collective pursues them as an avowed part of an artistic practice, placing them in the lineage of participatory conceptual art.

While the re-recording portion of *Taylor's Versions* was completed exclusively by Swift and a team of music professionals, the uptake portion, which was essential to Swift's aim of regaining control over her work, required active participation by the audience, rather as the success of *Free Beer* required uptake from brewers to produce and market the guaraná beer. Moreover, while many of these conceptual art projects invite people to do something fun or undertake a new experience, Swift is asking fans to give up something that matters to them. As Katie Goh puts it, *Taylor's Versions* "asks a tough task of her fans: to renegotiate their love for original recordings that Swift says are now toxic."[42] Fans clearly recognize this as a loss. After the 2021 release of the first re-recording, *Fearless (Taylor's Version)*, Goh observed:

> Something is missing for me on the re-recordings of the most juvenile-in-theme songs: Swift's near-yelp on Fifteen's climax … has been smoothed out and she's no longer straining with frantic desperation on You Belong With Me's choruses. These might be objectively better vocal performances, but the unpolished inflections of the original songs have become a sense memory. I hear them and I see my younger self sitting on the bus clutching a blue iPod nano.[43]

Another fan Goh spoke to finds that the song "Change," originally recorded in 2008, lost its historical connection to "youthful optimism" about the impending Obama presidency when it was re-recorded years later, partly due to "Swift's more mature vocals." "It's the one song from Fearless (2008) that she'll still listen to, but on CD, not via the Braun-benefitting streaming services."[44]

Swift has used a variety of strategies to mobilize her fan base and overcome sources of resistance. She has built enthusiasm for each release by dropping Easter eggs on social media, prompting speculation about which album will come next. She has seeded the albums with new material: reworked and extended versions of original songs as well as first-time releases. And the subtle differences between the originals and the faithful re-recordings have led to a focused intensity in fan reception as listeners notice and remark on changes in intonation, breath, and vocal timbre. Even where a change was experienced as a loss, this attracted listeners to attend carefully and engage in public discourse. Olivia Novato observes:

> Following the release [of *Speak Now (Taylor's Version)*], superfans were quick to note the absence of *the* shaky breath in "Long Live" .... Memes mourning the loss of the shaky breath started popping up around social media moments after the release as fans expressed their sadness about the updated, *sans*-breath recording. R.I.P.[45]

Of course, using creative strategies to attract fans to your new work is commonplace in the music industry. Swift also used strategies to mobilize them *against* the originals. Crucial to this effort is Swift's self-presentation as a victim of misogynistic bullying and music industry exploitation, and as a champion of better opportunities for emerging artists in the future. Joe Coscarelli notes, "You could teach an entire marketing class around the way she's made an esoteric fight among multimillionaires feel intimate and important, demystifying arcane contract minutiae and setting up the decision to stream 'Taylor's Version' over the original like an ethical choice."[46]

Ben Sisario summarizes the participatory element in observing that *Taylor's Versions* reveals one of Swift's "key skills: her effortless mastery of connecting with (and leveraging) her audience .... It's hard to imagine any other star engaging in an act of business retribution while also making it seem so joyful and so participatory for her fans."[47] Swift has enlisted her fans in a form of collective activity they understand as activism in pursuit of an ethically and politically desirable goal.

Conceptual Art (Taylor's Version)

I've pointed out that *Taylor's Versions* exhibits three hallmarks of conceptual art: appropriation, institutional critique, and audience participation. Does this make the project a work of conceptual art? I will offer some considerations that point toward a positive answer. I'll also consider some virtues as well as some shortcomings of *Taylor's Versions* viewed from this perspective.

Philosopher Kendall Walton discusses the fact that placing an artwork in a relevant artistic category, such as conceptual art, affects how we appreciate it.[48] He also notes that some category assignments are correct or appropriate, while others are incorrect: *Fearless (Taylor's Version)* is not an opera or a collection of poetry. Walton identifies four considerations that help to determine category assignment:

(1)   The work has many of the qualities that are standard for works in the category.
(2)   The work "is better, or more interesting or pleasing aesthetically, or more worth experiencing" when seen in relation to the category "than it is when perceived in alternate ways."
(3)   The artist "intended or expected" the work to be seen in relation to the category, or "thought of it as" a member of the category.
(4)   The category "is well established in and recognized by the society in which" the work was made.[49]

Walton notes that the considerations sometimes diverge; but an appropriate category assignment must always involve either consideration (3) or (4), since these are the considerations that give the category historical relevance in relation to the context of the work's making.

We can acknowledge immediately that there is no reason to think Swift intends or expects *Taylor's Versions* to be seen as a conceptual art project. However, conceptual art is historically well established as a category in the twenty-first-century United States (consideration (4)), and I've noted that *Taylor's Versions* has several hallmarks of conceptual art (consideration (1)). So let's focus on consideration (2). I suggest that *Taylor's Versions* has notable merits when seen as a conceptual art project, and seeing it this way directs our attention to features we might otherwise have glossed over.

Thinking of *Taylor's Versions* as a project of appropriation brings into relief three compelling achievements. First, as we've seen, *Taylor's Versions* has prompted very close listening that is aimed at comparing and contrasting the new recording with an earlier version—and, specifically, with that earlier version as remembered rather than as listened to, since fans are encouraged to stop engaging with the earlier recordings. Popular music is sometimes dismissed as a shallow form that does not encourage or reward deep listening, but the response to *Taylor's Versions* demonstrates that fans are carefully assessing specific sonic qualities and their impact. Second, their appropriative nature imbues *Taylor's Versions* with a distinctive aesthetic quality: the uncanny. As Joe Coscarelli describes it:

> The original "Fearless" is one of those albums that I've never stopped listening to, and so I know every breath, pluck and hiccup by heart, and I anticipate the exact sounds to come split-seconds before they happen. But the rerecordings are as if someone came into my room and replaced all the dinged-up furniture I've had forever with spotless versions.[50]

New recordings of the same songs that did not strive to replicate their sonic qualities, and thus engaged not in sonic appropriation but in the far more common practice of recording new and different versions of earlier hits, would not have this uncanny quality.

Third, by prompting close comparison of quasi-simulacra produced in different contexts, *Taylor's Versions* highlights the role of context and authorship in determining the aesthetic quality and impact of a work. "Change" doesn't function the same way when re-recorded long after the context of the Obama presidency. And "a woman in her early 30s getting in the head space of her 18-year-old self to sing about the awkwardnesses of her 15-year-old self," as Jon Caramanica puts it, is very different from the eighteen-year-old woman singing those songs in the first place from the vantage of only a couple of years of reflection and maturity.[51] Joe Coscarelli observes that "the meta-quality and knowingness of hearing her now, at 31, sing lines like [those about achieving more in life than just dating a football player, or the confusion of being a fifteen year old] … can't help be feel more winking than gutting, as they originally played."[52]

When we simply hear a song as performed by a particular person at a given moment, it can be difficult to know what role the person's age, status, or life experience are playing in our response. Hearing two recordings with very similar sonic qualities performed by an artist at two different life stages reveals how entwined our response to the music is with our understanding of the artist. These reflections on authorship and context are in line with those prompted by well-known projects of appropriation art like those of Sherrie Levine and Sturtevant.[53]

I suggest that the participatory element of *Taylor's Versions*, too, is a notable original achievement. While attracting fans to your new work is a standard business or marketing project, motivating them to abandon original recordings that they are profoundly attached to and know breath-by-breath is much more original. With some initial prompting from Swift, this was taken up as a collective project by fans who cultivated a shared sense of moral duty to renounce the earlier recordings. The collective aspect of the project involved fans sharing strategies to avoid accidentally streaming the originals while also creating a sort of mutual accountability to resist temptation to listen to the originals, being prepared instead to engage in public discourse about the re-recordings.

The institutional critique aspect of the project is, in my view, the weakest. Positioning the work as a critique of music industry hierarchies and gendered relations of domination was key to Swift's participatory strategy. However, as legal theorist Anjali Vats notes, Swift's project appropriates and builds not only on her own earlier recordings, but also on a long history of strategies by artists of color to reclaim rights to their music in contexts of racialized and gendered domination.[54]

While the teenaged Swift freely entered into a contract whose standard terms allowed her to amass extraordinary fame and wealth, many songwriters and recording artists of color experienced extreme forms of racialized financial exploitation that left them in poverty despite writing or recording transformative hits. As Vats discusses, Black artists, many of them women, have been active and creative in resisting this exploitation. In 1921 Juanita Stinnette Chappelle made the "revolutionary move" of becoming the first Black woman to hold an ownership stake in a record label. She thereby "claimed ownership of her master recordings through the co-ownership of her business" and paved the way for other women to own or co-own labels.[55] Dionne Warwick, too, used ownership of a record label as part of a strategy to increase her financial leverage and regain control over her master recordings in the wake of what she referred to as a "slave contract" with a label owned by a white woman.[56] Moreover, Prince preceded Swift in what we might plausibly regard as a conceptual art project when he renamed himself as a symbol in an intellectual property struggle against Warner Bros.[57] Swift doesn't acknowledge the historical precedent provided by the long struggle of earlier artists against conditions that were often far more exploitative; nor does she openly recognize their role in allowing her to secure more favorable terms even as a teenaged newcomer.

Moreover, as Vats argues, Swift's whiteness is part of the landscape that allows her to present herself in an uncomplicated way as a victim of exploitation. Black women do not benefit from the presumption of innocence and discourse of protection that surround white womanhood. While white women certainly experience gendered harassment and violence, they are more likely than Black women in similar circumstances to be recognized as victims and to benefit from efforts at redress, and less likely to be blamed for the surrounding circumstances. Swift can arouse her fans' ire about Kanye West's so-called "revenge porn" video in part because, as a white woman, she is not presumed to be hypersexual and may be seen as needing protection from West, given the historical positioning of Black men as sexual aggressors against white women. Though Scooter Braun, who Swift identifies as her bully, is white, the Blackness of West, his client, may be implicitly heightening the perception of Braun's culpability.

As we noted earlier, powerful acts of institutional critique have been mounted by artists like James Luna and Fred Wilson who belong to groups overwhelmingly disenfranchised and excluded in art contexts. Self-appropriation, as we saw in discussions by Martín Martínez and Serrano Zamora, has been used by people of color to resist racialized and gendered exploitation. And Black women in the music industry have used creative business strategies to reclaim power, recognition, and profit in the face of severely inequitable treatment. For Swift—whose net worth was $360 million in 2019,[58] when she declared the intention to re-record—to use self-appropriation and institutional critique to mobilize an intensive rescue effort might be seen as a form of audacity, or indeed *caucasity*.[59] But it would be hard to deny the strategy's success: she is reportedly now a billionaire.[60]

Swift is clearly a master of self-appropriation, as she cultivates a persona that motivates intense and lucrative loyalty from her fans. The victim persona that underpins her institutional critique is the extension of the underdog persona she continues to manifest in her music, including through such new hits as "Anti-Hero" from 2022's *Midnights*, where she sings about how she and everyone agree that she is the problem.[61] Her ongoing construction of a vulnerable, relatable girl-next-door persona—periodically engaged in acts of revenge as satisfying as they are petty—is perhaps its own conceptual achievement.

Taylor Swift is a highly successful popular music artist, and the *Taylor's Version* albums belong first and foremost to the category of pop music. To declare that *Taylor's Versions* is a clear exemplar of conceptual art would outstrip the evidence. But considering the project in relation to the conceptual art category helps both to shed light on distinctive aspects of its aesthetic innovation and success—especially in the domains of appropriation and participation—and to reveal that when it comes to Swift's avowed intention of institutional critique, commercial success may have occurred at the expense of greater integrity and attention to historical precursors. Perhaps a convergence of popular and academic discourse about *Taylor's Versions* will raise awareness of the pathbreaking work of Black feminists and other artists of color striving for intersectional liberation on both gender and racial fronts.[62]

Notes

1   Tim Ingham, "Taylor Swift Plans to Re-record Her Hits. Here's What She Might Be Facing," *Rolling Stone*, December 9, 2019, https://www.rollingstone.com/pro/features/taylor-swift-plans-to-re-record-her-hits-heres-what-she-might-be-facing-923019/ (accessed August 8, 2023).

2   Ibid.

3   Peter Goldie and Elisabeth Schellekens, *Who's Afraid of Conceptual Art?* (London: Routledge, 2010).

4   "Marcel Duchamp, *In Advance of the Broken Arm*. August 1964 (fourth version, after the lost original of November 1915)," *Museum of Modern Art*, https://www.moma.org/learn/moma_learning/marcel-duchamp-in-advance-of-the-broken-arm-august-1964-fourth-version-after-lost-original-of-november-1915/ (accessed August 8, 2023).

5   "4'33"," *JohnCage.org*, https://johncage.org/pp/John-Cage-Work-Detail.cfm?work_ID=17 (accessed August 8, 2023).

6   "Robert Rauschenberg, *Erased de Kooning Drawing*, 1953," *San Francisco Museum of Modern Art*, https://www.sfmoma.org/artwork/98.298/ (accessed August 8, 2023).

7   "On Kawara: Date Paintings," Guggenheim Museums and Foundation, https://www.guggenheim.org/video/on-kawara-date-paintings (accessed August 8, 2023).

8   Alexandra Nicolaides, "Robert Barry: All the Things I Know … 1962 to Present," *The Brooklyn Rail*, https://brooklynrail.org/2015/03/artseen/robert-barry-all-the-things-i-know-1962-to-present (accessed August 8, 2023).

9   "Post-Partum Document," *MaryKellyArtist.com*, https://www.marykellyartist.com/post-partum-document-1973-79 (accessed August 8, 2023).

10 Sherri Irvin, "Artwork and Document in the Photography of Louise Lawler," *Journal of Aesthetics and Art Criticism* 70, no. 1 (2012): 79–90.

11   "Posters, Stickers, Billboards, Videos, Actions: 1985–2023," *GuerrillaGirls. com*, https://www.guerrillagirls.com/projects (accessed August 8, 2023).

12   Adrian Piper, "My Calling (Card) #1," *Walker Art Center*, https://walkerart. org/collections/artworks/my-calling-card-1 (accessed August 8, 2023).

13   "Marina Abramović: The Artist Is Present," *Museum of Modern Art*, https://www.moma.org/learn/moma_learning/marina-abramovic-marina-abramovic-the-artist-is-present-2010/ (accessed August 8, 2023).

14   Christopher Bagley, "Sturtevant: Repeat Offender," *W*, May 8, 2014, https://www.wmagazine.com/story/sturtevant-moma-retrospective (accessed August 8, 2023).

15   For further discussion, see Sherri Irvin, "Appropriation and Authorship in Contemporary Art," *British Journal of Aesthetics* 45, no. 2 (2005): 123–37.

16   Bill Arning, "Sturtevant," *Journal of Contemporary Art* 2, no. 2 (1989): 39–50; 46.

17   Irvin, "Artwork and Document," 80.

18   Justo Serrano Zamora, "Overcoming Hermeneutical Injustice: Cultural Self-Appropriation and the Epistemic Practices of the Oppressed," *Journal of Speculative Philosophy* 31, no. 2 (2017): 299–310. Macarena Martín Martínez, "Corporeal Activism in Elizabeth Acevedo's *The Poet X*: Towards a Self-Appropriation of US Afro-Latinas' Bodies," *Revista de Estudios Norteamericanos* 25 (2020): 1–23.

19   Martín Martínez, "Corporeal Activism," 1.

20   Larisha Paul, "'Better Than Revenge (Taylor's Version)': Why Taylor Swift Shouldn't Rewrite Her Own History," *Rolling Stone*, May 15, 2023, https://www.rollingstone.com/music/music-features/better-than-revenge-taylor-swift-speak-now-taylors-version-problematic-song-recording-1234732910/ (accessed August 8, 2023).

21   "Acquisition: James Luna," *National Gallery of Art*, January 28, 2022, https://www.nga.gov/press/acquisitions/2022/luna.html (accessed August 8, 2023).

22   "Mining the Museum: Pedestals, Globe, and Busts," *Maryland Center for History and Culture*, https://www.mdhistory.org/resources/mining-the-museum-pedestals-globe-and-busts/ (accessed August 8, 2023).

23   "Mining the Museum: 'Metalwork, 1793–1880,'" *Maryland Center for History and Culture*, https://www.mdhistory.org/resources/mining-the-museum-metalwork-1793-1880/ (accessed August 8, 2023).

24   "'This Is Propaganda,' Tino Sehgal, 2002," *Tate*, https://www.tate.org.uk/art/artworks/sehgal-this-is-propaganda-t12057 (accessed August 8, 2023).

25 Vivian van Saaze, "In the Absence of Documentation. Remembering Tino Sehgal's Constructed Situations," *Revista de História da Arte* 4 (2015): 55–63.

26 David Browne, "Remaking Your Old Songs Used to Be Considered Lazy, Shady, and So Uncool. What Changed?," *Rolling Stone*, January 18, 2023, https://www.rollingstone.com/music/music-features/album-remakes-u2-taylor-swift-1234660335/ (accessed August 8, 2023).

27 "Def Leppard Re-recording 'Forgeries' of Old Hits," *Rolling Stone*, July 3, 2012, https://www.rollingstone.com/music/music-news/def-leppard-re-recording-forgeries-of-old-hits-247079/ (accessed August 8, 2023).

28 Taylor Swift, "For years I asked, pleaded for a chance to own my work," *Tumblr*, June 30, 2019, https://taylorswift.tumblr.com/post/185958366550/for-years-i-asked-pleaded-for-a-chance-to-own-my (accessed August 8, 2023).

29 Taylor Swift, "Taylor Swift on 'Lover' and Haters," interview by Tracy Smith, *CBS News*, August 25, 2019, https://www.cbsnews.com/news/taylor-swift-on-lover-and-haters/ (accessed August 8, 2023).

30 Ibid.

31 Swift, "For years I asked."

32 Sherri Irvin, *Immaterial: Rules in Contemporary Art* (Oxford: Oxford University Press, 2022), chap. 4.

33 Artist's statement translated by Licia R. Olivetti and reprinted in Cornelia Butler and Luis Pérez-Oramas, *Lygia Clark: The Abandonment of Art, 1948–1988* (New York: Museum of Modern Art, 2014), 160.

34 Irvin, *Immaterial*, 210.

35 "Adrian Piper. The Probable Trust Registry: The Rules of the Game #1–3," *Staatliche Museen zu Berlin*, https://www.smb.museum/en/exhibitions/detail/adrian-piper-the-probable-trust-registry-the-rules-of-the-game-1-3/ (accessed August 8, 2023).

36 Nato Thompson, ed., *Living as Form: Socially Engaged Art from 1991–2011* (New York: Creative Time, 2012), 172.

37 "Edible Estates," *FritzHaeg.com*, http://www.fritzhaeg.com/garden/initiatives/edibleestates/main.html (accessed August 8, 2023).

38 "Haircuts by Children—Mammalian Diving Reflex," *Mammalian.ca*, https://mammalian.ca/projects/haircuts-by-children/ (accessed August 8, 2023).

39 "Guaraná Power—Superflex," *Superflex.net*, https://superflex.net/works/guarana_power (accessed August 8, 2023).

40   Free Beer, "Free Beer—Performa Version," *FreeBeer.org*, https://freebeer.
     org/blog/ (accessed August 8, 2023).

41   Thompson, *Living as Form*, 226.

42   Katie Goh, "'I Made My Peace': Fans Divided over Taylor Swift's
     Re-recording Project," *The Guardian*, April 15, 2021, https://www.
     theguardian.com/music/2021/apr/15/i-made-my-peace-fans-divided-
     over-taylor-swifts-re-recording-project (accessed August 8, 2023).

43   Ibid.

44   Ibid.

45   Olivia Novato, "Here's What Changed in *Speak Now (Taylor's Version)*,"
     CR Fashion Book, July 7, 2023, https://crfashionbook.com/heres-what-
     has-changed-in-speak-now-taylors-version/ (accessed August 8, 2023;
     emphasis in original). A meme linked in the article can be found here:
     https://twitter.com/swifferwins/status/1677181791105437697

46   Jon Caramanica, Joe Coscarelli, Jon Pareles, Ben Sisario and Lindsay
     Zoladz, "Taylor Swift Remade 'Fearless' as 'Taylor's Version.' Let's
     Discuss," *New York Times*, April 9, 2021, https://www.nytimes.
     com/2021/04/09/arts/music/taylor-swift-fearless-taylors-version.html
     (accessed August 8, 2023).

47   Ibid.

48   Kendall L. Walton, "Categories of Art," *The Philosophical Review* 79, no. 3
     (1970): 334–67.

49   Ibid., 357.

50   Caramanica et al., "Taylor Swift."

51   Ibid.

52   Ibid.

53   Irvin, "Appropriation and Authorship."

54   Anjali Vats, "Owning Your Masters (Taylor's Version): Postfeminist
     Tactical Copyright and the Erasure of Black Intellectual Labor," in *The
     Routledge Companion to Intersectionalities*, ed. Jennifer C. Nash and
     Samantha Pinto (London: Routledge, 2023), 552–73.

55   Ibid., 558.

56   Ibid., 559.

57   Ibid., 561.

58   "Taylor Swift," *Forbes*, updated February 13, 2024, https://www.forbes.
     com/profile/taylor-swift/ (accessed February 13, 2024).

59 *Dictionary.com*, s.v. "Caucacity," December 21, 2020, https://www.dictionary.com/e/slang/caucacity/ (accessed August 8, 2023). 'Caucasity' is a widespread alternate spelling.

60 Devon Pendleton, Claire Ballentine, Marie Patino, Chloe Whiteaker and Diana Li, "Taylor Swift Hits Billionaire Status as Net Worth Surges with Eras Tour," *Bloomberg*, October 26, 2023, https://www.bloomberg.com/graphics/2023-taylor-swift-net-worth-billionaire/ (January 8, 2024).

61 I'm grateful to Jeremy Fried for this observation.

62 I'm grateful to Cheryl Frazier, Jeremy Fried, Stephanie Holt, and Babak Khoshroo for helpful feedback on an earlier version.

4

The Art and Craft of (Re-)recording

Michael Thomas Connolly

Introduction

When news of Taylor Swift's re-recording project began to spread, my social media feeds bubbled with discussion from many of the musicians, audio professionals, and Swifties in my friend circle. In mainstream discussions, people sensed that the idea of re-recording an entire discography was an ambitious and thought-provoking project—but fewer, I think, had a concrete sense of what the actual process might entail.

The next time you press "play" or drop the needle on your favorite Taylor Swift album, I invite you to put on a great pair of headphones and reflect for a moment on what you're hearing. In an imagined space before you, you perceive a woman performing a song, with a killer band behind her, supporting each dramatic turn in the song's story. Countless choices in preproduction, recording, editing, mixing, and mastering are invisible to you; you simply experience "Taylor Swift"—a beautiful illusion that life and emotional connection are somehow released from plastic and metal, appearing in the empty space before you.

I am not a philosopher. I am a recording engineer, producer, and musician. The ability of a recording to summon life in front of our minds—even to bring people back from the dead—has always fascinated me. Over the past twenty-five years or so, it's been my privilege to record and mix thousands of songs, and to spend time with all manner of artists as we jointly shepherd their projects into the world. I've come to realize that recording is fundamentally more "construction" than "capture." Just as moviemaking requires more than a lead actor and a script, a recording project requires the output of an entire creative team working together. My goal is to walk you through the process of making an album, step-by-step, and in doing so provide insight into just how many opportunities there are for creative contributions from all involved parties.

So, what exactly happens inside a recording studio? If we look to movies and television, we know how the scene goes: A musician slumps over her guitar, frowning because inspiration hasn't yet struck. She's missing that critical spark—the one key hook that will make the song come together. Suddenly, our hero remembers a conversation with a kindly mentor, and the missing song lyrics appear, fully formed, in her mind. The song writes itself—and now all it takes is a trip to the studio to capture it faithfully. We cut to a montage of concerts performed to ever-growing audiences, rubbing shoulders with world leaders, and eventual Grammy Award acceptance.

It's an appealing fantasy of how music is made—but one that leaves out a number of steps. Scientists know that TV science emphasizes test-tubes of brightly colored fluids while downplaying long hours of grant-writing. I imagine that boxing trainers would tell you that Rocky would need more than a brisk run up the Philadelphia Museum of Art's steps to be fully prepared for his fight. And as a recording engineer and producer, I can report that the inside of a recording studio is a little different than it appears on television.

So, what's realistic and what's fictional in the made-for-TV version of the recording process I described? You might guess that the flash of inspiration is a myth. But those certainly do happen. While songwriters may sometimes toil over song lyrics for months or years, other songs certainly seem to emerge fully formed with very little conscious effort—at least, if we discount the years or decades of practice that precede those "spontaneous moments."

Actually, the key premise I'd like to dispute is that one brings a song to the studio and captures it faithfully. There is no fact of the matter when it comes to recorded music; instead, a recording is the result of a long series of choices by the entire creative team—musicians, engineers, and producers—resulting in the finished musical object that reaches our ears via speakers or earbuds.

A Photographic Interlude

To understand this better, imagine you are a photographer tasked with capturing a portrait of your town's new mayor. On the surface, it's a straightforward task. But consider the choices which must be made. Where will you take this photo? Inside at the mayor's desk? At the town's scenic waterfall? Perhaps in front of a point of civic pride such as the newly built hospital. Instinctively, we know that the choice of setting influences the story we are telling. At her desk, the mayor asserts power and influence. At the waterfall, she is "just like us" and enjoys the town's natural beauty. In front of the hospital, the mayor shows her willingness to move the town into the future through exciting development projects.

We can go through the same exercise with the mayor's choice of clothing for the photo, and then again with the pose. What do the position of her hands tell us? Is she joined by a partner, a family, or the town's beloved parrot? Is she wearing a hard hat? Is her expression stern and commanding, or warm and open?

But the choices don't end there. Photographers know that the height of the camera will significantly influence how the picture feels. Does the mayor tower above the viewer, looking down? Are we eye-to-eye with her? Or even looking down on her, the scene dominated by the hospital or waterfall?

Subtler still is the choice of lens and camera settings. A photographer can be two feet away from a subject and fill the frame with their face using a wide-angle lens, or thirty feet away, zooming in with a telephoto lens to achieve the same framing. But these pictures will not look the same: the wide-angle lens and close distance will make the subject's nose look bigger, with their ears appearing to recede far into the distance, while the zoomed-in photo shot from far away will appear to flatten the face so that the ears and nose are in the same plane of depth. The effect is quite shocking, and illustrates the point: there is simply no fact of the matter in photography.

After the photoshoot, you review the pictures and see that they all contain different expressions on her face. Which expression is the "correct one"? Will you edit any blemishes from her skin, or leave them as they are? Will you adjust the color and lighting of this photo? Subtly emphasize the ripples of water on the waterfall behind her? Edit out the sign in the background pointing to the town dump?

The novice photographer may not be aware of the existence and impact of these choices—they may take a photo without considering them, and simply accept any result. But for the professional, consideration of these choices begins when the assignment is accepted. The critical question is: "What do I (and the mayor) want this photo to convey?" The photo doesn't just document the subject, but it also communicates a host of values and aesthetic preferences of the team that created it. The number of decision points in creating a "simple photograph" is staggering!

As you may now see, any particular photograph represents a vanishingly narrow slice of the whole reality it purports to capture. We created a two-dimensional image from a fixed vantage point of a living, three-dimensional person who exists through time, moves from place to place, and changes values and opinions. Of all the possible photographs that could have existed, we chose to make this one, and in doing so, we inform the viewer not only of the subject, but of who we are and what we value. No photograph, then, can ever be true or complete—it's only a datapoint recording the intersection of subject and creator at that moment.

But there's one final point to make in this example: to the casual viewer of the final photograph, the photographer's choices are invisible. The subjective choices which built the impression of our mayor are not recognized as choices at all; rather, for a successful photograph, the impression of our mayor as powerful, approachable, or concerned with the environment will be taken as the fact of the matter. When the job is done correctly, the photographer disappears and we see in the photography only what the creative team hoped we would.

In the Recording Studio

Armed with this framework, let's imagine Taylor Swift's process in the studio. The year is 2009, and Swift and producer Nathan Chapman are working on the album which will become *Speak Now*. She has written the words and music to her songs, and is ready to record them. (Note that I can claim no insider knowledge about the particulars of the album's production process, so this account may be considered "technically informed fiction." However, I can state that, in broad strokes, these are the steps which must be considered.) From our photography example, you can probably see where this is going: let the choices begin!

Step 1: Recording

As Swift and Chapman consider the song "Mine," which will become the lead single for *Speak Now*, they consider the instrumentation for the final recording. Swift wrote the song while playing her acoustic guitar. Should they leave it as a solo performance, or add additional instrumentation? This could be a few tasteful piano chords, a rocking full band behind her, or layers of programmed synthesizers. Should they add harmony vocals? They can thicken and add power to a vocal performance, but can also make a song feel less personal. (It's hard to be alone with your thoughts when six backup singers are sharing theirs with you.) Is the tempo of the song "correct"? A faster tempo to the song can add energy, drive, or urgency. But a slower tempo can leave space for more musical expression or a sense of feeling grounded. What about the musical key of the song? Both instruments and voices change qualities across their range of available notes. The choice of musical key will fit the song's melody onto a certain section of Swift's vocal range, which might make the song dark and quiet (at the bottom of her vocal range) or powerful and strident (if placed higher in her range). Should the musical performances be simple and straightforward? Or maybe virtuosic and complex? Should there be a ripping guitar solo, or understated long notes on an upright bass? A guiding principle Swift might consider is often expressed this way: "How do we want the listener to feel when hearing this song?" Should they be uplifted and energized? Should they feel contemplative and drawn inward? Invited to grieve? Invited to party all night long?

Recording projects are most successful when the performing artists, engineers, and producers are all aligned on these "feelings" goals. When we view the musical and technical choices through this lens, they become more straightforward. A music producer's primary job, in fact, is to help the team clarify the emotional or energetic goals of a song (or often, an entire album as a whole) and make sure that intent is considered at each step along the way. And it's certainly easy to lose sight of that intent as the choices continue to multiply.

Having decided on an appropriate tempo, key, and instrumentation (possibly through first recording demos and evaluating their impact), it's time to record the final version of the song. Should Swift and the team bring in all the musicians into the studio at once and have them play together? This is how I believe most people envision the recording process, but it's not how most pop records are created. In fact, the musicians may never even meet in some cases, having recorded their parts on different continents and potentially months apart from each other. There are tradeoffs in each case. It's hard to beat the energy of a live performance, allowing the musicians to all vibe with each other, but there can be a number of technical challenges for the recording engineer in keeping sounds from bleeding into other performer's microphones. Microphone bleed makes it more difficult to separately process sounds during the mixing phase to come, so engineers like to avoid it where possible, but sometimes the energy of a live performance makes it worth the trouble. It's also easy for musicians performing live together to get caught up in the moment and potentially take the song in a new and unexpected direction. Whether that itself is a good thing depends on the results, of course!

As Swift's team sets up for a recording session, the recording engineer sets up microphones near each performer. Like camera lenses, there is no single best microphone which accurately captures the source as it really is. All microphones capture different narrow slices of reality—even moving a microphone by a few inches in front of a singer or instrument will drastically change the sound it captures. The professional recording engineer will be making these choices of microphone and placement based on their understanding of the song's intention. While there is no microphone in my collection that is specifically marketed as a sad song microphone, I will certainly choose a darker, smoother sounding microphone like a Neumann U47 or a bright, strident one like the Telefunken 251 depending on which better suits the song's intention.

As humans, we are particularly sensitive to the qualities of the human voice, so engineers and producers often devote great care to selecting a vocal microphone. Again, there is no single best microphone for all singers—or even a particular singer. Instead, we might ask a singer to sing a verse of a song through several different microphones and then review the results. What we find is that each microphone captures a different presentation of the same voice. Again, it's always a reductive process. There is the sense that each microphone is leaving behind aspects of the voice while emphasizing other aspects. But some choice must be made, using the song's mission as our guide.

Experienced audio engineers know that the tonal choices don't stop with the choice of microphone. Microphones are plugged into preamps, which boost the microphone's tiny signal to a more usable level and then sometimes into additional signal processing equipment such as compressors or equalizers before the signal makes it to the recording medium itself. And don't get me started on digital versus analog recording![1]

Each piece of equipment, from mic, to preamp, to signal-processing outboard gear, imparts a distinct tonal footprint onto the recorded sound. Engineers and producers spend countless hours online discussing the merits of a "thick, meaty" preamp such as the Neve 1073 versus a "punchy, aggressive" API 312, or a "clean, glassy" Grace Designs m801. Audio neophytes ask which preamp is the best, while experienced engineers know that the answer is "whichever best accomplishes the intention for this part of this song." Painters debate paints and brushes; we argue about circuit designs from the 1960s.

Having selected and placed microphones and chosen outboard processing gear, it is now time to record the song. Here, too, the Hollywood idea of recording a song in a single take is mostly a fiction. Like Hollywood movies themselves, pop songs are generally pieced together from multiple takes to create the best composite (or "comp") possible. On the day of recording, a producer's job is to listen to the musicians as they perform the song time after time, making suggestions to try and help everyone remember the song's intent. The producer may notice the musicians getting tired and suggest taking a break, or coach a vocalist to dig for genuine emotion in a situation in which that may be hard to access.

Note that while an engineer and at least one performer must be present at every recording session, Taylor Swift herself might not be. Swift's performance credits on "Mine" are acoustic guitar and vocals—but acoustic guitar plays a relatively minor role in the sound of the finished song (and producer Nathan Chapman and guitarist Brian Sutton are also credited with acoustic guitar performances). So, it's not clear which sessions Swift attended. Final vocals are often recorded long after the band has finished recording their instrumental parts—often weeks, months, or even years later, and potentially in a different studio altogether. Engineers may record as many as twenty takes of a vocal if technical perfection is the goal, or only a take or two if continuity and vibe are more important.

When the recording process is done, we are sitting on a mountain of raw material: multiple takes of instruments and vocals, potentially multiple microphones used to record a single instrument (which could be chosen from or even blended together during mixing), and possibly entire instruments or harmony vocals which will end up not being used at all.

Step 2: Editing

It's now time to edit this recording. This involves first selecting the best takes and stitching them together into something that sounds like a single, coherent performance, and then editing those takes for rhythm, tuning the pitch of vocals, and potentially adding additional musical parts to flesh out sections that sound too empty.

Again, in editing we are faced with a series of choices. Should vocals be tweaked to be perfectly in tune? If a certain vocal syllable has a tinge of "grit" in it, should it be replaced with another take, or does that grit actually sell the song's emotion in that moment? How "dirty" or "real" should we allow the band's performances to be? If the drummer rushed the final moments of each chorus does that read as excitement or just bad drumming? There are no objective facts here—just the tastes, prior experiences, and preferences of the entire creative team.

At this point, you may exclaim: "This seems like so much work! Why not put a few microphones in front of the band and let them work their magic?" Well, you certainly can. But just as a single camera filming a play doesn't turn it into a Hollywood movie, a few microphones in front of a live band doesn't turn it into a modern pop record. Dating back as far as the Beatles' *Sgt. Pepper* era, the larger-than-life experience of listening to a modern pop record simply cannot be captured through simple studio techniques. Artists, engineers, and producers since the late 1960s have actively used the studio as a creative instrument through the exercise of these many choices.

It's also important to note that Taylor Swift may not have been present for the many hours of editing and take selection—even though this process significantly affects the presentation of her vocals to the world. More often than not, musicians look for outside perspective from trusted engineers and producers to help edit their performances.

Through relationships built over years, artists may trust a specific producer or engineer to understand their intention and create a composite performance which reflects that intention. But these tasks are certainly subjective and require significant creative decision-making. The work of a movie star rests on the foundation of hundreds to thousands of crewmembers to create a finished piece. Similarly, the completion of an album requires a team to turn Taylor Swift into "Taylor Swift," the *persona* heard on the song and perhaps the entire album—a concept which Ley David Elliette Cray examines in Chapter 8 of this volume.

As in our photographic example earlier, generally the team's work is invisible. If an editor chooses vocal takes which stitch together to convey emotional vulnerability, the *Billboard* review will praise the artist's interpretation. Of course, the source material has to be workable—the artist needs to deliver the takes which can be shaped into a final product—but the average listener might be shocked at the latitude possible through editing to shape even the emotional character of a performance. Working in audio production is not for the narcissist! We stretch, tune, shape, and persuade audio to convey the team's intention, but done correctly, the work will never be consciously witnessed.

Step 3: Mixing

Swift's team has now finished recording and editing "Mine." Are they done? No. In fact, they're about to enter the most subjective part of the entire process: mixing.

The art of mixing is taking all of the instrumental and vocal sounds which comprise a song and arranging them into a coherent, listenable whole. You can think of this process as arranging the various parts in three-dimensional space—which audiophiles might call the "soundstage." Our exquisite senses of hearing allow us to discern the placement of various parts in a stereo recording. A mix engineer can move a guitar or voice to appear to emanate from the left side of your headphones, the right, or any point in between. A little more surprisingly, a mixing engineer can also make a sound seem like it's coming from any point in three-dimensional space—it could be far away, slightly to the right of you, or down by your feet!

Along with arranging instruments in perceived space, a mix engineer will choose to alter the tone of each instrument to create a set of puzzle pieces which fit together. In most pop songs, the lead vocal is of primary importance; however, another element (say, an electric guitar) may have a very similar tonal fingerprint, obscuring the vocal in the way an overly busy background might distract the viewer in a portrait photograph. Years of ear training help mix engineers identify these conflicts and use appropriate tools to carve out auditory space for the important elements in the mix.

Mixes aren't static. The appropriate balance between instruments, their tonalities, and positions in space can change through the course of a song. Think of the lighting at a rock concert. It might change from a cool blue to an exciting red at a pivotal moment in the song, or a spotlight might call attention to a particularly soulful trombone solo. Similarly, mix engineers will change these parameters as the song progresses in order to shape the listener's experience, calling attention to the most interesting parts of the song as it unfolds. I have even used this technique many times to cover up mistakes in recordings I've mixed: Did the mandolin hit a particularly bad note? No problem; let's momentarily boost the volume of the tambourine on the other side of the soundstage, in effect saying, "Hey, look over here!" It really works.

The final aspect of mixing we should discuss is the use of effects, such as reverb (which can place our vocalist in a huge cathedral or a broom closet), delay, compression (evening out loud and soft notes), and many, many others that stretch, shape, and squeeze sounds to fit individual tastes. The history of recorded music is also the history of musical technology, and different eras of music can be identified by some of the distinctive sounds of the musical effects, especially reverb. Originally, extra reverb was added to recordings through the use of an echo chamber—basically, a sealed concrete room with a loudspeaker on one end and a microphone on the other. Aficionados of early rock'n'roll records can sometimes even identify the particular studio used for a recording by recognizing the distinct sound of its echo chamber. Fast-forwarding a few decades, the first digital reverbs which appeared in the late 70s made a huge splash in the pop music world, serving as a kind of status symbol. If you had spent the money on a Lexicon digital reverb, you would definitely use it lavishly, and as a result pop music from the early 80s often has far more reverb than the comparatively "dry" 70s sound that preceded it.

So, the aesthetic choices of mixing, as with all other choices in the recording process, don't exist in a vacuum; instead, they are highly informed by the time and context in which they take place. In the early 80s, the sound of a prominent Lexicon digital reverb was a rejection of the reverb-free sound of 70s rock, but the exact same sound used today seems dated and explicitly references the 80s themselves. Computer-based recording has made the reverb technology itself eminently affordable, so the sound no longer explicitly says "I am well-funded."

More recently, the use (or some would say, abuse) of AutoTune to create highly "stair-stepped" vocals first achieved mainstream popularity in Cher's 1998 song "Believe," became the cornerstone of T-Pain's signature vocal sound, and now, similarly, reads as a bit dated. Simply put, the distinctive sound of AutoTune no longer evokes the same response it did in 1998; so, it cannot be used in the same way to achieve an emotional goal, but can now be used if the goal is to evoke early-2000s nostalgia.

Coda

I mention this point as we turn our attention to the topic of re-recording. In "duplicating" a song, one may be forced to choose between making the same technical choices, or making choices to evoke the same feelings of the original work. A wonderful example of this appears in Baz Luhrmann's 2013 film adaptation of *The Great Gatsby*. Instead of a period-accurate soundtrack of early jazz music, the movie is scored with a contemporary hip hop soundtrack. In its time, early jazz seemed subversive, utterly modern, and possibly a bit dangerous, but it's nearly impossible for a modern listener to hear it that way. In scoring the film with today's most "modern" genre, Luhrmann chose to preserve the emotional, rather than the literal truth.

So, as we've seen, innumerable subjective choices go into the process of recording a song. For most pop music, these choices are the result of a team effort. Even if a song is composed in the blink of an eye, tens to hundreds of person-hours are spent for each finished minute of a pop song—largely in the choice-making process itself. The choices are often guided by an imagined emotional experience on the listener's part; yet, in order for that experience to be achieved, the listener must share a cultural context with the original creators.

Into the Re-recording Studio

As an engineer and producer, when I sat down to listen to Swift's re-recordings and compare them against their original counterparts, I was especially interested in her team's approach to re-recording itself. How much would be duplication versus reinterpretation? And if duplicating, which elements would the team duplicate as closely as possible, and which would they instead attempt to duplicate the emotional end rather than the technical means?

Before listening, I had imagined that Swift might take this opportunity to re-interpret the songs. Artists often find that lyrics written in their early adulthood take on new depth and meaning with the passage of time. Joni Mitchell's 2023 concert at the Gorge Amphitheatre in Washington State was a tear-inducing illustration of this for many, as the 79-year-old sang "Both Sides Now" with the perspective gained from a lifetime's worth of experiences.

Many musicians perform covers of other artists' songs, but artistic integrity is often held to hinge on whether a musician has contributed something of their own by reinterpreting the song, adding their own spin on it. This type of cover is taken to have artistic merit in a way not extended by many to cover bands themselves. Cover bands judge success by their fidelity in recreating the original sound (and in many cases, look) of the source material as closely as possible, but for this reason they're often seen as lacking any artistic merit of their own.[2] I believe a similar thought process visits musicians contemplating re-recording their own material. They don't want to become a cover band of themselves; rather, they want to retain artistic integrity through adding something new this next time around.

But within a few seconds of playing tracks from *Speak Now (Taylor's Version)*, it became clear that Swift's intentions leaned far more toward duplication than reinterpretation. Recall the number of choices which factor into each stage of the recording process—here, those choices were largely replicated a second time. The new versions of "Never Grow Up," "Haunted," and "Last Kiss" all are recorded in the same keys and tempos as their original 2010 versions. The same instruments appear, playing the same parts, solos and all. Even their positions in the soundstage from left to right are preserved closely.

From our analysis of the recording process, we know that these choices cannot align between the 2010 and 2023 versions through coincidence—nor, as you might have originally imagined, do they represent the only way to record the song. Instead, Swift seems to intend not to create a reinterpretation of the original material, but a complete replacement for it, saying, "This new version can replace the old in every way." This makes sense considering that the impetus for re-recording was more financial than artistic in nature.

Pop recordings at the budget and scale of Swift's tend to be efforts of a large team of producers, engineers, assistants, musicians, arrangers, vocal coaches, and more. It's in the interest of everyone involved to forward the idea of the singer-songwriter as auteur. But as on an auteur's movie sets, it takes many people's efforts *and* original creative work to produce a finished album. Thus, when we consider the duplication of a record, we are looking at the duplication not only of many choices made by Swift the first time around, but also of the choices made by her team of musicians, engineers, and producers. Copyright law allows a composer to take their song and "just perform it again" in a new recording session, but it offers little if any protection to many of the other creative choices which comprise the production. Swift has been silent on who arranged and composed all the accompanying instrumental parts for the original recordings, but the absence of producer Nathan Chapman from the Taylor's Version of *Speak Now* is notable. As the primary producer of the original recording (outside of Swift's own producer credit), Chapman likely contributed significantly to the translation of bare song to final track in ways which have been reproduced in the 2023 release.

There is one noticeable way, at least to an experienced audio nut, that Taylor's Versions differ from their original counterparts. The mixes themselves sound different. Even with the same instrumentation and spatial arrangement of instruments in the mix, there are still plenty of decisions a mix engineer must make. While the original version of *Speak Now* feels somewhat congested, with multiple instruments tightly surrounding the vocal vying for the listener's attention, in the Taylor's Version, the mix engineer has carved out more space around the vocal, creating a more relaxed and spacious presentation of the sound. Rather than the excitement of a full band crowded onto a small club stage, this is the Carnegie Hall presentation, with plenty of room for each instrument to breathe.

Interestingly, the tonal differences on the original version of *Red* (2012) are less pronounced when compared to its 2021 counterpart, but this is because the spacious feeling is already there on the 2012 version. Mix engineer Șerban Ghenea has the primary mixing credit for both versions of *Red*,[3] and I suspect that the consistency between the two version's mix presentation speaks to Ghenea's preferences themselves. In contrast, *Speak Now*'s original mix engineer Justin Niebank did not mix the 2023 version; instead, it was Serban Ghenea again. He also mixed the first Taylor's Version release, *Fearless*, originally mixed by Nathan Chapman. Here, Swift and the team seem to be prioritizing a consistent tonality across the re-recorded albums as opposed to maintaining the original feel and tonality of each original record.

In light of such careful efforts to duplicate so many aspects of the recording itself, why would the team not want to replicate the quality of crowdedness and the more pointed, urgent tonality of the original?

I believe that in this choice, Swift is stating what each song is and what it is not: the song's identity includes the words and music, the instruments and their parts (likely shaped by Nathan Chapman in the original release), the tempo and key, and even the instrument's arrangements from left to right in the soundstage, but it does not include the tonality or crowdedness of those instruments (also shaped by Chapman through his mixing work, but abandoned in the new mix). Mixing aesthetics change over the years and can in many cases be as clear a giveaway for a certain era, as AutoTuned vocals are for the early 2000s. It seems that rather than allow the re-recordings to sound dated at a level that might remain subconscious for many listeners, the team elected to update the mix itself—similar to producing a remaster of each original album—to create a contemporary consistency across albums.

Conclusion

When I first became aware of the re-recordings, I had imagined Taylor's Versions to be something like a director's cut of a film: "Here are the ways I would have recorded these songs if not for the influence of my label and management." Swift wrote or co-wrote all of the songs on the re-recordings, and the public often takes songwriting and performance to be the whole of all creative contributions to a record, imagining the recording process itself to be a mere capture of what the musicians have done in the studio. But as we've seen, so many choices go into all aspects of a recording. *Speak Now (Taylor's Version)* lists a total of fifty-seven participants, split roughly equally between musicians and technical contributors. Imagine the number of creative choices outside of Swift's direct control in creating this work! I had originally seen the "Taylor's Version" designator as dismissive of the whole team's efforts. (As I imagine *The Great Gatsby*'s production team might feel about my referring to it as Baz Luhrmann's film above.) But I misunderstood her intent.

Swift's televised interview with Seth Meyers from November 11, 2021, allows her to speak about it in her own words.[4] In the interview she never mentions any updated artistic aims for the project, or the idea of "re-interpretation" I often associate with re-recording. Instead, Swift states, "When something says '(Taylor's Version)' next to it, that means I own it, which is exciting." Given this aim, the decision to duplicate as many aspects of the recording as would be noticeable to the average fan, while updating the mix aesthetics to conform each to a 2023 "Taylor Swift sound" is perfectly sensible. To the average listener, the re-recordings sound "the same, but better," having updated sonic elements which might risk feeling dated, and crucially for Swift's stated purpose, having eliminated any need to continue listening to the original recording. Thus, the addition of "Taylor's Version" to each song and album does not indicate that they are solely Swift's creations, but rather her property.

Swifties may see the re-releases as those of an auteur at work, as Swift creating her music singlehandedly while sticking it to traditional power structures—and it benefits Swift and her team if they do. But we can see that while the "Taylor Swift" persona is an auteur, the real-world Swift is not. Through countless choices, the team of musicians, engineers, producers, photographers, graphic designers, social media managers, and videographers has created the illusion of life in the recorded "Taylor Swift." Swift now owns that persona and its appearance in the re-recordings outright—as she should.

Notes

1   For my take on the digital versus analog debate, see Michael Thomas Connolly, "On the Record: An Audio Professional's Take on Vinyl," *Aesthetics for Birds*, April 7, 2021, https://aestheticsforbirds.

com/2021/04/07/an-audio-professionals-take-on-vinyl/ (accessed January 10, 2024).
2   For a careful examination of the relationship between Swift's re-recordings and cover versions of songs, see Chapter 2 of this volume.
3   You can find Ghenea's complete discography on his website here: https://serbanghenea.com/discography/.
4   Taylor Swift, "Taylor Swift Full Interview on Late Night with Seth Meyers," interview by Seth Meyers, *Late Night with Seth Meyers*, November 14, 2021, https://www.youtube.com/watch?v=DYIOaifhjQU (accessed August 17, 2023).

5

Re-recording as Reclamation

Metaphysics, Metaphor, and Taylor's Versions

Brandon Polite

Introduction

In the action-packed music video for "I Can See You," a From the Vault track from *Speak Now (Taylor's Version)*, a star-studded crew of thieves break into a highly fortified museum vault. But this isn't a standard art heist; it's a rescue mission. The thieves rescue Taylor Swift and the cover art for *Speak Now (Taylor's Version)* and make their escape, blowing up the museum for good measure. In an Instagram post about the video, Swift describes how "I … really wanted to play out symbolically how it's felt for me to have the fans helping me reclaim my music."[1] Swift is referring to her project of re-recording her first six studio albums after Scooter Braun acquired the rights to the albums' masters when he purchased Swift's former label, Big Machine Records, in 2019. Yet, in what sense has Swift "reclaimed" her albums by re-recording them? Has she only reclaimed them in a *metaphorical* way, meaning her victory over Braun is purely symbolic? Or has she *literally reclaimed* them, meaning there's a sense in which she's genuinely gotten her albums back?

The question of whether Swift can literally reclaim her albums by re-recording them is a *metaphysical* one.[2] Specifically, it's an *ontological* question, as it has to do with the identities of things, their relationships to one another, and how to classify them. The particular question before us is: are the original versions and the re-recorded versions of

Speak Now, and all of the rest, identical works of art? If they are, then Swift will have produced instances of the albums that are legally hers and thereby robbed Braun of the ability to produce and financially benefit from the only legitimate instances of them—seemingly the best possible revenge within the confines of copyright law.

In this chapter, I will examine and evaluate the two theories of the ontology of art according to which Swift could literally reclaim her albums by re-recording them. Finding them both unacceptable, I will conclude that the only way for Swift to literally reclaim her albums would be to acquire their masters. Her victory against Braun, then, can only be symbolic. But Swift's metaphorical reclamation of her albums, I will argue, has actually gone better than had she literally reclaimed them; thus, by re-recording her albums, Swift has gotten something better than revenge! To reach this conclusion, we first need to understand the nature of *re-recorded music*. And this requires that we get up to speed on the nature of *recorded music*. I turn to that task now.

The Nature of Recorded Music

Because they contain the same songs in the same order (ignoring the From the Vault tracks), you might be tempted to think that Swift's re-recorded albums aren't different works of art than the original ones. But albums aren't mere collections of songs. If they were, then Ryan Adams's *1989*, a cover album containing alt-rock renditions of every song on *1989*, would count as one and the same work of art as Swift's *1989*, meaning they would be perfectly interchangeable with one another in any relevant context.[3] But we treat them as distinct albums in practice. This is because we properly distinguish between *songs* and *tracks*.

As philosophers working on the ontology of music describe them, songs are "ontologically thin," meaning they specify relatively little of how their instances must sound.[4] A song is basically a combination of lyrics, a vocal melody, and a chord progression, and it can be realized in a wide variety of ways. Changing the key, tempo, instrumentation, genre, style, musicians, etc., usually won't affect whether a performance or recording counts as a genuine instance of a given song. Every time Swift performs "Bad Blood" live, for example, it will sound subtly different from each of her other performances of the song. And Ryan Adams's cover version sounds radically different than Swift's original version. Yet, despite these differences, all of these versions, both live and recorded, count as instances of the song "Bad Blood."

Although they may be instances of the same *song*, Swift's and Adams's recordings are nevertheless distinct *tracks*.[5] This is because tracks are "ontologically thick," meaning they specify nearly every aspect of how their instances must sound. Their thickness comes from the fact that tracks reside in *recordings*. Within the popular music tradition, which is our focus here, tracks are typically multitrack studio recordings. Michael Thomas Connolly offers us a detailed account of the process of producing a track in Chapter 4 of this volume, but a brief synopsis of how tracks come into being will be helpful here to get clearer on their nature.

The tracks we buy, stream, and listen to aren't typically recorded in a single take, but are rather built up (Frankenstein-style) out of parts of several (sometimes dozens of) takes. A musician records take after take of a specific part, such as a bass line or lead vocal; the best bits of each take are selected, spliced together, and then balanced, equalized, and so on, to sound like a single, continuous performance. A mix engineer then takes all of the tracks for each part and mixes them together, changing how loud each part is and what their spatial locations are, among other things, at each point of their respective durations, assembling them into the form we'll eventually hear in the finished track. They mix and remix the track numerous times until the producer and the artist— and maybe the record company—are satisfied with how it sounds. The final mix is then given to an audio engineer for mastering, where the track is further refined and polished in a variety of ways (equalized, compressed, etc.) into its finished state: the *master recording*. The master is then prepared to be mechanically or digitally transferred to the various formats it will be released on: vinyl records, cassette tapes, compact discs, and a variety of purely digital formats, like MP3s and FLAC files.

We access a track by listening to *copies* of its master recording across these formats. But the track itself is not identical with the master recording. The master recording is merely a length of polarized magnetic tape or else the series of ones and zeros comprising a digital file. Instead, the track is what has been *encoded* into the master recording and all of its subsequent copies: namely, the audio signal of the mastered final mix. Instances of the track are produced by *decoding* the encoded audio signal in the right way, specifically, by playing copies of the master recording on playback devices appropriate for their format—vinyl records on record players, CDs on CD players, etc.[6] By putting the needle down or pressing "play" on your playback device, you reproduce the audio signal of the mastered final mix and thereby hear the track.

An *album*, then, is fundamentally a *collection of tracks*. Albums are also collections of songs, but only because the tracks instantiate those songs. This is how we treat them in actual practice. We can appreciate the quality of Swift's songwriting by listening to Adams's version of *1989* just as much as we can by listening to the original album. But we appreciate more than just songwriting when listening to albums. We also appreciate their production values, the quality of the assembled vocal and instrumental performances, and other aspects of how the album *sounds*, which are aspects of the recorded tracks that make up the album. As a result, Swift's *1989* and Adams's *1989* are distinct albums, even though they instance the exact same songs, because those songs are realized in different tracks.

The question before us now is whether *1989 (Taylor's Version)* isn't merely the same collection of songs, but also the same collection of tracks as the original *1989*. If it were, then it would be identical with the original album—the two would actually be one and the same work of art. The preceding discussion points us toward an answer: we have to determine whether re-recording an album in the way Swift has can ever count as a means to producing legitimate instances of the album. This way of producing instances of an album (by re-recording it) would obviously be different than how their current owners produce them (by mechanically or digitally copying the original master recordings). But why not think that this is a legitimate way of reproducing an album? If it were, then it would be a way for Swift to produce copies of her original albums that she owns, and thereby literally reclaim them, without needing to own the original masters. In doing so, she would circumvent the laws surrounding copyright and benefit financially from selling, streaming, and licensing copies of the albums that genuinely belong to her.

Formalism

According to a classic twentieth-century aesthetic theory, re-recording would be a way for artists to reclaim their albums. The view, known as *formalism*, which was advocated most strongly by Clive Bell and Monroe Beardsley, maintains that any two works of art that are *perceptually indistinguishable* are *ontologically indistinguishable*.[7] In simpler terms, two albums that sound exactly the same (two paintings that look exactly the same, etc.) are instances of one and the same aesthetic object.

If formalism were correct, it would offer a path for any recording artist in Swift's situation to literally reclaim their work. They could produce new instances of their albums by meticulously recording new versions that perfectly replicate their finest sonic details. Of course, the law is such that the original masters would still be owned by someone else who would still profit from selling and licensing copies of them. But the new masters the re-recording artist has produced and the original masters would encode ontologically identical artworks, meaning they'd provide access to one and the same aesthetic object. Copies produced from both the original and re-recorded masters would thus count as instances of the same work of art—the masters of each version would be interchangeable in every relevant context and thus identical. As a result, owning a master recording would not mean that one has legal rights to a unique aesthetic object, rendering copyright protections effectively meaningless.

This may seem like a terrific outcome for Taylor Swift—indeed, to any recording artist who doesn't own their masters. It strips power from the corporate overlords who own their catalogs by revoking the special status that original masters have to provide exclusive access to recorded music. Original master recordings would not be metaphysically special, and would thus be far less economically valuable, if artists could produce genuine instances of their albums that are legally theirs, which they can thus profit from, by perfectly replicating the original recordings.[8]

Of course, Swift has chosen *not* to perfectly replicate the original versions of her albums. The Taylor's Versions she's released so far sound incredibly similar to the original recordings, but they aren't perfect clones. Subtle and occasionally not-so-subtle differences exist between each original and re-recorded track. From the formalists' perspective, therefore, Swift's project of reclaiming her albums by re-recording them would be a failure. But if the formalists are right, then Swift absolutely *could* still get her albums back. If she wants to achieve this goal, she'd need to re-record the albums *again*—only faithfully this time. This would result in a literal (and not merely metaphorical) victory for Swift. She'd now actually own—really, co-own—her albums and not just imperfect (even if economically viable) knockoffs of them.

But this victory would come at a major cost. This is because formalism doesn't entail that only the artists themselves can produce authentic instances of their albums by re-recording them; it entails that *anyone can*. If I had the time, ability, and inclination to record a perfect replica of, say, *Fearless*, I would thereby produce *Fearless*. The original *Fearless* and my sonic doppelganger would be ontologically identical and thus, for the formalists, one and the same album.

Imagine that I do record such an album. I reproduce each instrumental part, every subtle nuance of Swift's vocal performance, and so forth, with absolute fidelity to those on *Fearless*. Not even experts using the most sensitive audio-analyzing tools can tell the difference between *Fearless (Brandon's Version)* and the original album. It's a perfect duplicate. Now imagine that, after achieving this feat, I secretly steal every single copy of *Fearless* on Earth (call me the Grinch Who Stole *Fearless*) and replace them with copies of *Fearless (Brandon's Version)*. If formalism were true, then my actions could be criticized in various ways, but not because I've robbed anyone of the ability to listen to *Fearless*. This would be true even if I destroyed every copy of *Fearless* that I've stolen and also its master recordings, meaning no further copies of the original album could be produced. This is because, for the formalists, listening to your copy of *Fearless (Brandon's Version)* is not merely a good "substitute" to listening to *Fearless*—the best you can do in an unfortunately *Fearless*-less world. Instead, your copy of *Fearless (Brandon's Version)* is genuinely a copy of *Fearless*. It doesn't matter that what you're actually hearing are my amazing imitations of Taylor Swift and her collaborators' efforts. Because the albums *sound the same*, they *are (instances of) the same album*.

I presume that most of you reading this would want to resist this conclusion. A world where only *Fearless (Brandon's Version)* exists really would be a world without *Fearless*. If this is what you're thinking, then you're in good company. Nearly every philosopher who has worked on the ontology of art for the past half century rejects the formalist principle that perceptual indistinguishability entails ontological identity.

Why Formalism Fails

To see why, consider the principle's flipside: that any two aesthetic objects that sound (look, taste, etc.) noticeably different are thereby ontologically distinct objects. How we access and experience recorded music poses problems for this claim. For one thing, the playback device we listen to an album on affects how it sounds. If I play my CD copy of *Fearless* on a high-end stereo system, it will sound noticeably different than if I then play it on a crappy boombox. The fine sonic details I'd hear the first time won't be available the second time. Because of this, formalism would entail that the two stereos are producing distinct aesthetic objects—essentially, instances of two different albums—even though they're playing the very same copy of *Fearless*.

It would also entail that anyone whose playback device has an equalizer could produce a new work of art *each time* they play a track. Equalizers allow users to adjust an audio recording's high, low, and mid-range frequencies in real time. Boosting or reducing the volume of these frequencies changes how it sounds. But we shouldn't accept, along with the formalists, that fiddling with the EQ produces a new work of art distinct from the track the artist released: the final mix encoded into the master recording. It simply gives me the ability to hear the track's sonic details across its full range of frequencies better than I otherwise could. This means that the recorded track, as the object of aesthetic attention, is something we hear *in* or *through* the auditory properties of the soundwaves produced by our playback devices; it cannot be reduced to or identified with them, as the formalists would have us believe.[9]

This claim is further supported by the fact that the format we listen to an album on also affects how it sounds. Analog formats sound different than digital ones. Vinyl records and cassette tapes sound warmer and fuller than CDs, which have a noticeably clearer audio quality. And digital audio formats come in varying degrees of fidelity to master recordings. High-quality digital formats like the WAV files found on CDs and the FLAC files that Tidal uses sound noticeably better than low-quality formats like the Ogg Vorbis files that Spotify uses and the MP3s that Amazon uses for their standard-definition offerings. The latter are referred to as "lossy" audio formats because the files are highly compressed, meaning they fail to preserve the masters' finer sonic details—the higher the compression rate, the more audio data is lost. Lossy audio files are smaller and thus more easily and cheaply transferable than their "lossless" counterparts, but at the cost of sounding noticeably worse.

When Taylor Swift and other artists release an album, they typically do so across numerous formats, including the ones I've just mentioned. Yet, we don't treat your CD copy, my vinyl copy, and the MP3 copy of *Red (Taylor's Version)* that our friend downloaded as instances of three distinct albums. Instead, we think that they give us access to one and the same album. If they were instances of distinct artworks, the three of us wouldn't be talking about the same thing when we discuss "the album." Worse still, the entire discourse surrounding popular music—from album reviews in music magazines, to analyses on blogs, arguments on social media, in-persons conversations, etc.—would make little sense if formalism were true. We could never be sure which album a person is talking about without knowing for sure what format they were listening to, as well as what sound system and EQ settings they'd used! Indeed, the only way we could ever be completely confident that we've listened to the same album as anyone else would be to listen to it together with them. But despite the real value of listening to music with others,[10] popular music, as a mass art form, is meant to be experienced and discussed by a mass audience—that is, by individuals who are distributed widely across the globe.[11]

In light of the preceding considerations, the costs of accepting formalism are simply too high. We should reject the formalist principle that works of art and other aesthetic objects are identifiable by their perceptual properties. The consensus among philosophers of art is that an artwork's identity depends instead on its "history of production": *when, where, how, by whom,* and perhaps even *why* an aesthetic object was made determines its identity.[12] According to this view, the *Mona Lisa* and a perfect copy are not interchangeable instances of the same painting, and *Fearless* and *Fearless (Brandon's Version)* are not the same album. Each reproduction was made at a different time, in a different place, in a different way, by a different artist, and/or for a different reason than the original and thereby counts as a separate work of art.

Two copies of *Fearless* are genuine instances of the same album, in contrast, because they share the relevant causal relationship to the definitive track: the final mastered mix encoded into the master recording, which itself has a unique causal history that can be traced back to the events in the recording studio that brought the album into existence. An album's genuine instances can be traced back to those events because they have been directly copied (either mechanically or digitally) from the original master recordings, which encode in the grooves of a vinyl record, the ones and zeros of an audio file, etc., the sonic results of the countless artistic decisions the performers, producers, engineers, and others made in the recording studio when creating the album.

If the preceding is correct, then re-recording a track—and, thus, an album as a collection of tracks—is not a way of producing genuine instances of it, no matter how faithfully you reproduce its sonic properties. The re-recordings that Swift has produced capture different decisions from different recording sessions and often by different personnel than the original recordings do.[13] And it is for this reason that most philosophers of art, myself included, would conclude that Taylor's Versions are distinct works of art from the original versions. Because of this, Swift cannot literally reclaim her albums— that is, possess and profit from genuine instances of them—by means of re-recording them. The only way to do so would be to acquire their masters, which, unfortunately for Swift, doesn't seem to be in the offing any time soon.

Intentionalism

But perhaps this conclusion is too hasty. There is another theory in addition to formalism according to which Swift could literally reclaim her albums by re-recording them. Like the consensus view, it treats works of art as objects whose identities fundamentally depend on their causal histories. Indeed, it pushes the "artworks as historically defined objects" line about as far as it can be pushed, treating artworks as entities that change continuously throughout their lifetimes, even sometimes in ways that lead them to be unrecognizable from their earlier selves, while still being one and the same work of art.

This view, known as *intentionalism*, which has been developed and defended by Guy Rohrbaugh, recognizes that artworks, like other entities, change over time in ways that don't impact their identities.[14] As an artist works on a particular artwork, it undergoes all sorts of revisions along the way to completion. For example, a track is laid down in the recording studio. It starts off as a solo acoustic number, but over time is transformed into a full-on symphonic pop ballad. It is mixed dozens of times until the artist and production team feel it's ready to be mastered and released. The artist could have decided that mix #8, in which the orchestra was entirely inaudible, was the finished track, but the fact that they mastered mix #39 doesn't mean that the two mixes are distinct works of art; instead, mix #8 and all of the other mixes are merely *earlier stages* of the finished artwork: the final mastered mix of the track you and I get to enjoy on our record players, car radios, and so on.

Artworks don't only change while they're being produced; they can also change after they've been released to the world. Some of these changes have natural causes. Photographs fade, paintings deteriorate, buildings erode, but we don't think of these changes as resulting in new works of art. Other changes are produced by human intervention. Some are made by individuals other than the artist. A vandal may damage a famous painting, but we don't think of the canvas as having contained two distinct artworks but instead a single, continuous work that has undergone change. But sometimes artists themselves change a work after they've "finished" it. Mary Shelley heavily revised *Frankenstein* between the novel's first (1818) edition and final (1831) edition. The 2012 Ultimate Collector's Edition of Ridley Scott's *Blade Runner* (originally released in 1982) includes five distinct versions of the film, including Scott's (2007) "Final Cut." Much to some fans' annoyance, Kanye West released *The Life of Pablo* four times between February and June of 2016, substantively revising the entire album throughout the process—altering lyrics, mixes, guest vocals, the track listing, and more. Taylor Swift replaced a homophobic lyric on "Picture to Burn" from her (2006) debut album soon after its release by recording a new one and editing it into the track; and this version has appeared on every subsequent release of the album and presumably will on Taylor's Version of the track.

Intentionalists aim to specifically accommodate cases like these in which artists change their minds about whether their works are finished after they've released them to the world. Rohrbaugh argues that an artwork is only complete when it has satisfied the artist's "plan" for it: once the work fully realizes their intentions, it is thereby complete.[15] But the artist's plan isn't static; it's inherently *revisable*, meaning it can always be changed.[16] It is also inherently *indeterminate*, meaning that, among other things, an artist may discover what their plan for a work was only after they've released it to the world.[17]

When Swift released her debut album, she presumably didn't want to hurt anyone with "Picture to Burn."[18] The intention not to be hurtful was thus part of her plan for the track, a part that she only discovered thanks to some fans or critics (or perhaps her PR team) helping her become aware of it. To change the offending lyric in the way she did, according to the intentionalist analysis, means that the edited and re-released track now better realizes her plan for it than the original release did and thereby constitutes the finished track.[19] Moreover, by editing and re-releasing "Picture to Burn," Swift reveals a fact about the original version that we, and likely even she, didn't know: namely, that it (and thus the album it appears on) was released as an unfinished work.[20] It thus has the same status as all of the other mixes made while the track was developing into its final state. None of them, according to the intentionalist, are independent artworks ontologically distinct from the finished track. Instead, similar to how ten-year-old me isn't a fundamentally distinct person from right-now me, the other mixes— including the original, seemingly final mix—are merely earlier stages of the now-finished track. To speak technically, they count among the finished track's *earlier temporal parts*.

To get clearer on what this means, consider that, while writing this chapter, I've revised this paragraph dozens of times to put it into what I believe is the best state to convey the ideas I want to communicate with it. Some of these revisions were subtle: adding a helpful adjective here, deleting another one there, etc. But some were more substantial. Indeed, I've deleted this paragraph and restarted it from scratch multiple times. But none of these changes seem substantive enough to affect the paragraph's identity. That is, it's implausible to think that every time I made a change I produced a brand new paragraph. Instead, I've been working on one and the same paragraph throughout the writing process. The same is true for artworks. Jane Austen's many drafts of *Emma*, for example, are not independent works of art (ontologically distinct novels) but merely earlier stages of the same novel. This would even be the case if she'd burned a completed manuscript and started over numerous times. So long as all of her actions are directed toward realizing one and the same plan, the intentionalists hold that each draft is part of one and the same work of art.

The intentionalists would analyze Swift's re-recordings in the exact same way. In an interview promoting the release of *Fearless (Taylor's Version)*, Swift said, "I really did want this to be very true to what I initially thought of and what I'd initially written. But better. Obviously."[21] This indicates that Swift is using the re-recordings as an opportunity to improve on the original versions of her albums and thereby better realize her plans for them. The fact that she has recorded the tracks again from scratch does not mean, for the intentionalists, that the re-recordings are new works of art. That Swift doesn't believe the original recordings were as good as they could have been and is making strides to improve them entails that *they had always been unfinished* and thus were earlier temporal parts of the now-finished albums: the re-recordings she's released as "Taylor's Versions."

If intentionalism were correct, then re-recording would count as a way for artists to produce legitimate instances of their albums. An artist would simply need to come to realize that the original versions fell short of their plans, as Swift has seemingly done, and respond by recording them again. Once satisfied that the new recordings fully realize their plans, the artist would have thereby completed their albums. This would entail, among other things, that the original master recordings *never were* a means to produce genuine instances of the finished albums, but only instances of their earlier stages—little more than demos of the now-finished albums. As a result, the artist would have literally reclaimed their albums without needing to legally acquire the original master recordings of them, since the finished and thus genuine works are encoded in the new masters.

Why Intentionalism Fails

But as with formalism, intentionalism promises more than it can deliver. The problem resides primarily in what intentionalists believe follows from the fact that artists' plans are inherently revisable and indeterminate. Specifically, that an artist could always, at any point, change their plan toward a seemingly finished work—perhaps one that's been out in the world and beloved for years—and thereby reveal (perhaps only to themselves) that it was, in fact, never finished: a mere work-in-progress. This is problematic for several reasons.

For one thing, it seems to grant artists weird metaphysical powers. By changing their plan, an artist reveals that their work was unfinished. As Rohrbaugh conceives of it, this change isn't a metaphysical one but an epistemological one: only the artist's *judgment* that the work was finished changes, its *ontological status* as unfinished remains unchanged.[22] Yet, whether an artwork is finished *right now* certainly appears, on his view, to be contingent on a choice the artist will make *in the future*. If the artist ultimately never decides to change the work after they've released it, then it's been finished at least since it was released. But if the artist ultimately decides, perhaps even decades later, that the work didn't fully realize their plan, then the work will have always been unfinished.

Swift's choice to re-record her albums was an historically contingent one. Scott Borchetta, who owned Big Machine Records prior to selling it to Scooter Braun, could have been nice and let Swift buy the rights to her albums with no strings attached. Alternatively, Swift could have agreed to Borchetta's deal of acquiring the masters for her first six albums, one at a time, by recording six new albums for Big Machine.[23] Or she could have simply done nothing in response to Braun buying her catalog. Since none of these scenarios involve Swift eventually changing her plans, the intentionalists would hold that Braun acquired the masters for the finished albums when he purchased Big Machine. So, it doesn't merely seem that Swift's judgment about her albums changed while their ontological status remained the same when she decided to re-record them. It very much appears as if her change of judgment literally changed the past and made it so that Braun acquired the rights to unfinished works.

It isn't clear that artists, or indeed anyone, has the causal power to change the past. We certainly change our beliefs and judgments about the past pretty regularly, but we don't actually change the past when we do. Unless some controversial theories about the laws of physics end up being true, the past very much can't be changed—at least, not through mere cognitive acts. Because of this, we should reject intentionalism.

A further problem for the theory is that it's radically at odds with our actual critical and appreciative practices. It matters to us whether we're engaging with a finished artwork or a work-in-progress. We respond to and evaluate drafts differently than finished novels, demos and rough mixes differently than finished tracks, rough cuts differently than finished films, etc. In particular, we treat them less as independent works of art to be regarded in their own right and more as documentary artifacts that can help us better appreciate and understand the finished works. But if intentionalists are right, then we can *never* be confident that any artwork we're engaging with is finished.

During the eleven years between its 2008 release and Swift's 2019 announcement that she was re-recording her back catalog, we all thought we'd been listening to, enjoying, and talking about the actual

Fearless. Yet, intentionalism entails that we were instead engaging with one of the album's earlier stages—effectively, a highly polished demo. We were thus appreciating and evaluating that version of *Fearless* in the wrong way. Worse still, we also can't be sure that we're engaging with *Fearless (Taylor's Version)* in the right way because Swift could, years from now, choose to re-record *Fearless* again, meaning that it will also have been, unbeknownst to us, a mere demo of the actual album. This process of revision and re-release could repeat every few years for the rest of Swift's life. Worst of all, Swift could form the intention to change the work to better realize her plan for it right before she dies (sorry for being so macabre) without telling anyone, and this would mean that the album always has been (and always will be) an unfinished work. If this were correct, then it would be practically impossible for us to ever engage with it in the right way.

The preceding story could be told for any work of art we ever engage with. As a result, intentionalism would entirely undercut our ability to appreciate and evaluate art, as we'd never know for certain whether the artworks we're dealing with are finished or unfinished and thus how to properly engage with them. Since intentionalism aims to clarify when artworks are finished so that we can appreciate and understand them in the right way, the theory fails on its own terms.

Intentionalism's failure provides us with a compelling reason to believe that artists cannot change a work after they've released it without thereby changing its identity. In actual practice, we're generally quite resistant to accepting artworks of this sort as the genuine works. Think of all the outrage George Lucas has sparked with the many changes he's made to the original three *Star Wars* films since their initial release. A large portion of the *Star Wars* fandom refuses to accept any of the altered editions as the true films; they think of them instead as being distinct (and inferior) films. Along similar lines, we treat remixes as distinct from original tracks. We appreciate and evaluate the remix of "Bad Blood" featuring Kendrick Lamar on the Deluxe Edition of

1989 differently than the original album mix. In general, we seem to think that once a work has been released to the world it cannot be altered in any substantive way without resulting in an ontologically distinct work of art.

This way of thinking is supported by Darren Hudson Hick. Like the intentionalists, Hick recognizes that the process of making art is usually a complex and messy one. Artists often continually revise their plans in response to how their work looks (sounds, etc.), which leads them to change how it looks, and so on—a feedback loop that continues until the artist is satisfied the work is done. Due to this complexity, Hick contends that it is impossible to identify the precise moment at which an artist has completed a work.[24] Fortunately, we don't need to know this for our practical purposes. To appreciate and evaluate an artwork in the right way we simply need to know that it is, in fact, finished. And we know that a work is finished, according to Hick, because it has been released to the public.[25] While the artist likely completed the work sometime before it was released, the fact that it has been released means that it is definitively finished.[26] Any change the artist makes to the work after this point results in a new work of art.

If Hick's view is right, and I believe it is, then we can confidently appreciate and evaluate pretty much all of the art we regularly engage with—the fact that a work has been released gives us a sufficient reason to treat it as finished.[27] As importantly for our purposes, Hick's view entails that Swift's re-recordings aren't identical to the original recordings of her albums. The fact that they were released at different times, paired with their distinct causal histories and sonic differences, is enough to guarantee that they're distinct works of art. This means that, contrary to the intentionalists, the original albums are not unfinished works (mere earlier stages of the Taylor's Versions); they were finished when they were originally released, just as we always thought they were. Each original album includes the same songs as its corresponding Taylor's Version, but because they're collections of distinct tracks, they are ontologically distinct albums.

Metaphorical Reclamation: Better than Revenge

Formalism and intentionalism offered the two best metaphysical routes through which Swift could literally reclaim her albums by re-recording them. But since both of them fail, it appears that re-recording isn't a means for artists to produce genuine instances of their albums. Swift's re-recording project, therefore, has only allowed her to reclaim her albums in a metaphorical sense.

But so what? The sort of literal reclamation that the formalists and intentionalists promised is a weird one. Imagine being in high school and your diary—into which you've poured all of your deepest hopes, dreams, fears, loves, hates, etc.—falls into your bully's hands. A formalist tells you not to worry, they'll get it back for you. They then proceed to write a word-for-word duplicate of your diary, copying your handwriting precisely, and give it to you. Then an intentionalist says they'll help you get it back. "All you have to do," they advise, "is revise some of your hopes, dreams, and so on, and rewrite it. The real diary will then be yours, and your bully will be stuck with a mere rough draft." In either case, you would be disappointed, to say the least! Your bully still has your diary and can do whatever they want with it.

The route to reclamation the formalists and intentionalists promised Taylor Swift is little different than this. Even if her re-recorded masters allowed her to produce genuine instances of the original albums, Scooter Braun would still stand to benefit financially from his stake in the hopes, dreams, fears, and more that Swift poured into those albums and that are encoded into their masters. (Not to mention all the blood, sweat, and tears she and her production team put into producing them.) A literal victory in which Swift doesn't actually acquire the original masters, therefore, would not be better than a symbolic one. Just as you'd actually want your diary back, Swift ultimately wants to acquire the rights to those masters.

While reclaiming her albums metaphorically rather than literally may have given Swift a "merely" symbolic victory, probably not in her wildest dreams could it be going better. Interest in Swift and her work increased dramatically because of her re-recording project. The four re-recorded albums released so far all debuted at number one on the Billboard charts; they've collectively sold over 4 million copies in the United States alone; and they've been collectively streamed over 14 billion times on Spotify,[28] with Swift having been named Spotify's Artist of the Year for 2023.[29] iHeartRadio, the nation's largest radio broadcaster, has committed to replacing the "stolen versions" of her tracks with Taylor's Versions, depriving Braun and others of millions of dollars in the process.[30] Her Eras Tour, which partly trades on both the nature of her re-recordings (as occasions to revisit her past selves, as Ley David Elliette Cray examines in Chapter 8 of this volume) and their success, is the second-highest earning of all time and is estimated to have added over $5 billion to the US economy.[31] And to round out 2023, she was named *Time*'s Person of the Year.[32]

The number of records Swift has broken and accolades she has received just since releasing *Fearless (Taylor's Version)* in April 2021 could probably fill more than an entire chapter in this book. But just as importantly, she's inspired other artists to follow her lead and re-record their own music,[33] or else demand greater control over their work.[34] It seems as if, to misquote Obi-wan Kenobi, by trying to strike her down, Scooter Braun has made Taylor Swift more powerful than he—and perhaps anyone but the most ardent Swifties—could have possibly imagined.[35]

Notes

1   Taylor Swift (@taylorswift), "WELL. SO. I've been counting down for months and finally the 'I Can See You' video is out," *Instagram*, July 8, 2023, https://www.instagram.com/p/CubIwi0ue3l/ (accessed December 18, 2023).

2   Metaphysics is the branch of philosophy interested in investigating the fundamental nature of reality.

3   I hate to bring up Adams here, given the credible allegations of sexual misconduct that have been made against him. Unfortunately, his cover

album is the most helpful example for my purposes in this section. (Joe Coscarelli and Melena Ryzik, "Ryan Adams Dangled Success. Women Say They Paid a Price," *New York Times*, February 13, 2019, https://www.nytimes.com/2019/02/13/arts/music/ryan-adams-women-sex.html [accessed December 18, 2023].)

4   See, for example, Stephen Davies, "The Ontology of Musical Works and the Authenticity of Their Performances," *Noûs* 25, no. 1 (1991): 21–41; Theodore Grayck, *Rhythm and Noise: An Aesthetics of Rock* (Durham, NC: Duke University Press, 1996); and Andrew Kania, "Making Tracks: The Ontology of Rock Music," *Journal of Aesthetics and Art Criticism* 64, no. 4 (2006): 401–14.

5   Copyright law also treats songs and recorded tracks as distinct entities, as Darren Hudson Hick shows in Chapter 1 of this volume. While Swift owns the copyright to her songs, she doesn't own the master recordings of the tracks that appear on the original versions of her albums. This is why—as allowed by her original contracts with Big Machine Records— she can produce new versions of the albums by re-recording her songs, but can't mechanically or digitally copy the original masters.

6   See Stephen Davies, "Ontology of Art," in *The Oxford Handbook of Aesthetics*, ed. Jerrold Levinson (Oxford: Oxford University Press, 2003), 155–80.

7   Clive Bell, *Art* (London: Chatto & Windus, 1914); and Monroe Beardsley, *Aesthetics: Problems in the Philosophy of Criticism*, 2nd edn (1958; repr., Indianapolis, IN: Hackett, 1981), 31–4.

8   The fact that record companies have responded to the success of Taylor's Versions by rewriting contracts to prevent artists from ever re-recording their albums suggests that they are troubled by exactly this possibility. (See Steve Knopper, "Labels Want to Prevent 'Taylor's Version'-Like Re-recordings from Ever Happening Again," *Billboard*, October 30, 2023, https://www.billboard.com/pro/taylor-swift-re-recordings-labels-change-contracts/ [accessed December 18, 2023].)

9   This is a commonly held view among philosophers of music. See, for example, Peter Kivy, *Music Alone: Philosophical Reflections on the Purely Musical Experience* (Ithaca, NY: Cornell University Press, 1990), 86–9; and Roger Scruton, *The Aesthetics of Music* (Oxford: Oxford University Press, 1997), chap. 2.

10 See Brandon Polite, "Shared Musical Experiences," *British Journal of Aesthetics* 59, no. 4 (2019): 429–47.

11 For discussion of the natures of mass art and mass consumption, see Noël Carroll, *A Philosophy of Mass Art* (Oxford: Oxford University Press, 1998), 188.

12 See, for example, Walton, "Categories of Art," 334–67; Jerrold Levinson, "Defining Art Historically," *British Journal of Aesthetics* 19, no. 3 (1979): 232–50; Arthur C. Danto, *The Transfiguration of the Commonplace: A Philosophy of Art* (Cambridge, MA: Harvard University Press, 1981); Amie L. Thomasson, "The Ontology of Art and Knowledge in Aesthetics," *Journal of Aesthetics and Art Criticism* 63, no. 3 (2005): 221–29.

13 My argument here is consistent with Michael Thomas Connolly's analysis of the recording process in Chapter 4 of this volume.

14 Guy Rohrbaugh, "Psychologism and Completeness in the Arts," *Journal of Aesthetics and Art Criticism* 75, no. 2 (2017): 131–41. See also his "Artworks as Historical Individuals," *European Journal of Philosophy* 11, no. 2 (2003): 177–205.

15 Rohrbaugh, "Psychologism and Completeness," 136–7.

16 Ibid., 138.

17 Ibid., 137.

18 This in no way excuses her use of the term, of course.

19 The edited version would also constitute the *finished song*, according to intentionalism, since a change to the lyrics is a change to the ontologically thin song as much as it is to the ontologically thick track.

20 Ibid., 139.

21 Taylor Swift, "Taylor Swift Says She Went 'Line By Line' on Every 'Fearless' Song | PEOPLE," interview, *People*, April 9, 2021, https://www.youtube.com/watch?v=QAnbsUz1fOs (accessed December 18, 2023).

22 Rohrbaugh, "Psychologism and Completeness," 139.

23 Taylor Swift, "For years I asked, pleaded for a chance to own my work," *Tumblr*, June 30, 2019, https://taylorswift.tumblr.com/post/185958366550/for-years-i-asked-pleaded-for-a-chance-to-own-my (accessed December 18, 2023).

24 Darren Hudson Hick, "When Is a Work of Art Finished?," *Journal of Aesthetics and Art Criticism* 66, no. 1 (2008): 67–76; 71–2.

25 Ibid., 72–4.

26 A couple qualifiers are needed here. First, since artists sometimes choose to release unfinished works (such as demos of tracks and early cuts of films), the work needs to be released without an explicit declaration by the artist that it's unfinished (ibid., 71). Second, since artists are sometimes coerced (by record labels, movie studios, etc.) into releasing unfinished works, the work must also be released with the artist's consent (ibid., 72–3). So long as those two criteria are met, a work that's been released to the public counts as finished in Hick's view.

27 That a work has been released is, to use a technical term, a "sufficient condition" for the work to be complete—that is, enough by itself to guarantee that it's finished.

28 "Taylor Swift—Spotify Top Albums," *Kworb.net*, last updated February 12, 2024, https://kworb.net/spotify/artist/06HL4z0CvFAxyc27GXpf02_albums.html (accessed February 13, 2024).

29 Chelsea Sanchez, "Taylor Swift Is Crowned as Spotify's Top Artist of the Year with 26 Billion Streams Worldwide," *Harper's Bazaar*, November 28, 2023, https://www.harpersbazaar.com/culture/art-books-music/a45975825/taylor-swift-most-streamed-spotify-artist-2023/ (accessed December 18, 2023).

30 Chris Willman, "iHeart Promises to Only Play Taylor Swift's New Versions of Her Songs, Once They're Out," *Variety*, November 17, 2021, https://variety.com/2021/music/news/iheart-taylor-swift-will-only-play-new-versions-1235114816/ (accessed December 18, 2023).

31 Connor Murray, "Every Major Event in Taylor Swift's Record-Breaking 2023—From the Eras Tour to Time Person of The Year," *Forbes*, December 6, 2023, https://www.forbes.com/sites/conormurray/2023/12/06/every-major-event-in-taylor-swifts-record-breaking-2023-from-the-eras-tour-to-time-person-of-the-year/ (accessed December 18, 2023).

32 Sam Lansky, "Person of the Year 2023: Taylor Swift," *Time*, December 6, 2023, https://time.com/6342806/person-of-the-year-2023-taylor-swift/ (accessed December 18, 2023).

33 Eleanor Dye, "Paramore Are Set to 'Re-record Their Music after Row with Bosses at Atlantic' in a Move Inspired by 'Supportive' Pal Taylor Swift," *MailOnline*, January 7, 2024, https://www.dailymail.co.uk/tvshowbiz/article-12935887/Paramore-rerecord-music-inspired-taylor-swift.html (accessed January 15, 2024).

34 Eamonn Forde, "Taylor-made Deals: How Artists Are Following
Swift's Rights Example," *The Guardian*, January 9, 2024, https://www.
theguardian.com/music/2024/jan/09/taylor-swift-deals-how-artists-
rights-example (accessed January 15, 2024).

35 I have presented early versions of the ideas that made their way into this
chapter to many audiences over the past couple of years. I would like to
thank all of them for their questions and insights. I would also like to
thank Darren Hudson Hick, Alex King, and Ley David Elliette Cray
for their feedback on earlier drafts of this chapter.

6

Meaning and Morals in Taylor's Versions

Alex King

Spot the Difference

Turning the corner in an art gallery in 1964, philosopher and art critic Arthur Danto sees a large stack of what appear to be shipping boxes full of dish scrubbing pads. Upon closer inspection, he realizes that they are painted facsimiles made of plywood. They were Andy Warhol's now-famous *Brillo Boxes*.

Danto recalls that "'Brillo Box' was instantly accepted as art; but the question became aggravated of why Warhol's Brillo boxes *were* works of art while their commonplace counterparts, in the back rooms of supermarkets throughout Christendom, were not."[1] Their outward features were basically the same. The plywood boxes look (more or less) identical to the actual shipping boxes. Both were made by people. Warhol's boxes didn't contain Brillo pads, but nor do the cardboard ones, until they're filled. So, we're left with a puzzle. Why are Warhol's boxes art while the others aren't?

Fifty-five years later, in an interview for CBS, Taylor Swift sits across reporter Tracy Smith. They discuss the personal feuds and legalities that surround the ownership of her "masters," the original set of studio recordings that form the basis of produced songs. The take-home point is that the masters of her first six albums don't belong to her, but she wishes that they did. Smith inquires, "Now, could you re-record?" Swift bursts into a wide grin, "*Oh* yeah," and reveals that she plans to do just that.[2]

As of this writing in early 2024, we find ourselves two-thirds of the way through Swift's project. She has released four re-recorded albums: *Fearless* (2008/2021), *Red* (2012/2021), *Speak Now* (2010/2023), and *1989* (2014/2023), and there are two more to go.

Like Warhol's *Brillo Boxes*, the re-recordings—officially dubbed "Taylor's Versions"—bear a very close resemblance to the originals. Of course, Swift's voice has matured and changed, but then Warhol's boxes were made of plywood. Even if the facsimiles aren't perfectly indistinguishable from their originals, they are very, very close. Both could, to the cursory or untrained audience, easily be mistaken for the original.

Danto's puzzle is how we classify Warhol's *Brillo Boxes* as art, but not the actual cardboard boxes made by the Brillo company. Our puzzle is not quite that. Both the original versions of Swift's albums and the re-recordings are artworks. Our puzzle has to do with the meaning of those works. It seems like Taylor's Versions *mean* something different from her originals. But how could they?

Red Squares

Danto offers his readers a related thought experiment: Imagine yourself in a museum, and lined on the walls are several red, square paintings. At first glance, they look the same, but when you look more carefully, you can spot some minor differences: one is on canvas, another on wood; one uses oil paint, another acrylic. They are also produced at different times and by different artists, and have different references and titles. One is a punning Moscow landscape called *Red Square*. Another is called *Israelites Crossing the Red Sea*, a sad reference to what the drowned Egyptians might have experienced once the Red Sea swallowed them up. Another, *Red Table Cloth*, is a clever still life.

Danto's concern is not our concern. He introduces these examples in order to contrast them with red squares of paint that are not art. But his discussion presupposes that all of these are art, and more importantly that they are different works of art with different meanings. They are to be interpreted differently, given the variations across their authorship, titles, genre, time period, and context of production.

Like the assorted red squares in the museum, Taylor's Versions and the originals they mimic appear superficially identical (or close enough). But like the assorted red squares, they don't seem to mean quite the same thing. For a closer examination, let's take Swift's red squares: *Red* and *Red (Taylor's Version)*.

The songs have the same songwriters and the same headline performers, though some of the other performers are different (studio musicians, as well as mixing and production personnel). The tracks have very similar if not identical titles: "22" becomes "22 (Taylor's Version)." The genre is the same—although here, too, we might have a slight difference, depending on how we understand the bounds of a genre. Maybe Taylor's Versions belong to a genre that we could call "corporate revenge music" alongside certain indie statement albums or Rage Against the Machine's corpus. Or maybe we could consider re-recordings their own genre, including Taylor's Versions alongside the re-recordings done by the Everly Brothers, Frank Sinatra, U2, Def Leppard, and other artists.

These minor differences may not affect the meaning of Taylor's Versions (though I'll complicate that assumption below). Even so, there are much more significant differences. The albums were released at different times and therefore in different contexts. And context is a crucial factor in the determination of meaning. To take a very simple case, calling someone tall in the context of the NBA draft suggests a significantly different height range than it does for someone you would call tall in the context of a kindergarten class. Or consider signs that inform us of mask-wearing practices. Not only did these signs develop changing meanings and associations during the months and years after the start of the Covid-19 pandemic in early 2020, but such signs would be nearly unintelligible before then. How would we have interpreted a store sign in 2015 that read "Masks recommended"? What kind of mask would we even have thought they were talking about? Is the store holding a masquerade ball? Or maybe a Halloween party? Context matters, and the rest of this chapter will explore the ways that context and other seemingly slight differences affect the meaning of Taylor's Versions.

Albums

Let's start by looking at albums, since Swift conceives of albums as an important economic and artistic whole.[3] Taylor's Versions are accompanied by new liner notes. In the liner notes to *Red (Taylor's Version)*, she writes that *Red* "was all over the place, a fractured mosaic of feelings," but adds: "I'm not sure if it was pouring my thoughts into this album, hearing thousands of your voices sing the lyrics back to me in passionate solidarity, or if it was simply time, but something was healed along the way."[4]

If she feels these things, she may sing the re-recordings in a subtly different way. If that's true, then it's easy to see how they would acquire new meanings. But if all that changes is her emotional state when she sings them or her communicative intent, and not anything we can directly perceive in the music, can we say that Taylor's Version has new meanings? I think we can.

Before digging deeper into this, it makes sense to take a brief step back. What is artistic "meaning" and what would it take for that "meaning" to change? Part of meaning is the literal meaning of words—an issue of *semantics*, if you want to be technical about it. "Fly" has multiple literal meanings: the action, the insect, or the zipper on jeans. Part of meaning is also determined by context—an issue of *pragmatics*, again to be technical. When I say "me," that refers to Alex King; but when you say "me," it refers to someone else. "Tall" works like this, too: tall people, tall buildings, and tall mountains have vastly different height ranges. A further part of meaning that I want to include in this discussion is emotional expression and effect. If I shout angrily and you are alarmed by my anger, that's pretty different from what happens if I calmly articulate the same sounds and you grasp them normally, with no alarm or shock. I want to say my shouting means something different from my calm articulation. This is especially true for music, where a line sung over minor chords can have a very different meaning than a line sung over major ones. With this in hand, now turn back to Taylor's Versions.

We cannot ignore the important context that Swift's life has changed and developed since she released the original albums. Musicologist Paul Théberge writes of *Fearless (Taylor's Version)* that "the songs can no longer be easily read as tentative statements penned by an earnest teenager, they are recordings of songs that have already proven their worth, made by an artist who has (finally) matured." [5] Although Taylor Swift is the artist behind both the originals and the re-recordings, different versions of Swift stand behind the two, as Ley David Elliette Cray discusses in detail in Chapter 8 of this volume. She is, as Théberge says, not an earnest teenager—or an earnest woman in her early twenties, looking to break out of the country scene and garner more mainstream appeal, as with *Red*; instead, she is an influential A-list celebrity with a net worth of over a billion dollars.

In 2021, when Swift released the re-recordings of both *Fearless* and *Red*, she was also in a stable, multi-year relationship. It is in this light and with the accompanying liner notes that we hear the re-recordings. When we listen to *Red*, we hear a Taylor Swift who sings of messiness and fracture; when we listen to *Red (Taylor's Version)*, we hear a Taylor Swift who sings with nostalgia and healing. This contextual information has the power to change the meanings, despite the similarity of sounds.

We also cannot ignore that, at the level of the album, there are actually very significant material changes. In addition to updated liner notes, *Red (Taylor's Version)*, like all Taylor's Version albums, contains many more tracks than the original album or its Deluxe Edition. The albums, in this case, are clearly just quite different works.[6] They don't resemble each other as closely as Danto's red squares; they resemble each other in the way that a full novel and its abridged versions resemble each other. As a result, the meaning that we take from these albums as full works will clearly be different.

Finally, we cannot ignore the very fact that they are re-recordings. I mentioned the titles earlier. *Red* and *Red (Taylor's Version)* are only slightly different. The difference may seem trivial, but it isn't. Retitling is absolutely indispensable to Swift's goal: industry professionals, streaming services, and consumers need to be able to tell the difference between the originals and her versions if they are to support her in a market where both exist.[7] Furthermore, as Danto says, "[A] title is more than a name; frequently it is a direction for interpretation."[8] The painting titled *Red Table Cloth* we correctly interpret as a still life, in contrast to the visually indistinguishable *Red Square*, which we read as a witty Moscow landscape. The former offers artistic commentary on the still life genre, where the latter offers, perhaps, political commentary on communism or the Soviet Union. Different interpretive avenues open up in light of the titles. In these cases, the titles are essential pieces of direction that we have for interpreting the paintings. Similarly, an essential part of what Taylor's Versions *are* is protest against the music industry. It is the reason without which they would not exist, their sine qua non. When an album or song has "(Taylor's Version)" appended to it, we have an important piece of direction for receiving and interpreting it. This is in part why it would be very strange to review any of Swift's re-recorded albums without at any point discussing them as re-recordings.

Songs

If we turn to the songs, we find similar considerations. The liner notes, Swift's evolved career, and the legal controversies in the music industry affect the meaning of *Red (Taylor's Version)* as a whole as much as the individual songs. But we can discover even more if we look at the songs themselves.

"Girl at Home" was not part of the sixteen songs released on *Red*, but was part of the additional content that appeared on the Target-exclusive Deluxe Edition, released at the same time in 2012. It was a demo for *Red* and is a fine, if somewhat boring, acoustic guitar-forward country pop ballad. By comparison, "Girl at Home (Taylor's Version)" is quite different. The lyrics and length stay roughly the same, but the production has transformed the song into a much more energetic, danceable electropop jam.[9]

Here, we see that Swift is willing to make substantial changes, and this set fans wondering whether she would make others in the course of other re-recordings. As it happened, one long-speculated change appeared on *Speak Now (Taylor's Version)*, in the song "Better than Revenge (Taylor's Version)." The song tells the story of the narrator, whose love interest is stolen from her by another woman. The original chorus discredits the thieving interloper in part by hinting at her promiscuity, but revised lines refer instead to the man's irresistible, moth-like attraction to her and suggest that the woman is seductively drawing him in. The original had received criticism for "slut shaming,"[10] and Swift had expressed regret over the lyric.[11] It seemed a perfect opportunity to revise, and she took it.

The revised line is in keeping with the original lyrics, which simply portray Swift's rival as a mean and insensitive snob. But the new line adds two subtle shifts: it paints Swift's romantic rival as a femme fatale—a more flattering because more agentially assertive position; and it paints her ex as a hapless doofus. These are both morally significant shifts. With the femme fatale element, Swift adds something to the woman's character portrayal beyond mean and snobbish. She is now infused with a bit of cunning—an admirable quality, even if it is used to hurt the narrator. More significantly, the earlier version fails entirely to deride the ex, focusing solely on the woman. In hinting that he behaved foolishly, Swift quietly corrects a common critique of (quasi-)adultery narratives cast under this gender rubric: that they pit women against each other, ignoring the man's responsibility.

In these cases, her changes undeniably alter the meaning of the songs. A country ballad doesn't express the same emotional tone or evoke the same response as an electropop jam. And the characters portrayed in "Better than Revenge (Taylor's Version)" have importantly different features than those portrayed in "Better than Revenge." But we don't have to reach for such overt cases to see meanings shifting.

Consider, from *Speak Now*, the song "Dear John." This song is widely believed to be about singer-songwriter John Mayer, whom Swift briefly dated. In late 2010, just under a year after their breakup, the album was released. John Mayer was on the public mind for an interview given earlier that year to *Playboy* magazine, in which he made a series of misogynistic and racist comments. It was in this context that fans heard Swift sing about how young she was during their relationship. But in 2021, a post-#MeToo world renders those lines much more disturbing. And it is hard not to hear Mayer, who was thirty-two at the time of his involvement with a nineteen-year-old Swift, lobbied with an additional predatory accusation.

This can get a bit confusing because there are actually two issues at play here. One: Do we now hear something different in the *original* version that we didn't before? Has its meaning changed? Two: Does the *new version* mean something different from the original? Regarding the first issue, when we watch movies or read novels with outdated moral frameworks, we often feel the twin impulses to excuse ("Well, things were different back then … ") and to condemn ("But, wow, this is pretty awful."). But does the meaning of these originals change over time, or is it fixed and only our reception that changes? I'm not taking a stand on this question.

What I am suggesting is that, with respect to the second issue, were those screenwriters and those novelists to *re-compose* their works verbatim and *re-release them now*, the meaning of those rereleases could not help but be different. Artistic intention matters to the meaning of an artwork. It's not all that there is to meaning (you can't just make words mean whatever you want them to, any more than you can simply *will* a minor chord to sound happy), but it isn't irrelevant. And Swift's artistic intentions for her re-recordings are different from her artistic intentions for the originals.

When Taylor Swift originally composed and sang the lyrics to "Dear John," she—like many of us—was probably not thinking about male power and privilege and the way that it systematically interacts with vulnerable young women. She, like many women before the #MeToo

Movement, may have conceived her situation rather innocently. She sings that she should have known better; she wonders if the bad relationship was her fault—the result of her being too blindly optimistic. These are the thoughts of someone who sincerely doubts herself.

When she sings these lyrics more than a decade later, issues adjacent to #MeToo cannot but be at the forefront of her mind. She has demonstrated very clearly, through interviews and even legal action,[12] that she thinks a great deal about sexual harassment and about men who abuse their power and privilege at the expense of women around them. Her more recent album *Midnights (3am version)* even contains a song that is much more explicitly critical of Mayer, "Would've Could've Should've," where she demands that he return to her the childhood and girlish innocence that she has since lost. So, when a 2023 Swift calls attention to her age at the time of their relationship, she infuses it with additional gravity. When she wonders whether everything was her fault, it is wryer and more biting, almost sarcastic—not a typical emotional posture for Swift, but one that, knowing her likely updated perspective on the situation, is doubtless implied.

To my mind the best example of this will be the imminent re-recording of "Look What You Made Me Do." The song appears on Swift's 2017 album *Reputation* and hasn't yet been re-recorded, but it is a revenge anthem for the ages. It was the lead single, released in advance of the album, and ended a roughly yearlong hiatus from major public appearances and releases. In it, Swift alludes to a number of different feuds, mistreatments, and past relationships, all revolving around the main refrain, an unapologetic "Look What You Made Me Do."

A very salient spurning will accompany the re-recording of this song: the cause of the re-recordings themselves, and the revenge that the re-recording project embodies. Swift will surely be thinking of and drawing from this experience when she re-records this song, and it will be impossible not to think of Big Machine Records, Scooter Braun, and the whole lot when we hear her sing about how they've taken her kingdom and tried to make a fool out of her. When she sings about how often she rises from the dead there will be an additional allusion—to her rising up with a set of new masters in hand (even if the project isn't yet complete at the time she releases Taylor's Version of *Reputation*). Such lyrics seem as though they were pre-written for this situation, and I will be astounded if she does not explicitly note the additional meaning in interviews, liner notes, or visual references during performances.

To Change or Not to Change?

The tangible changes Swift has made to individual songs shift their meanings in pretty significant ways. Swift has also chosen to add new liner notes and other new resources (new titles, additional tracks) for us to use in interpreting her music. And, though she hasn't chosen this, the updated context affects how we interpret songs like "Dear John" and the eventual "Look What You Made Me Do." In some cases, the shift in meaning that comes from context will only be slight, but in others—like the cases I've discussed—it will be more significant.

Interestingly enough, the fact that she has made some tangible changes affects even those cases where she hasn't changed anything. Maybe this sounds paradoxical: her actual changes change things that haven't changed. But think about it this way. Imagine that every day, you wake up and someone else makes your breakfast. That sounds great, but imagine that you're not choosing what to eat. It's just made for you, and that's your breakfast. You eat it because you're hungry—maybe you like it fine, maybe you love it, maybe you would really rather have something else. (If this sounds far-fetched, remember that this is the life of many children.) One day, you wake up and whoever it is that makes your breakfast asks you what you want. You're taken aback! Suppose, as seems likely, that you decide to switch it up. You've been getting eggs every day. Today, on the first day you get to choose your breakfast, you request Cinnamon Toast Crunch. You eat it—maybe you like it, maybe you love it, or maybe you regret the decision. The next day, you wake up, and whoever makes your breakfast asks what you want this morning. Suppose you go back to eggs—maybe you liked the cereal, but not for today, or maybe you didn't like it at all. *The fact that you had eggs for breakfast* signifies something different today than it did before. You know you can have something else. Just yesterday, you did have something else. Before, eggs were chosen for you. But this time, *you* chose them.

Now look at Swift and the re-recordings. She has shown us that she can and will make changes. This inevitably makes us wonder what she might change in the future. But it also affects any cases where she *might* make changes that she *doesn't*. When she leaves things the same, it's not because she's obeying some unwritten rule of re-recordings; it's because she chooses to.

For example, when Swift re-recorded the sleeper hit "All Too Well" from *Red*, she recorded both the mimic track "All Too Well (Taylor's Version)" and an extended ten-minute version that was the final bonus track on *Red (Taylor's Version)*. She has done this with other songs, too, releasing a doppelgänger track along with a remix, acoustic version, or extended version. This makes a corresponding decision for "Girl at Home" a live possibility, one that some fans wish she had pursued. But she chose not to take it. And her decision to re-record "All Too Well (Taylor's Version)" with her usual fidelity to the original is something many fans and radio stations are surely very happy about.

One among many Reddit fan threads discussing this situation is titled: "What songs have the possibility of getting the girl at home treatment?" Speculation in this and threads like it is a mix of users discussing what they *hope* she changes and what they *expect* her to change, but also what they *dread* she might change and will be relieved if she doesn't. In the original post, user graysonsix writes: "I think Taylor changing the production of girl at home really sets the standard of what Taylor's version means."[13] And they are absolutely right. That she leaves certain songs untouched comes to signify something—perhaps an additional respect for the past or for the fan relationship with the song (as we might read in "All Too Well [Taylor's Version]"), or a doubling-down on the message (as we might read in "Dear John [Taylor's Version]"). Especially when songs present the same conundrums as those cases where she has made significant changes—if, for instance, they contain questionable lyrics or artistic choices she wouldn't now make—her choice to *not* alter anything has heightened significance. Or consider how she altered "Style (Taylor's Version)" for 2023's *1989 (Taylor's Version)*: she did this not radically but still noticeably. Among other things, it's much louder, the balance has shifted to emphasize the bass and higher frequencies (including a noticeably more prominent synthesizer line in the chorus), and her vocal articulations have changed. Given the preservation of "All Too Well (Taylor's Version)" and many other of her major hits, it's clear that she has some respect for preservation. But her changes also show that this respect knows some bounds. I won't speculate further on why she decided to make the tradeoffs she has in "Style" or any other particular case. The point is simply that her choice to alter some re-recordings seeps out and affects the meaning of even those that remain largely unchanged.

But maybe this all looks a bit overblown, a case of reading too much into things. Maybe the re-recordings aren't *that* special or interesting. They're just a simple political statement, a way for her to re-appropriate her music. The idea that we should reinterpret her entire re-recorded body of work, down to the most identical-sounding song, may seem ridiculous—as the authors of Chapter 2 in this volume argue. It's just pop music; it ain't that deep. For those plagued by such worries, remember that Swift has already taught her fans to scrutinize her work to the tiniest detail. She is famous for including "Easter eggs" in her work (and outside of it), hidden messages that fans can unravel to discover different bits of information or hints at what's to come.[14] To suggest that paying attention to subtle differences between the originals and re-recordings is simply a case of reading too much into things is to forget that Swift is a practiced expert in subtle messaging.

Meaning and Doing

We have so far focused on the meaning of Taylor's Versions, but there is more to communication than what we mean. Communication is also about what we *do*. This is the heart of what's called *speech act theory*: that when we *speak*, we also *act*—not in the sense that we pretend something, but in the sense that we perform an action. When I say, "Would you please pass the salt?" I utter something with meaning. But if you grasp my meaning, then you understand me as *doing something*, in this case, making a request of you. And in this case, I ask you to do it in a way that is *polite*. If I said, "Hey, gimme the salt already!" I would also be communicating a request, but in a pretty different style. In a very real way, I am *doing* something different. In response to my polite request, you will, if you're nice, pass me the salt. That's another layer of doing: I do something, and if I've done it successfully, then you'll do something in return.

Taylor's Versions are very complex pieces of communication. They have meaning and context, yes, but those are made more complex by a number of other facts. They are mimicking previous pieces of communication from earlier eras in Swift's life. They have surrounding *paratexts*—things that go beyond the songs themselves (the "texts" we're examining): amended titles, additional liner notes, new music videos, accompanying social media, public appearances and interviews, performances and tours, and even merchandise. When I ask you to pass the salt, I don't typically slip you a secret note as I do so, nor am I wearing a "Pass the salt!" t-shirt, nor do I have a website where I sell "Pass the salt!" t-shirts. But Swift is often doing exactly this, and these factors add dimension to what Taylor's Versions do—and what any of Swift's songs do. In short, they're doing many more things than I'm doing when I ask you to pass the salt. And what's more, they're trying to get hearers to do many more things than, well, pass the salt.

So, what do Taylor's Versions do? What acts does she perform with them? And what is she trying to get others to do?

Most obviously, there is a *legal act*. The re-recordings help her reclaim songs whose masters don't legally belong to her. They don't actually help her reclaim ownership over the masters—she still does not own them. But her cloned recordings aim to displace demand for the originals on the open market. She wants us to stream and purchase those instead.

Taylor's Versions also make her money. A lot of it. By re-recording her albums, she performs a series of very significant *financial acts*. She redirects streaming and other royalties to herself. Maybe more importantly, her re-recordings offer the opportunity to bring each album back to center stage in public discourse. There's more content: Taylor's Versions of *Fearless* and *Red* each have five corresponding EPs. And there's more associated media: Each release affords a fresh round of press tours and social media. And there's more merch: Swift can merchandise apparel adorned with re-recorded album covers, but also accessories like books or jewelry that appear in new music videos.[15] It's similar to what the Harry Potter movies did for the books, or what additional spinoff films do for the franchise: they keep the public eye on Harry Potter and draw new and sustained engagement with all of its commercial output—books, movies, merchandise, social media, performances, even amusement park rides and souvenirs. And because Swift is a sharp businesswoman, she sees and seizes these opportunities.[16] What she is trying to get us to do, in this case, is very clear.

The re-recordings are also a site for pointed *parasocial acts*. Taylor's Versions strengthen the relationship she has with her fans and the sense of community they have with each other. The music industry has taken advantage of her, and she shares that information with her fans the way one would share it with friends. She re-records albums, and asks her fans to respect her wish to listen to *those* rather than the originals. The parasocial acts are layered: she wants us to listen to the re-recordings, but she also aims to build honesty and integrity into her brand and to instill loyalty in her fans. Fans have largely, it seems, happily obliged— at least when it comes to streaming.[17] Swift gratefully accepts this and in turn lets their feedback inform her own artistic choices, further tightening the parasocial relationship between her and the "Swifties."[18] They are a famously loyal bunch.[19]

This shades into a set of intertwined *political and moral acts*. Swift's re-recordings change the politics of the contemporary music industry. Re-recording isn't new, but Swift's fame and the systematicity with which she pursues her re-recordings project mean that her re-recordings receive much more attention than others. Shedding light on some of the unpleasant behind-the-scenes business of music is itself a political act. Her re-recordings may tangibly affect the way artists and labels negotiate and draw up contracts, as the Everly Brothers' re-recordings did in the 1960s. (Ironically, perhaps the likeliest outcome is a tightening of restrictions on the part of record labels.[20]) Her open letter condemning Apple Music's trial period payment policy produced immediate and beneficial changes for both her and the rest of the musicians streaming there, so we might expect something similar here. (However, her multi-year boycott of Spotify did not fare so well, ending with her eventually caving in—as with many other musicians who've boycotted the service.) She certainly seems to hope that her project will at least empower artists by informing them.

Swift's re-recordings also inject audience choices with moral pressure. If you care about exploitation and systematic harm in general, and especially if you care about those injuries befalling Taylor Swift, then you will avoid listening to originals instead of their re-recordings. (Except for those in special circumstances: you listen to hard or digital copies that you already own, you pirate digital copies, or—maybe—you are writing a chapter on Taylor Swift that compares the re-recordings to the originals.) In fact, the re-recordings present fans with an even thornier moral predicament: whether to stream not-yet-re-recorded albums. Here, the moral scruples pull in both directions. On the one hand, she still receives money for the not-yet-re-recorded album streams, just not as much as she would if she owned the masters, and continued listening keeps those albums on streaming charts; but on the other hand, it funnels money to people framed as her enemies and disincentivizes them from ever selling the masters to her.

The very presence of Taylor's Versions on the market changes the array of choices for listeners. One set of moralized acts that Swift performs has to do with the workings of the music industry: legality, politics, exploitation, and harm. The other moralized act Swift performs has to do with us, the audience. She presents listeners with new, moralized choices. Choosing to listen to *Red* in 2015 is one thing; choosing to listen to *Red* after 2021 is another. The presence of re-recordings inescapably moralizes and politicizes our individual choices. Even those fans who continue to stream the originals acknowledge that there's some reason not to do so. The presence of re-recordings makes those choices no longer straightforward and costless. And choosing the re-recordings is even costlier for those fans dedicated enough to detect the difference.

After all, some people can't detect any sonic differences between the originals and the re-recordings. Others can, but only for some songs, and only if they're played back-to-back. But some fans can detect the differences without any assistance. Those fans face an especially difficult tradeoff. When those fans hear, say, "Style (Taylor's Version)," they feel less nostalgia, less familiarity, less emotional resonance. The choice they face when considering whether to listen to originals or re-recordings is not the same one the rest of us face. Their choices have become moralized in a way that actually sits in tension with their relationship to Taylor Swift and her music. In a way, Swift puts them in a tough spot. Their loyalty is bred largely from their relationship to her original music, and she now asks them to give up that music for the uncanny re-recordings. In some cases, this is no real sacrifice (the original "Girl at Home" is not especially widely liked). But in cases like "Style," it is the source of serious heartache and moral uncertainty.[21]

There are several decisions here that seem identical but are not. The decision to listen to *Red* when *Red (Taylor's Version)* is available is very different from the decision to listen to it in the absence of alternatives. And that decision, for those who can't tell the difference between the originals and re-recordings, is yet different from the decision that faces those who can tell the difference, especially when that difference affects their emotional experience of the music. What we have here is another setting in which things that look identical are not actually the same. Red squares, *Red* albums, *Red* songs, and now *Red* listening choices: all phenomena that would be invisible to us if we didn't look more carefully, not just at the art itself, but at everything that surrounds it.[22]

Notes

1   Arthur C. Danto, *The Transfiguration of the Commonplace: A Philosophy of Art*, (Cambridge, Mass.: Harvard University Press), vi.

2   Taylor Swift, "Taylor Swift on 'Lover' and Haters," interview by Tracy Smith, *CBS News*, August 25, 2019, https://www.cbsnews.com/news/taylor-swift-on-lover-and-haters/ (accessed August 1, 2023).

3   See, for example, her remarks in Taylor Swift, "For Taylor Swift, the Future of Music Is a Love Story," *The Wall Street Journal*, July 7, 2014, https://www.wsj.com/articles/for-taylor-swift-the-future-of-music-is-a-love-story-1404763219 (accessed August 1, 2023).

4   Taylor Swift, Liner Notes for *Red (Taylor's Version)*, Republic Records, 2021, compact disc.

5   Paul Théberge, "Love and Business: Taylor Swift as Celebrity, Businesswoman, and Advocate," *Contemporary Music Review* 40, no. 1 (2021): 41–59; 57.

6   Brandon Polite offers additional reasons to believe that Taylor's Versions and the original versions of Swift's albums are distinct works of art in Chapter 5 of this volume.

7   In a 2012 article for *The Hollywood Reporter*, a lawyer discusses how important yet difficult this is in a digital era: "I'm not sure how you differentiate between [the original and the re-recording]." (Shirley Halperin and Eriq Gardner, "Pour Some Sugar Again: Why Def Leppard Is Rerecording Hits," *The Hollywood Reporter*, August 1, 2012, https://www.hollywoodreporter.com/news/general-news/def-leppard-universal-recording-hits-356397/ [accessed August 1, 2023].)

8   Danto, *The Transfiguration of the Commonplace*, 3.

9   She similarly re-recorded "Babe," originally a collaboration with the country duo Sugarland, as a solo track that sounded significantly different, which she then released as a From the Vault track on *Red (Taylor's Version)*.

10 Lisa Respers France, "Taylor Swift Changes Controversial Lyrics for 'Better than Revenge'," *CNN*, July 7, 2023, https://www.cnn.com/2023/07/07/entertainment/taylor-swift-better-than-revenge-lyrics/index.html (accessed August 1, 2023). Also, though Swift had earlier changed a homophobic lyric on "Picture to Burn" from her 2006 self-titled debut album, that was much earlier than and entirely independent from the re-recordings project.

11   Hermione Hoby, "Taylor Swift: 'Sexy? Not on My Radar,'" *The Guardian*, August 23, 2014, https://www.theguardian.com/music/2014/aug/23/taylor-swift-shake-it-off (accessed August 1, 2023).

12   In 2016, she donated $250,000 in legal funds to help support a sexual harassment lawsuit fellow singer Ke$ha filed against her producer Dr. Luke. (Todd Leopold, "Taylor Swift Donates $250K to Kesha, Offers Support during 'Trying Time,'" *CNN*, February 23, 2016, https://www.cnn.com/2016/02/22/entertainment/taylor-swift-kesha-feat/index.html [accessed August 1, 2023].) In 2017, Swift herself filed and won a (counter) suit against a DJ, David Mueller, who was found to have groped her (Andrew Flanagan, "Taylor Swift Wins Sexual Assault Lawsuit against Former Radio Host," *NPR*, August 14, 2017, https://www.npr.org/sections/therecord/2017/08/14/543473684/taylor-swift-wins-sexual-assault-lawsuit-against-former-radio-host [accessed August 1, 2023].)

13   graysonsix, "What Songs Have the Possibility of Getting the Girl at Home Treatment?," *Reddit, r/TaylorSwift*, March 28, 2022, https://www.reddit.com/r/TaylorSwift/comments/tq441x/what_songs_have_the_possibility_of_getting_the/ (accessed August 1, 2023).

14   For my extended take on Swift's Easter eggs, see Alex King, "How Swiftomania Turns Fans into Professors," *Aesthetics for Birds*, October 26, 2023, https://aestheticsforbirds.com/2023/10/26/taylor-swift-easter-eggs/ (accessed January 10, 2024).

15   You can—or could—buy, as an empty journal, the book that appears at the end of "All Too Well: The Short Film" and the locket that appears in the "Run (Taylor's Version)" lyric video on Swift's website.

16   For sustained discussions of her business acumen, see James Perone, *The Words and Music of Taylor Swift* (Santa Barbara, CA: Praeger, 2017), and Théberge, "Love and Business."

17   Glenn Peoples, "Have Taylor's Version Re-recordings Crowded out the Originals?," *Billboard*, July 21, 2023, https://www.billboard.com/pro/have-taylor-swift-re-recordings-hurt-originals-streaming-sales/ (accessed August 1, 2023).

18   As an *Entertainment Weekly* cover story says, "She shares updates about her life and drops hints about new music, which fans then gobble up and re-promote with their own theories, which Swift then re-shares on her Tumblr or incorporates into future clues." (Alex Suskind,

"New Reputation: Taylor Swift Shares Intel on TS7, Fan Theories, and Her Next Era," *Entertainment Weekly*, May 19, 2019, https://ew.com/music/2019/05/09/taylor-swift-cover-story/ [accessed August 1, 2023].)

19 Interested readers should look at Chapter 7, where Irene Martínez Marín explores Swift's relationship with her fans in more depth.

20 The primary effect of the Everly Brothers' re-recordings was to strengthen labels' restrictions on re-recordings. (See Mark Beaumont, "Taylor Swift's New 'Fearless' Is a Success, but Beware the Dangers of the Re-record," *NME (New Musical Express)*, April 12, 2021, https://www.nme.com/blogs/nme-blogs/taylor-swifts-fearless-beware-of-the-rerecord-2918002 [accessed August 1, 2023].) Music lawyer Tamera Bennett writes that many contract re-recording restrictions have already been extended from five to seven years, in light of Swift's re-recordings project. (Tamera Bennett, "Will Taylor Swift Change the Re-record Clause?," *Create Protect Blog*, December 22, 2021, https://www.tbennettlaw.com/blog/2021/12/22/will-taylor-swift-change-the-re-record-clause [accessed August 1, 2023].)

21 Mary Beth Willard, *Why It's OK to Enjoy the Work of Immoral Artists* (New York: Routledge, 2021), argues that it is morally permissible for fans to engage with the art of morally problematic artists when they are especially personally attached to those works. A similar argument could be made here for fans especially attached to Swift's originals.

22 For helpful discussion, I am grateful to participants in a summer reading group at Simon Fraser University (Elliot Schwartz, Mete Han Gencer, Celia Gentle, Gavin Victor, and Iman Ferestade), as well as to Nayancee Shrivastava, Nic Bommarito, and Samantha Matherne. I'm especially grateful to Brandon Polite for very thoughtful feedback on prior versions and many Taylor Swift conversations, texts, and gifs.

7

Appreciating Taylor's Versions

An Aesthetic Love Story

Irene Martínez Marín

Appreciation and Changes in Aesthetic Taste

A central aspect of Taylor Swift's re-recordings has to do with the kind of valuing or appreciation these albums demand, especially among her longtime fans. The question is: how should fans relate to these albums? Although Taylor's Versions are regarded as almost sonic duplicates of her earlier albums, there are still notable differences, both aesthetic and moral, that suggest a need for a renewed appreciation. However, altering or revising one's taste can be challenging, especially when it involves the creations of one's favorite artist. The aim of this chapter is to examine the contrasting "old" and "new" love for Swift's music as experienced by her fans in light of the re-recordings.

As I will argue, Taylor's Versions invite longtime fans to reevaluate their emotional attachment to the original albums and engage in an active aesthetic investigation of their aesthetic merits. This dual exploration will delve into the complex and transformative journey of taste experienced by both the artist and her audience. Throughout the discussion it will become clear that some of the main difficulties concerning the appreciation of the re-recordings stem from (1) the nature of the attitudes involved in our valuing activities and (2) the intricate relationship between such attitudes. Let me clarify these two points.

First, appreciating an aesthetic object, such as an album, is a matter of exercising one's aesthetic taste. As some scholars have argued, aesthetic taste has a dual character: perceptual and emotional.[1] Taste, on the one hand, refers to the ability to perceptually recognize the features that make an object worthy of aesthetic appreciation and to judge it as worthy on the basis of such perceived features. On the other hand, it is commonly thought that those aesthetic objects that we tend to value positively are those that reflect our ideals and personal commitments. Taste, in that sense, is also partial, personal, and highly selective. Thus, a full-blown act of appreciation is a hybrid process that encompasses a particular combination of attitudes: a positive judgment based on the perceived merits of an item and a kind of affection toward it. Fans are deep appreciators in this sense, given their capacity to form judgments about the value of the products of their favorite artists in an autonomous way and their strong affectionate connection to these same products.

Second, what we *judge* to be valuable and what we *like* are importantly connected in the process of valuing. This is because exercising our aesthetic taste involves a relational interplay between perception and emotion, where they mutually influence one another. We can say that "in exercising taste, aesthetic agents *attune* themselves to an aesthetic object insofar as they align or calibrate their emotional sensibilities to the perceived aesthetic character which that object exhibits."[2] However, there are instances where our attitudes fail to influence each other, impeding proper engagement with aesthetic objects. Substantive changes in taste are an example of such breaks, leading to an internal conflict as our previous valuing attitudes clash with newly formed ones. To illustrate this point, consider the following example.

Imagine discovering, thanks to the art history and media studies courses you have been taking, that your favorite TV show lacks significant aesthetic merit. Despite this realization, you still enjoy it. While acknowledging its limited aesthetic value and forming a new judgment about it, you might continue to experience certain pleasure watching it. However, it wouldn't be accurate to say you now *fully* appreciate the show, considering the changes you have experienced in your perceptual sensibility. In this case you would have to abandon your liking for the show in order to align it with your newly formed negative judgment of it. Now that you can identify the show's flaws, sustaining the same level of affection for it may prove challenging. One might also question the "aesthetic" nature of the attachment given the negative judgment formed. Moreover, your newly formed negative judgment about your favorite show could motivate you to explore other aesthetic objects, potentially leading to a shift in your aesthetic preferences. During this transition, you may experience an internal conflict, questioning whether abandoning your previous likes means losing something important about yourself or whether there's something to gain from changing your taste.

I believe that Swift's fandom in coming to appreciate the re-recordings may experience this sort of conflict. By closely examining some of the features of Taylor's Versions and how they have been received by Swift's fans, it will become clear how their appreciation of these albums can result in an incoherent combination of attitudes: between the earlier likings of Swift's original albums and the newly formed judgments regarding the importance of the re-recording project. Appreciating the re-recordings thereby entails aligning one's judgments about them with one's felt responses to them. This will include exploring the relation between fan loyalty and personal authenticity, as well as the role of biographical taste. Ultimately, the aim of this chapter is to shed light on this particular challenge that longtime fans encounter when trying to come to appreciate Taylor's Versions while also offering a potential resolution to the conflict.

The Challenge: Fan Loyalty vs. Personal Authenticity

The motivations behind Swift's decision to want to own her master recordings are well-known. In brief, after her former label, Big Machine Records, sold her first six albums to music manager Scooter Braun,

Swift publicly expressed that her re-recording project was a response to bullying,[3] manipulation,[4] and a means of gaining artistic control over her music.[5] However, there is a less discussed aspect that is crucial in understanding the underlying rationale for this project (and its success, so far). This has to do with the unique nature of Swift's fandom. It is safe to say that the feasibility of Swift's project, as Sherri Irvin discusses in Chapter 3, owes much to her devoted fanbase. Now, what is so special about Swift's fans?

Taylor Swift's fandom, affectionately known as Swifties, stands out as one of the largest, most active, and devoted communities in today's music industry. In addition to the relatable and confessional qualities of Swift's lyrics, her innovate use of social media and technology has been key in cultivating this fiercely loyal following.[6] This loyalty and trust in Taylor Swift's persona offers insights into the artist's unprecedented decision, and monumental task, to re-record an important portion of her catalog. From a fan's perspective, particularly for longtime fans, this project offers an opportunity to revisit valued memories, discover new material "From the Vault," and deepen their connection with their beloved artist. Moreover, the re-recordings encourage fans to play an active role in their appreciation of Swift's music. Fans can exercise their agency by choosing to stream the re-recorded albums instead of the original ones, thereby showcasing their loyalty through direct action.

This is not the first time that Swift has called on her fandom to take action. Most notably, after she broke her political silence in an Instagram post revealing who she would vote for in the 2018 US midterm election, Swift encouraged her audience to register and exercise their right to vote. In that post, she openly criticized Marsha Blackburn, a Republican senate candidate with a voting record against equal pay for women, the reauthorization of the Violence Against Women Act, and gay marriage. The post resulted in 65,000 new registrants and garnered more than 2 million likes.[7] As highlighted by Simone Driessen, the discussions among Swifties after the artist's political statement revealed an emotional investment in Swift's persona that went beyond her music.[8] While a certain part of her fandom was critical of Swift's declarations, and interpreted it as a potential career strategy, others considered it a necessary act in America's turbulent political landscape. Either way, the ways in which fans navigated Swift's declarations in her transition from pop-star to "celebrity politician" demonstrated a deep caring for Swift that transcended her music.[9]

This response can be attributed to what are known as "parasocial attachments," which refers to the kind of one-sided relationship that individuals can develop with media figures.[10] This same parasocial relation can also help us better understand how Swifties have been responding to the re-recordings, even though there are important differences between these two moments in Swift's career. When the artist revealed her moral stance on important social issues, this act either strengthened or weakened the connection between Swift and her fans on a political level. This act influenced our perception and understanding of Swift as an individual. In contrast, Swift's decision to re-record her albums has had a direct impact on the appreciation of her music. While the project undoubtedly has serious political and ethical implications, the central focus in this case remains on the music itself. In this situation, the audience can perceive themselves as being *aesthetically* empowered because of their capacity to actively support Swift's decision to regain control over her musical works. However, things are not that simple from a fan's perspective.

A conflict arises for longtime fans as they feel compelled to stop listening to the original albums that Swift herself deems problematic and instead embrace Taylor's Versions. The tension can be described as follows: On the one hand, for fans, engaging with Taylor's Versions is an important way of demonstrating their support for Swift and her ethical campaign about music rights. On the other hand, one might worry that the re-recordings prevent fans from engaging with the original recordings of songs they love, preventing them from accessing cherished memories and nostalgic feelings associated with these tracks.

Preserving and privileging aesthetic experiences and objects that are dear to us has important benefits; it can help explain the enduring relationships that we form with particular aesthetic objects as well as provide a sense of self.[11] As Felix Bräuer puts it: "our aesthetic tastes are central to our conception of who we truly are and, correspondingly, that imagining a radical change here goes hand in hand with a feeling of loss of self. In short, it seems to us that, in part, we are what we like and that radically changing what we like would change who we are."[12] On this basis, fans have a reason to cultivate their engagement with those aesthetic objects that are related to (or reflect) their current aesthetic interests—in this case, Swift's original albums.

To be more precise, the worry is that longtime Swifties might struggle to develop an authentic attachment to Taylor's Versions. If fans merely *evaluate* the project positively, they will not be able to fully appreciate the re-recorded albums. *Liking* or *coming to love* Taylor's Versions is crucial, as mentioned in the previous section, since liking is an essential component of aesthetic appreciation. But why exactly is liking so important for appreciation?

While our aesthetic judgments are linked to our reasoning skills and our capacity to being receptive to certain aesthetic qualities via perceptual means, our aesthetic likings reveal something more personal about how those objects relate to us and our broader system of beliefs. Aesthetic liking also aims to make sense of the idea that valuing, in general, entails an overall caring for what is considered valuable from an appreciator's perspective. Furthermore, if Swifties are not affectively moved by Taylor's Versions, it will be difficult for them to participate in several appreciative practices that depend on the motivational dimension of liking. It is our likings that drive us to want to experience a song repeatedly, recommend it to friends, or invest energy and time in better understanding it. When our aesthetic engagement lacks liking and is solely based on a judgment about the object's worth, our aesthetic experiences are impoverished, as liking is what ignites our curiosity, interest, and love.

In summary, fans may feel like they are being pulled in two opposite directions—torn between cultivating their love for the original albums *and* remaining loyal to their favorite artist. To put it differently, Swifties may find themselves in a situation where they have good reasons to assess the artist's re-recordings positively and yet to continue engaging with the original albums. While Swift has not explicitly asked fans to cease engaging with the original albums but rather to stop buying and streaming them (thus preventing any further enrichment of Scooter Braun), a sense of solidarity with Swift is likely to make fans feel less like true fans if they persist in listening to the originals. It is important to note that, in this scenario, a fan's conflicting attitudes are not logically incompatible (as it is possible for them to hold both simultaneously) but rather incoherent. This incoherence is relevant because it impedes fans from fully appreciating Taylor's Versions. Only when fans positively judge and also come to love Taylor's Versions can we consider them as truly appreciating the aesthetic worth of the re-recordings. The question, then, is how fans can balance their motivation to support Swift while developing a personal attachment to Taylor's Versions. For the rest of the chapter, I will explore issues related to aesthetic improvement and personal growth as a means of alleviating this tension.

Revising One's Aesthetic Judgments

For fans, one way of coming to align their evaluation about the worth of the re-recordings and their affective relation to them starts by revising their original aesthetic judgment of Swift's albums. Fans need to "see" for themselves the aesthetic merits or demerits of the new recordings if they want to be in a good position to appreciate, or not, this project. It is not only important to share Swift's idea about music rights or to care about her well-being, but also to fully engage with the different re-recordings in an autonomous manner.

Taylor's Versions are not mere indiscernible sonic duplicates; rather, listeners, especially longtime fans, can perceive important differences between them and the originals. Critics and fans have pointed out variances in phrasings and vocal inflections, but also richer vocals and an improved quality in the musical production. As critic Katie Goh writes:

Swift's vocal performance is stronger on the re-recording, and she's freshened up some originally muddy enunciation. The fidelity is also considerably cleaner: guitar riffs are more isolated, given space to shine, like on You Belong With Me, and the drumming is more roundly finished, occasionally tuned a degree lower than the original to match Swift's deeper, more mature tones.[13]

From a fan's perspective, the act of comparing Taylor's Versions with the original recordings can be viewed as a collaborative appreciative enterprise. Fans assist each other in identifying the most subtle differences within the songs. Online discussion forums on *Reddit* and elsewhere are filled with extremely detailed aesthetic descriptions of the distinctions between the albums. This valuing practice is of special significance, not only because it allows fans to enhance their aesthetic skills but also because it contributes to the ongoing development of connections and relationships among Swifties.

Another important aspect to consider when revising one's aesthetic judgments about Swift's music is how the advantageous epistemic standpoint from which the adult artist sings alters the meaning of certain songs, a claim Alex King supports in Chapter 6 of this volume. If you once found it hard to take seriously the insights and advice shared by a young Swift, her mature voice lends a heightened sense of realism to her storytelling and conviction to some of the lyrics. These changes add depth and nuance to the re-recordings and infuse them with a newly acquired emotional undertone, a "she knows what she is talking about" experience. Some of her most popular heartbreak songs, like "All Too Well" or "Dear John," hit different in Swift's adult voice. The distance from where they are being sung conveys less anger and frustration, due to the gracious way in which she appears to be treating her younger self.

Furthermore, being aware of the motives behind the re-recordings reshapes some of Swift's songs. Her persona—a concept Ley David Elliette Cray examines at length in her chapter in this volume—comes across as stronger, more secure, and in control of her own life, giving tracks like "Mean" a prophetic, if not comical quality. These differences are also noticeable in the album covers of *1989* and *1989 (Taylor's Version)*. In the former, we don't see her entire face, and the image is dark and faded, resembling an old Polaroid. In the new cover, we see her whole face, she is smiling, and the image is bright and clear. These visual differences not only signify the different place, both personally and professionally, where Swift finds herself now but also help set the tone of the new recording. The new album, featuring Swift's smiling face in clear detail on the cover, exudes a luminous quality, whereas the original album carries a more angsty vibe.

Despite numerous positive instances, singing about the past from a present-day perspective can also lead to some aesthetic losses. For example, particular emotions such as the hope and optimism found in the original "Change" (2008), which appeared right after Obama's first election, are impossible to fully recreate due to the different historical moment we live in now. Additionally, certain lyrics that felt witty, wise, and sophisticated when sung by a teenager may now appear naïve and even prejudiced and un-feminist. One could see the controversial change to the lyrics of "Better than Revenge" as a response to this very problem. Vrinda Jagota in her *Pitchfork* review of *Speak Now (Taylor's Version)* notes how the loss of some of the teenage angst that marked this record makes the songs "slightly anonymous, more like lullabies and folk songs than expressions of pressing concern."[14] On a similar note, critic Laura Snapes worries that Swift's skilled voice has killed her "youthful twang" which "made these songs kick harder in all their dressing-downs and rabid desires, emphasizing the sense of a girl wading into adult waters."[15] Swift's sound might be less vindicative and affected by the themes and events that inspired her original writing. However, it remains open to discussion whether this is a positive or negative aspect of the re-recordings.

What is clear is that both sonic differences and variations in artistic meaning carry significant aesthetic weight. Moreover, these changes are not unintentional; they directly respond to Swift's desire to enhance the overall aesthetic quality of her recordings. As a result, by paying close attention to certain aesthetic features of Taylor's Versions, we can determine that there are good reasons for longtime fans to judge them positively—and even to prefer them to the older versions—based on their aesthetic merits. Or, as one critic eloquently stated about the re-recording of *Speak Now*: "If you loved the original album, then you'll love *Taylor's Version* even more."[16]

Aesthetic considerations play a key role in helping fans navigate the conflict between their personal attachment to Swift's previous albums and their loyalty to her as an artist. By revising their original judgments and realizing that, in many instances, Taylor's Versions are aesthetically superior, fans have found an additional reason to appreciate the re-recordings. This reason is significant because it is grounded in the aesthetic value of the music itself rather than in one's allegiance to Swift as an individual. However, a worry remains: Can these judgments about the aesthetic merits of Taylor's Versions truly replace or alter longtime fans' appreciation of the original albums?

We can imagine a scenario in which a longtime fan is able to judge positively Taylor's Versions, based on their aesthetic superiority, and still feel unmoved by them.[17] As mentioned earlier, acknowledging the aesthetic merits of an artwork is not enough for a full appreciation; there's a need to also emotionally favor or like the work. If that's the case, recognizing the aesthetic value of the re-recordings marks just the initial step for fans to establish a meaningful connection with their value. Therefore, the next question we must address is: How can fans develop a genuine love for Taylor's Versions?

Biographical Taste

Taylor's Versions provide longtime fans with a unique opportunity to actively compare the different features of Swift's old and new recordings. This aesthetic investigation invites for collaborative interactions within the Swiftie community and leads to richer aesthetic experiences. However, fully appreciating the re-recording project requires not only acknowledging the aesthetic merits of the new versions, but also reassessing one's personal attachment to the original ones. Fans can find a way of coherently relating to their value and thus incorporate them into their life when they understand how to *both* positively judge *and* affectively respond to Taylor's Versions. In this last section, I intend to provide an answer to the delicate question of why fans may want to revise their love for the original albums in favor of the re-recordings.

As previously discussed, our attachments to objects of value play a role in shaping our identities. The things we love and care about, including artworks, reveal much about our ideals and ourselves. Consequently, longtime fans may fear losing a significant part of themselves in the process of appreciating Taylor's Versions. This apprehension derives from Swift's petition to her fans to refrain from streaming the original recordings—an act that symbolizes a cut-off from certain experiences associated with those tracks. But what makes these experiences so meaningful?

For many fans, Swift's original tracks served as the soundtrack of their adolescence—a formative period characterized by moments of joy and freedom, but also by loneliness and confusion. Not every period in one's life is as easy to relive. Teenage memories are often best left untouched; revisiting them is much like the uneasy and cringy sensation of re-reading one's personal diary. What is intriguing about Taylor's Versions is that they offer more than an opportunity to reopen that diary; they are also an opportunity to rewrite it and transform those memories. We can see Swift as (intentionally or not) inviting fans to revise their attitudes toward who they were in the past, in the same way that she's revising her past self through the re-recordings. *Were you a good friend? Did you forgive too readily? Were you too young to be messed with? Do you still believe it when somebody tells you they love you?*

As mentioned earlier, the cover for her album *1989 (Taylor's Versions)* is another clear example of the very different relationship Swift has with these songs. Interestingly, she maintains the same cover style for the other three Taylor Version's released so far. It will be exciting to see if there are any differences with her debut album, *Taylor Swift*, and with

Reputation (which, in an important sense, is an album about reclaiming one's image).

Appreciating the re-recordings also involves a revision of one's own biographical taste. Fans are being asked to reevaluate their caring and love for the songs as they were originally recorded, while carefully attending to the memories associated with each record. This process is not merely an exercise of nostalgia, but also one of personal change and growth. As Tara Chittenden has argued, Swift's music is a case of "nostalgic reverse" for younger fans who have not experienced most of the "firsts" mentioned in her songs (romantic relationships, break-ups, leaving home).[18] Instead, these fans substitute their own missing past with Swift's.

What I find more interesting about the re-recordings is that longtime fans now have a former self to draw upon when making sense of those songs. It is time to include their own knowledge and place it at the center of their appreciation. Placing ourselves at the center of appreciation comes with a new sense of understanding and intimacy. As longtime fans listen to an adult Swift as adults themselves, they gain a new perspective on how to best interpret and evaluate some of the situations described in Swift's songs. Fans who were too young when the original albums were released now have the tools and knowledge to make sense of them. This newfound understanding can help create a deeper bond with the albums and even with the artist. Rather than seeing Swift as an older sister figure or an "oracle of experiences," fans can now relate to her as a friend—not just with sympathy, but also with understanding. This is an understanding built upon a common ground of shared emotions and experiences, something which was perhaps lacking in the earlier albums due to a young audience's limited lived experiences and, in some case, a perceived lack of authenticity on Swift's retelling of such experiences—not to mention her young age.

In the same way that the revision of one's aesthetic judgment involves collaboration with other fans, revisiting one's past through the re-recordings can be positively enhanced within this same community setting. Swifties do not need to face their past alone, which, as mentioned above, can be quite daunting. Given the common lived experiences that Swift refers to in her songs, it is easy for fans to revisit their pasts together when discussing Taylor's Versions. Engaging in this shared retelling of one's past can hopefully lead to a certain clarity and a communal feeling of belonging. This outcome would be far more challenging to achieve if one were to understand this process merely as an individualist and personal endeavor.

In sum, fans do not need to worry about the re-recordings representing a break with their past selves, but should see them as an opportunity to build new memories by gaining a deeper understanding of their pasts. These new memories are key, since they can help fans ground their love for Taylor's Versions and also ease the worry that they might be putting their identities at risk by ceasing to cultivate their love for the original versions of songs they grew up with.

Conclusion

From a fan's perspective, appreciating Swift's re-recordings is a complex and demanding task. The strong parasocial relationship that Swifties experience with their favorite artist gives them reasons to engage with Taylor's Versions. However, for longtime fans, it might be too much to ask them to stop streaming the original albums, given their emotional attachment to these songs. So, we can imagine cases in which fans simultaneously evaluate positively the re-recordings but prefer the original versions to Taylor's Versions.

To appreciate is a matter of both perceptually responding to the good-making features of an object and favoring or liking that same object. This is because aesthetic appreciation requires the cooperation of both one's perceptual and emotional capacities. Both need to be in place to account for the estimative and partial dimensions of valuing. The concern, then, is that fans holding incoherent attitudes toward

Taylor's Versions wouldn't be able to fully appreciate them. A proper aesthetic appreciation of the re-recordings demands both a positive judgment based on their aesthetic features and actually liking them.

Addressing this conflict reveals a dilemma between fan loyalty and personal authenticity. I have attempted to provide a solution to this dilemma by highlighting two considerations in favor of appreciating Taylor's Versions. The first consideration has to do with the aesthetic merits of the re-recordings. I have emphasized how Swift's richer vocals, improved musical arrangements, and variations in artistic meaning contribute to an enhanced aesthetic experience. The second consideration revolves around the personal growth that arises from critically reassessing long-standing relationships with objects of value. While this revision risks longtime fans cutting themselves off from certain cherished past memories, it also enables them to place their present selves at the center of appreciation and to relate to Swift's music in a more authentic manner.

Ultimately, with this chapter I have tried to show that for a longtime fan, coming to fully appreciate Taylor's Versions is a challenging and messy exercise. As we have seen, it demands not only an aesthetic openness to revise one's previous aesthetic judgments, but also an acknowledgment that our identities, including our aesthetic selves, are not static. Change and improvement are fundamental aspects of our aesthetic educations, and engaging with Taylor's Version offers a valuable opportunity to practice and embody these transformations.

Notes

1   See, for example, Jerrold Levinson, "Aesthetic Properties, Evaluative Force, and Differences of Sensibility," in *Contemplating Art* (Oxford: Oxford University Press, 2006); Carolyn Korsmeyer, "Taste," in *The Routledge Companion to Aesthetics*, ed. Berys Gaut and Dominic McIver Lopes, 3rd edn (London: Routledge, 2013), 257–66; and Irene Martínez Marín and Elisabeth Schellekens, "Aesthetic Taste: Perceptual

Discernment or Emotional Sensibility?," in *Perspectives on Taste: Aesthetics, Language, Metaphysics, and Experimental Philosophy*, ed. Jeremy Wyatt, Julia Zakkou and Dan Zeman (London: Routledge, 2022), 58–74.

2   Martínez Marín and Schellekens, "Aesthetic Taste," 70.

3   Swift holds Scooter Braun partly responsible for Kanye West's controversial song "Famous" and its music video.

4   Swift revealed on Tumblr that Big Machine Records extended her an offer to gradually regain ownership of her old masters, one album back at a time, in exchange for every new album she turned in. (Taylor Swift, "For years I asked, pleaded for a chance to own my work," *Tumblr*, June 30, 2019, https://taylorswift.tumblr.com/post/185958366550/for-years-i-asked-pleaded-for-a-chance-to-own-my [accessed June 21, 2023].)

5   Swift accused Braun and Big Machine head Scott Borchetta on social media of preventing her from playing a medley of her older songs at the American Music Awards of 2019 and of making use of older songs or performance footage in her Netflix documentary *Miss Americana* (2020). (Taylor Swift (@taylorswift13), "Don't know what else to do," Twitter, November 15, 2019, https://twitter.com/taylorswift13/status/1195123215657508867 [accessed June 21, 2023].)

6   Perone, *The Words and Music of Taylor Swift*, 78–81.

7   Gwendelyn Nisbett and Stephanie Schartel Dunn, "Reputation Matters: Parasocial Attachment, Narrative Engagement, and the 2018 Taylor Swift Political Endorsement," *Atlantic Journal of Communication* 29, no. 1 (2021): 26–38.

8   Simone Driessen, "Taylor Swift, Political Power, and the Challenge of Affect in Popular Music Fandom," "Fandom and Culture," ed. Ashley Hinck and Amber Davisson, special issue, *Transformative Works and Cultures* 32 (2020), https://doi.org/10.3983/twc.2020.1843; and "Look What You Made Them Do: Understanding Fans' Affective Responses to Taylor Swift's Political Coming-Out," *Celebrity Studies* 13, no. 1 (2022): 93–6.

9   Driessen, "Look What You Made Them Do."

10 Donald Horton and R. Richard Wohl, "Mass Communication and Para-social Interaction," *Psychiatry: Journal for the Study of Interpersonal Processes* 19, no. 3 (1956): 215–29.

11   Anthony Cross, "Aesthetic Commitments and Aesthetic Obligations," *Ergo: An Open Access Journal of Philosophy* 8, no. 38 (2022): 402–22.

12   Felix Bräuer, "Aesthetic Testimony and Aesthetic Authenticity," *British Journal of Aesthetics* 63, no. 3 (2023): 395–416.

13   Katie Goh, "I Made My Peace: Fans Divided over Taylor Swift's Re-recording Project," *The Guardian*, April 15, 2021, https://www.theguardian.com/music/2021/apr/15/i-made-my-peace-fans-divided-over-taylor-swifts-re-recording-project (accessed November 29, 2023).

14   Vrinda Jagota, review of *Speak Now (Taylor's Version)*, album by Taylor Swift, *Pitchfork*, July 12, 2023, https://pitchfork.com/reviews/albums/taylor-swift-speak-now-taylors-version (accessed November 29, 2023).

15   Laura Snapes, review of *Speak Now (Taylor's Version)*, album by Taylor Swift, *The Guardian*, July 7, 2023, https://www.theguardian.com/music/2023/jul/07/taylor-swift-speak-now-taylors-version-review (accessed November 29, 2023).

16   Tom Lowe, "Better than Revenge, and the Original? Speak Now Taylor's Version Review," *The Boar*, July 23, 2023, https://theboar.org/2023/07/speak-now-taylors-version-review (accessed November 29, 2023).

17   Note that Swifties do not need to like the versions as much as they like the originals, being coherent in their aesthetic judgment and aesthetic liking about their value is enough. It's only problematic when they judge them to be good but dislike them.

18   Tara Chittenden, "In My Rearview Mirror: Female Teens' Prospective Remembering of Future Romantic Relationships through the Lyrics in Taylor Swift Songs," *Journal of Children and Media* 7, no. 2 (2013): 186–200.

8

Taylor's Versions and Versions of Taylor

Ley David Elliette Cray

Introduction

Ever since moving from the somewhat large Dallas-Fort Worth metroplex to the smaller, quieter city of Las Cruces, New Mexico, in July 2022, countless people have asked me the same question: "why?" At this point, my routine response is nothing more than a smirk along with a declaration that I'm just now "in my sleepy desert town era." Not only is it an easy answer that tends to generate a quick chuckle, but I also like what it reinforces about me and my current conception and performance of self: I'm calmer now, perhaps a little more contemplative, looking less for excitement and more for subtle, quiet contentment. I'm finding joy, not in an abundance of happenings, but instead in a relative lack—a sort of less-is-more alternative to my previous living situation. This now habitual response of mine isn't just a way of avoiding further conversation about the full (and much more complex) reasons for my relocation; it's also one part among many in the never-ending process of constructing or updating a public-facing persona.

My clever little answer is, of course, indebted to Taylor Swift. Anyone familiar with her career is familiar with this talk of *eras*: overarching periods in her life and artistic trajectory, shifting in ways that represent evolutions in style, personality, ambitions, subject matter, and more. Although they've tended to correlate with album release and touring cycles, these eras incorporate more than just collections of songs and the performance of such, comprising also interviews, clothing and adornment, even public political stance and sentiment. Compare, for example, the curly haired, conservative-friendly country spirit of the Debut Era to the apolitical high-waisted sparkles of the 1989 Era, and both to the more overtly liberal-leaning indie-pop storytelling of the Folklore Era. Such shifts represent not just new albums, but also new aesthetics, new invitations for engagement, and—just as in my case—new maneuvers in the never-ending process of constructing or updating a public-facing persona, perhaps culminating in the record-shattering Eras Tour from 2023 to 2024.

Somewhat akin to David Bowie before her, Swift's procession and progression of eras and their accompanying personas are noteworthy parts of her dynamic artistic presentation. Arguably, consideration of these eras is inseparable from engagement with her oeuvre: when engaging with a song like "Tim McGraw," it *matters* that we hold in mind the fact that this song was a product of the Debut Era rather than, say, the 1989 Era. This point largely generalizes: the various eras provide lenses, frames, and contexts through which to situate and understand—both aesthetically and artistically—Swift's output over time.

All of these considerations highlight yet another area in which Swift's (at this time of this writing, still ongoing) re-recording project becomes increasingly interesting: how should we understand the presence and roles of these different personas when, say, *Fearless (Taylor's Version)* is both created and released during the middle of the Evermore Era? Is it most helpful for us, as listeners looking for an informed and enriched aesthetic experience, to hear this as an updating of the persona Swift sang through during the original *Fearless* album cycle? Or instead as a layering of the Fearless Era persona on top of or alongside the Evermore Era persona? Maybe as a temporary suspension of the Evermore Era persona, with the Fearless Era persona making its brief and temporary return?

Throughout this chapter, I'll argue (among other things) that these questions really do matter. In doing so, I'll explore what some philosophers of music have had to say about this notion of *performance personas*, and adapt and extend the more limited frameworks developed with a particular focus on the notion of *performance* into the realms of *recordings*. After applying this extended framework to Swift's growing collection of re-recordings, I'll wrap up with some brief, forward-looking considerations of loose-ends.

Performance Personas: A Basic Framework

In a discussion of performance personas and the roles they play in our engagement both with musical artists and with their output, Jeanette Bicknell writes:

> A singer's public persona is the face, body, and personal history he or she presents to the audience. It includes such factors as gender, race, age, and ethnicity, as well as quirks of personality .... This information is conveyed by the singer's appearance, clothing choices, and the statements and activities reported by the media or circulated among fans. A public persona may transparently reflect a singer's true personality; more likely, it will be highly mediated and constructed.[1]

Building from what Bicknell says here, we can see that the presence of such a persona is not so much a mere artistic option or embellishment, but is instead an inevitability: any time a performer performs in public, there *is* a face, a body, and some degrees of both personal history and quirks of personality presented to the audience. Also inevitable is the fact that this history and these quirks will be, in some sense, *curated*: though there may be some aspects of both that the artist cannot help but to share, there will also be aspects of both that they *choose* to share and those that they choose to *not* share.

When we look at Swift's Debut Era, we see a very different physical presentation—in terms of hair, make-up, clothing, and other adornment—than we do in later eras, especially those such as the 1989 Era. In offering disclosures—either direct or indirect—about her own experiences with romantic relationships over time, Swift further curates her persona through glimpses into her personal and "private" history. At the same time, there are certain other facts—such as, say, her blood type, favorite substitute kindergarten teacher, preferred breakfast cereal—that remain genuine bits of personal history despite being not at all foregrounded and hence playing no (current) role at all in Swift's persona(s).

It's reasonable to assume, of course, that the apparent agnosticism about Swift's preferred breakfast cereal as it relates to her performance persona(s) is not exactly "highly mediated and constructed," but is instead due to nothing beyond the fact that such trivia is irrelevant to the music she makes. Other aspects of her persona, however, *are* mediated and constructed in exactly the way gestured at by Bicknell—and have been shown to be so. For example, in Netflix's *Miss Americana* documentary (released in January 2020), Swift is seen arguing with her father and other members of her team about the potential effects of, for the first time after years of consistent "apolitical" presentation, publicly criticizing Donald Trump. The worry regarding publicity was that such criticism might draw backlash—backlash that could prove to be detrimental for her brand. In a moment of what could be read as principled defiance, Swift responds: "I'm sad I didn't say it two years ago" and that she "want[s] to be on the right side of history."[2] Within Bicknell's framework, we can understand what's going on here as a negotiation of public persona, a decision as to whether to include particular political convictions into the public-facing character that Swift invites her audience to see, conceive, and experience her as.

Later, in May 2020, Swift offered direct criticism (via tweet) of Trump.[3] This tweet quickly became her most "liked" tweet (at the time), and in the months that followed, her opposition to Trump became more and more a part of her public presence—and hence, her persona. One way or another, the apolitical nature of her previous persona(s) was, quite deliberately, no more.

Whether these shifts in persona over time result in genuinely new and distinct personas or simply a single persona going through a process of evolution is not an issue I'll address here. We can say with confidence, however, that our understanding of an artist's persona absolutely impacts the ways in which we aesthetically engage with and appreciate their output. In arguing for this point, Bicknell writes: "[A]udiences accept certain songs from some singers but not from others. If there is too great an incongruity or mismatch between a singer's public persona and what is conveyed in a particular song, audiences will fail to be convinced. They will not accept this song from this singer and so will be inhibited from taking pleasure in the performance."[4] On Bicknell's understanding, a key component in our typical appreciation of musical performances is that we be *convinced*: that the performer performs in a manner that leaves us *believing* them. This sense of believing is broad: it's not so much that we expect them to be intoning literal truth through song lyrics, but instead that the sentiments and emotion expressed through the sung word do not leave us skeptical of the performer's authenticity. Such skepticism, it is thought, would preclude most listeners from really being able to "drop in" to the performance: while a convincing performance might reach the level of being rightly called sublime, moving, or awesome, an unconvincing performance would almost certainly fail to merit any such praise. In this way, being convinced by a performance is perhaps the first step toward experiencing its further aesthetic virtue.

Conceiving of personas, again, as characters a performer invites the audience to think of them as, we can understand them as providing a sort of "range" of songs that that performer could more-or-less convincingly perform. The quirks, history, and other traits of a particular persona might feel an odd and unconvincing match with certain lyrics or even certain musical styles, for example. The glitter-clad pop icon Taylor from her 1989 Era is perhaps less suited to convincingly perform a faithful rendition of her Debut Era material, just as Debut Era Taylor performing a song like "Welcome to New York" would have likely left audiences at the time not so much drawn in as perplexed. The same goes for the revelation of her political convictions: once such beliefs became integrated into her performance persona, her lyrics and sentiments expressed through them can no longer be convincingly heard as espousing, celebrating, or even aligning with contemporary (i.e., Trump Era) conservative values. Since much of Swift's output focuses on love and relationships, and given that such topics are often highly value-laden and even implicitly politicized, the effect of such a shift could be quite substantial.

Such considerations were surely on the mind of her interlocutors during the aforementioned scene from *Miss Americana*: if Swift goes publicly anti-Trump, then a certain not-insubstantial subsection of her audience would likely no longer find her music to be, in the sense discussed here, *convincing*. If the music is no longer convincing, it will likely no longer be experienced as *enjoyable*—and, hence, no longer be seen as something to buy, stream, or otherwise financially support. In choosing to publicly highlight this exchange in *Miss Americana*, Swift further constructs her persona: inviting audiences to conceive of her as someone who defiantly chooses to prioritize integrity over financial risk. It is, somewhat straightforwardly, a way of presenting and performing an image of authenticity.

Recording Personas: A Slightly Extended Framework

As we shift our focus to Taylor's Versions and her ongoing project of re-recording her previously released albums, it's worth noting a limitation on the application of Bicknell's framework: to avoid complications, Bicknell states that she will only "concentrate on public performances of song, rather than singing in the shower, along with the car radio, to children at bedtime, and so forth."[5] As she further develops her account, Bicknell restricts her focus to just live, solo performance of popular song. There is nothing methodologically suspect about this, of course: sometimes we restrict our focus and ambition so that we can further ensure that we are saying true things about our subject matter, without assuming that those true things generalize to cases outside of the scope of discussion. Since Bicknell's account does not—or, at least, is not intended to—apply to recordings of songs, this leaves us unable to move forward into discussion of Taylor's Versions without extending the framework, if only slightly.

The first step toward such an extension is to clarify that *performances of song* and *recordings of songs* are quite different things. Furthermore, our typical modes of engagement with each also diverge substantially. Getting clear on these differences—that is, on the differences between our engagement with something like Swift's live, in-concert performance of "Love Story" and our engagement with something like Swift's 2021 recording, "Love Story (Taylor's Version)"—will help us to develop and understand the nature, roles, and effects of personas in a broader, more expansive sense.

Recordings of songs are designed for a process of playback through which we can listen to and engage with them, often at our convenience. By *recordings* here, though, I mean not just *any* recording of a song. Instead, I focus more narrowly on *studio recordings*: that is, recordings that are quite literally assembled in the studio.[6] We can distinguish studio recordings from *live recordings*: that is, recordings directly of live performances themselves. Admittedly, this is neither a strict nor easy distinction to draw: some studio recordings take place outside of conventional studios (I myself have recorded many tracks in my living room, bathroom, and even car) and some live recordings are heavily manipulated through studio post-production. Similarly, some studio recordings involve a live performance (in studio) with minimal or no post-production at all. Despite these complications, paradigm cases of both studio recordings and live recordings are easy to identify: although both appear on the *Speak Now (Taylor's Version)* album, the fifth track, "Dear John (Taylor Version)," is a studio recording while the twenty-third track, "Dear John (Live from Minneapolis)," is a live recording. Our focus will be on recordings that are more like the former, rather than those that are more like the latter.[7]

With this clarification in place, we can begin to observe the different ways through which we engage with studio recordings as opposed to live performances. When it comes to recordings of live music performances, we tend to listen *through* the recording and instead *to* the performance that it is a recording of—perhaps, in some cases, going even further and listening *through* the performance and *to* the song that is being performed. Recordings thereby serve as documents, tools through which we gain access, one-step removed, from the actual target of our attention. (If we think of some live performances as tools through which we gain access to songs as the actual target of our attention: *two*-steps removed.) For *recording-based* music—what Andrew Kania, Theodore Gracyk, and other philosophers of music have broadly called "rock"[8]—however, we instead listen *to* the recording itself, insofar as the recording is the actual target of our attention. Given that many (most, even) studio recordings are assembled in studio without corresponding to any full (or even partial) performance of the song in question, instead being assembled from multiple takes, this means that what we are attending to when we engage with recording-based music is simply *not* a performance.[9]

It would prove helpful, then, to distinguish between *performance* personas (as already discussed) and *recording* personas, perhaps taking both to be varieties of a more general notion of an *artistic persona.* When on stage, performers quite literally embody their performance persona—their movements, mannerisms, and physicality all become parts of, or extensions of, the persona. This is not straightforwardly the case in the context of studio recordings: a recording persona is not a character we physically *see* embodied in front of us, but is instead one that we *imagine.* Here, our imaginings are informed by what we know (or infer, or guess) about the performer's embodied physicality, mannerisms, history, etc., but also by aspects of the recording— including sonic elements internal to the recording as well as external elements such as associated artwork, liner notes, and so on. Consider, for example, a Swift fan who first encounters her music through a vinyl album without any previous exposure to live concerts (or recordings thereof); in the framework being developed here, the image of Swift in this fan's mind would be that of a recording persona, rather than performance persona.

Perhaps the most striking difference between a performance persona and a recording persona is what we might call the *temporal fixity* of the latter. When Swift performs her songs live, we most naturally hear those songs through whatever persona she is embodying at the time.[10] But when we listen to a studio recording, we most naturally hear that song through the persona fixed at the time of the recording, as if the persona itself is encoded in the recording right alongside the song itself. Put another way: when Swift performs "Shake It Off" in 2023 as part of the Eras Tour, we are hearing the song as *performed* by Taylor-2023. By contrast: when, even in 2023, we listen to the sixth track on 2014's *1989* album, we inevitably hear the same song as *recorded* by Taylor-2014. In this way, the association of persona with live performances of the song enjoys some fluidity, whereas the association of persona with the studio recording is temporally fixed. Fittingly, this tracks with conceptions we might have of live performances as being living, dynamic spaces and of recordings as fixed documents of a particular point (or stretch) of time.

To sum up so far: since studio recordings aren't performances (in the relevant sense), we need to subtly tweak our notion of personas when attempting to apply them to such recordings. Two key differences are: (1) live performances of songs inherit, at least to some degree, the performance persona of the performer at the time of performance, whereas studio recordings come with a temporally fixed recording persona; and (2) engaging with live performances of songs involves perception and consideration of a physically embodied persona, whereas engaging with studio recordings involves perception (in some sense) and consideration of an imagined persona. Even with these differences acknowledged, however, Bicknell's key point remains true: insofar as a recording persona might feel incongruent with the recorded song in a manner that makes the listening experience unconvincing, considerations of artistic personas—of either variety discussed throughout this chapter so far—remain aesthetically relevant.

Which Version of Taylor in Taylor's Versions?

When we listen to "Love Story"—recorded for and released on the 2008 album, *Fearless*—the recording persona imagined is presumably that of Fearless Era Taylor: an innocent, perhaps somewhat naive (due to relative inexperience with life) yet still insightful (due to being wise and reflective beyond her years), apolitical and emphatically polite country girl focusing mostly on the emotional processing of high school relationships. Temporally fixed by the recording, this persona is what is most naturally imagined when listening to "Love Story," whether at the time of its debut or at the time of this writing in 2024. This persona impacts and filters our interpretations of the song: the invocations of Romeo, Juliet, and scarlet letters coming from the perspective of someone who had perhaps lightly studied such texts at a middle- or high-school level relatively recently; and the reminiscence about how young she was when she first saw her love interest carrying a hint of irony, given the concurrent and comparable youth of the persona delivering the line. The resulting listening experience is, many would presumably agree, not just convincing but also compelling: a young and naive reflection on love reinforced in its sincerity by being sung to us by someone imagined as young and naive.

When we hear the same song performed live on, say, the 2023 Eras Tour, we hear—and see—an older, wiser, post-Midnights Era Taylor. This is a Taylor who has surely moved past the simple and straightforward romanticization of *Romeo and Juliet*. She is a comparatively much more political Taylor who can contextualize a particularly teenage variety of love against a backdrop of global capitalism, rising fascism, and the complexities of near-unprecedented stardom. Without even yet taking into account strictly *musical* differences, this shift in persona affects the way we might hear the song: less as an exuberant expression of youthful love, but instead as a *reflection on* such—a perhaps bittersweet encapsulation of nostalgia for (what seemed to be) a simpler time, with simpler struggles and simpler priorities. The performance is still convincing—compelling, even—but it convinces us of something far more nuanced, more reflective, and perhaps more tragic. Maybe you can relate: Swift's flashback to her teenage relationship simply hits *different* when sung (of the same experience) by a 32-year-old rather than a nineteen-year-old.

What do we say, then, about "Love Story (Taylor's Version)," recorded for and released on 2021's *Fearless (Taylor's Version)*? Given what has been said so far, we have options. Here are some of them:

(1) **The temporally fixed recording persona in "Love Story (Taylor's Version)" is the same as that in the original recording (namely, the Fearless Era Persona).** While perhaps an initially plausible assessment, this option might start to seem at least a little odd after some brief reflection: it would, after all, involve Swift suspending her current persona and instead adopting a former persona that would be easily recognizable as such. In that way, she would be inviting audiences not to hear her as *her*, but as a *character* based on her past self. She would be quite obviously play-acting as her teenaged self, and inviting us to hear her as such. This suspension of the transparency so often associated with Swift's personas seems an odd fit with her artistic tendencies.

(2) **The temporally fixed recording persona in "Love Story (Taylor's Version)" is the same as the persona publicly adopted at the time of the recording, namely, the Evermore Era persona.** While also potentially intuitive, this option might still not be the most comfortable fit. The Evermore Era Taylor is simply too mature, too reflective, too experienced, and too learned (compared to Fearless Era Taylor) for the song to be as believable as when we hear it through the Fearless Era persona. Evermore Era Taylor simply wouldn't identify with Juliet in the way that Fearless Era Taylor did. In making the song less believable, this would have the effect of making the recording aesthetically worse than the original—a conclusion we perhaps ought not to lean into on these grounds.

(3) **The temporally fixed recording persona in "Love Story (Taylor's Version)" is some piecemeal amalgamation or averaging-out of the Evermore Era and the Fearless Era.** I suspect that this option enjoys even less initial plausibility (and appeal) than either of the above options, and also that upon reflection, it becomes even more difficult to either state or comprehend. It might be best, then, to leave it to the side.

> **(4) The temporally fixed recording persona in "Love Story (Taylor's Version)" is neither the Fearless Era persona nor the Evermore Era persona (nor any amalgamation of the two), but is instead a new and distinct persona—one coupled with all of the Taylor's Version re-recordings.** On this view, we have a new persona on our hands: perhaps that of principled, defiant, and determined artist-yet-businesswoman, one whose current work is not only a comment on her previous work but also a recalcitrant reaction toward cynical and exploitative business practices. This persona is itself a bit of a paradox, melding *punk* with *I am more powerful than you, so I will do what I want*—with that tension providing a unique and compelling (to some) protagonist.

Of the four, I suspect that Option 4 enjoys the most plausibility. Of course, despite still being a consciously constructed (and hence, to some degree, artificial) persona, this Versions Persona (for lack of a better term) would highlight the ultimate artificiality of all of Swift's other personas. It does so, too, in a manner that seems importantly different from the results of Option 1: with the advent of the Eras Tour, it seems that Taylor herself is consciously and explicitly leaning into the same notion of a *post-persona* persona, deliberately highlighting the "eras" as a series of characters she has played on the way to where she finds herself now.

We see further evidence of this reading through the frequent costume changes on the Eras Tour—something like sixteen times over a 3.5-hour duration—with outfits selected to represent (and cue the audience in on) which era is being highlighted at the time. And just as Swift has commented on persona shifts in her lyrics previously (consider the claim that the old Taylor's dead in "Look What You Made Me Do" from 2017's *Reputation*), one can also read her updated lyric or vocal performances on some among her re-recordings as coming from the perspective of this wiser, more mature Versions Persona. Examples include the change to the lyrics of "Better than Revenge" on *Speak Now (Taylor's Version)* to avoid implications of "slut shaming," or the shift in vocal performance on "Dear John (Taylor's Version)" to give more of a feeling of a mature woman looking back on her past rather than a twenty-year-old in the throes of heartbreak.[11]

To return to the question asked at the beginning of this section: which version of Taylor is the Taylor of Taylor's Versions? Since the adoption of at least some persona is—as argued earlier—inevitable, it simply isn't plausible to conclude that this is some "unmasked," transparent Taylor, completely without persona. Instead, it seems that our best understanding of Swift's current persona is that of the Versions Persona, marking an ostensibly "post-era" era during which Swift—recognizing all of the above—puts her mastery of personas as aesthetic tools on full display while simultaneously—and somewhat defiantly—crafting a "no persona" persona. Beyond mere play-acting, this is an artistic act with aesthetic impact: to return to an earlier example, hearing "Love Story (Taylor's Version)" while holding this Versions Persona in mind lends the recording the aesthetic of a middle finger, especially given the relative fidelity to the original recording.[12] And personally speaking, all other philosophizing aside, this seems to be sufficient reason for approaching the recording in exactly that way.

Conclusions and Further Considerations

Understanding Swift's re-recordings, as well as the Eras Tour, through the lens of the Versions Persona leads us to a Taylor that is, while still constructed, one step closer to reality: a curated persona that, along with the audience, is "in" on the persona bit. In maneuvering in this way, Swift is able to foreground and highlight this aspect of her artistic capacities and strength. Just as with Bowie before her, Swift's ability to navigate and utilize personas as artistic tools is not just admirable and perhaps enviable, but also a contributing factor to her well-deserved praise and acclaim.

Much more discussion is warranted, of course. What additional obligations related to the construction and curation of persona are incurred as the artist reaches near-unprecedented levels of fame, wealth, and cultural influence? To what degree are the frequently expressed worries about potential "queer-baiting"—that is, the cynical act of gesturing at and suggesting queer identity while retaining enough plausible deniability so as to retain appeal (and, hence, marketability) both for queer audiences *and* queerphobic audiences—worth taking seriously, and in what ways are they comparable to Swift's own expressed worries about the tensions between remaining publicly apolitical, on the one hand, and being "on the right side of history," on the other?[13]

These are all good questions, and questions worth exploring. We can explore them later, however. In the meantime, we can instead take the time to enjoy the constructed and curated performance of the wizened, paradoxical, middle-finger, *no-persona* persona singing to us songs of teenage love.

Notes

1   Jeanette Bicknell, "Just a Song? Exploring the Aesthetics of Popular Song Performance," *Journal of Aesthetics and Art Criticism* 63, no. 3 (2005): 261–70; 262–3. For further discussion and development of these ideas, see also Jeanette Bicknell, *A Philosophy of Song and Singing: An Introduction* (London: Routledge, 2015); Theodore Gracyk, "Performer, Persona, and the Evaluation of Musical Performance," *Contemporary Aesthetics* 15 (2017), https://digitalcommons.risd.edu/liberalarts_contempaesthetics/vol15/iss1/13/; and Wesley D. Cray, "Transparent and Opaque Performance Personas," *Journal of Aesthetics and Art Criticism* 77, no. 2 (2019): 181–91.

2   *Miss Americana*, directed by Lana Wilson (Los Angeles, CA: Tremolo Productions, 2020), https://www.netflix.com/title/81028336.

3   Taylor Swift (@taylorswift13), "After stoking the fires of white supremacy and racism Your entire presidency," *Twitter*, May 29, 2020, https://twitter.com/taylorswift13/status/1266392274549776387?lang=en (accessed July 31, 2023).

4   Bicknell, "Just a Song?," 266.

5   Ibid., 261.

6   Michael Thomas Connolly discusses at length how studio recordings are assembled in Chapter 4 of this volume.

7   This is, in part, due to considerations offered in Christy Mag Uidhir, "Recordings as Performances," *British Journal of Aesthetics* 47, no. 3 (2007): 298–314, according to which the mode through which we engage with recordings of live performances is sufficiently similar to the mode through which we engage with live performances for our earlier account of performance personas (from this chapter's second section) to more-or-less straightforwardly apply without need for extension.

8   See, for example, Gracyk, *Rhythm and Noise* and Kania, "Making Tracks," 401–14. See also Brandon Polite's chapter in this volume for further discussion of the nature of studio recordings.

9   Or, at least, not a performance in the relevant sense. For a framework in which the act of constructing a studio recording is, in a fact, a species of performance—though one still importantly different enough from live performance for the remarks here to stand—see Stephen Davies, *Musical Works and Performances: A Philosophical Exploration* (Oxford: Clarendon Press, 2004).

10 Although see Cray, "Transparent and Opaque" for the additional complication of the *song persona*, which I leave to the side here in order to keep things from getting *too* complicated.

11 A related but importantly different case is that of "Picture to Burn," released on Swift's debut album. This song originally contained a lyric that Swift soon after re-recorded and edited into the otherwise unaltered track, so as to avoid homophobic connotations. This differs from the other cases discussed so far insofar as this was an edit and re-release of a track, rather than a full re-recording, and was likely also done primarily for strategic, commercial reasons (i.e., not alienating gay fans) rather than as an intentional and robust, persona-driven commentary.

12 For more on how the meanings of songs might change across re-recordings, see Alex King's chapter in this volume.

13 For applicable discussion, see Wesley D. Cray, "Aesthetics from the Closet," *American Society for Aesthetics Newsletter* 4, no. 1 (2021): 1–3, and Jeremy Fried, "Ally Aesthetics," *Journal of Aesthetics and Art Criticism* 77, no. 4 (2019): 447–59.

9

The Rights of the Living Dead

Taylor Swift's Zombie Army

Elizabeth Cantalamessa

Introduction

In the music video for her song "Look What You Made Me Do," Taylor Swift rises as a zombie from a grave marked "Taylor Swift's Reputation" while singing about how little she likes to be messed with. She goes on to sing about how she has grown smarter and more resilient, before warning that karma is all she thinks about. Swift's transformation into a zombie rising from her reputation's grave serves as a useful illustration for her transition into a public figure. To become a public figure or celebrity, I claim, is to exist alongside a zombie version of yourself. This zombie shares the same name and physical likeness but operates independently of its flesh-and-blood counterpart. In fact, public figures do not have any special authority over the zombie version of themselves, and in some contexts they enjoy less authority over their zombie counterparts than others do.[1] In the United States, for example, public figures are not legally entitled to protections against criticism via parody, which can include unauthorized use of their likeness for offensive images, insulting jokes, and other forms of public mockery.

Further, a public figure or author's name serves multiple different functions, in addition to referring to the concrete individual. For example, someone can be the author of a song while not enjoying the legal and economic entitlements of ownership. As Michel Foucault observed, a work is entitled to become the "murderer" of its author, which suggests that the author's name exists among the living dead.[2] An artist's works can bear their name yet operate independently of their attitudes or mental states. In the United States, music copyrights are divided between production rights, which cover the actual composition of a song, and master rights, which govern the recording of a composition and how it is used or sampled by third parties. In June of 2019, the master rights to Taylor Swift's first six albums were sold without her knowledge or consent, effectively "murdering" her rights as their author. Swift's 2019 decision to re-record her first six studio albums can thus be understood as an act of institutional revenge, a way to get back at the people who have wielded power over her and the institutions that enable exploitation—a battle with her zombified works: the "stolen" original albums. In this chapter I sketch an institutional theory of celebrity names to explain the institutional, personal, and political significance of self-appropriation, using Taylor Swift's act of re-recording her own music as a paradigm case.

What's in a Name? Barthes and Foucault on the Author Function

Philosophers have traditionally assumed that an account of proper names is an account of their semantic meaning and the nature of reference in a manner that also captures how sentences involving a proper name can be true.[3] On this account, proper names do little more than refer (or point) to a particular persons, places, or things. For example, the name "Taylor Swift" refers to the famous singer who was born in West Reading, Pennsylvania, in 1989. Or, "the Grand Canyon" refers to a large chasm in southern Arizona. The philosophical work involves specifying how the relevant linguistic items successfully refer to non-linguistic entities out in the world. Reference is a word–world relation that contributes to a proposition's truth value. If a term fails to refer, then the proposition is either false or meaningless. Two names are identical when they refer to the same object, or when they can be substituted in the same sentence without modifying its truth value. On the earliest view, reference is fixed by a definite description because the description can be substituted for a name without modifying the truth value of the sentence.[4] Take the sentence, "Taylor Swift attended the MTV Video Music Awards." Since I can substitute the proper name "Taylor Swift" with the definite description "the famous singer born in West Reading, Pennsylvania, in 1989" without modifying the truth value of the sentence, both expressions share the same referent.

While this account conceives of reference as the sole or essential function of proper names, it isn't the only account available to us. In the context of public artistic production or authorship, proper names serve multiple functions in addition to referring to concrete individuals. The account I support considers a consequence of the postmodern insight that authors do not have a special relationship to their name *or* to their work. In what follows, I use "author" as a placeholder for particular authors, artists, or public figures in general. Rather than offering a theory of the semantic meaning or nature of proper names, I am interested in exploring how proper names function in institutional contexts. In the next section I will suggest that authorial names function to license a set of entitlements, permissions, prohibitions, and obligations.

During the mid-twentieth century, literary criticism underwent a major shift in how it understood the relationship between an author's mental states and the aesthetic properties or meaning of their works. According to the so-called *intentional fallacy*, it is a logical mistake to assume that an artist's psychological states determine the meanings of their works.[5] In his seminal 1967 essay "The Death of the Author," Roland Barthes argues that an author does not play a special role in determining the meaning or aesthetic properties of their work.[6] Critics, journalists, fans, and legal agents can all play a role in determining the aesthetic properties of the work independently or in tension with the author's own beliefs about them. Barthes referred to the primacy of the audience in determining the features of a work as the "death of the author."[7] Previously, an author's intentions, experiences, or biographical facts played an important role in fixing a work's aesthetic properties, of which there was only one "correct" interpretation. For Barthes, the "death" of the author is really the "birth" of the reader, which is to say aesthetic meaning was no longer "out there" in the world and determined by an author's intention, but the responsibility of the reader. As I'll argue in the following section, Swift's loss of ownership over the masters of her first six albums suggests as well that the death of the author enables the birth of the *music-industrial complex*, where people (or institutions) that play no role in creating a work can still reap the economic benefits one would typically associate with authorship.

Michel Foucault in his 1969 lecture "What Is an Author?" extends Barthes's thesis to argue that the concept of the author should be understood as a discursive function. For Foucault, writing bears a special relationship to death because the text has a right to "kill" or "murder" its author.[8] According to Foucault, an author's name no longer functions in the same way as other proper names, which can be determined through reference or description. Instead, the author "is a certain *functional principle* by which, in our culture, one limits, excludes, and chooses."[9] Foucault characterizes this function in terms of permissions, obligations, presuppositions, and inferential implications.[10] For example, to say that "Homer does not exist" functions to express the claim that the name "Homer" does not refer to anyone. However, this does not imply that claims involving the name "Homer" are meaningless, as it does on the traditional view. Instead, the name serves to unify a set of texts, including the *Iliad* and the *Odyssey*, a unification that is always, in principle, open to debate.

While Barthes and Foucault are concerned with literary criticism, I think their account of proper names (e.g., the author) offers an illustrative contrast to the traditional view and its metaphysical account of a proper name as identical to a definite description. If the author does not bear any special relationship to their work, then an author's name is something like a tool we use to unify a set of works but not to tether them to any non-discursive entity. For example, to claim that various works were written by "Plato" is to license inferences about the relationship between them, as permitting critical discourse to make claims about the relational properties between the works. In other words, in the context of critical discourse an author's name no longer performs a referential function.

Notably, Foucault restricts his analysis to literary authorship and claims that the author as a function of discourse "does not have a legal status" and "a contract may well have a guarantor—it does not have an author."[11] At the same time, Foucault admits that there "exist properties or relationships peculiar to discourse" that go beyond considerations of grammar or extension, into various "modes of existence."[12] He suggests that there are modes of existence appropriate to different cultural and historical periods. Thus, I think a possible extension of his idea is an analysis of the "contractual" mode of existence, as one of the institutional functions of an author's name (and the function of authorship more broadly). Swift's case reveals that authorship can be (legally) contested, where people who do not share any traditional creative relationship to a work or set of works can reap the benefits that were once reserved for the author. Moreover, Foucault sees the referential function of the author as a reflection of "our era of industrial and bourgeois society, of individualism and private property."[13] Similarly, I will argue that in the context of the music-industrial complex, the author of a composition is someone who instigates a process of commercialization. In other words, the author function legitimizes certain texts as a component of their body of work, which plays an important economic function: profit-making. However, Foucault fails to recognize how authorship was largely reserved for (white) men, and for economically marginalized authors economic entitlement becomes a substantial political issue as well. Swift's situation highlights Foucault's closing consideration that questions of authorship will evolve from reference to appropriation, and due to institutional rules or practices we can legitimately evaluate "who" can "assume the various subject functions" and who cannot either do so or do so as easily.[14]

My point here is to suggest that in the context of commercialization, the referential function of proper names is replaced by an institutional or contractual function.[15] In other words, we can model proper names as not merely designators for concrete individuals, but also as tools for establishing entitlements, permissions, and prohibitions.

Authorship, Zombification, and the Music-Industrial Complex

So far, I have argued that proper names perform multiple communicative functions, in addition to referring to or describing non-linguistic entities "out there" in the world. I will now extend my argument to show how becoming a public figure is one of the social-historical conditions that cause an artist's name to perform a different, institutional function.

As a reminder, becoming a public author is a form of "death" because one's name no longer serves a merely referential function.[16] Further, the author no longer enjoys the privilege of controlling how their works, name, and likeness are replicated or used in critical discourse. I call this process "zombification." I do so because this process takes place after the "death" of the author. Consider zombification as the process of becoming a public figure such that one is no longer entitled to prohibit others from using their image, name, or works, such as for the purpose of commentary, parody, and the like—the same processes involved in the death of the author. The zombie is an entity that resembles some concrete, living person but does not have any of its own mental states, desires, or plans. Instead, it is merely a discursive representation of a living person. Public figures undergo a process of zombification where their image and name are used in ways that they need not endorse, accept, or even know about. For example, I have zombified Foucault in this very chapter by using his claims, ideas, and their consequences to express my *own* interpretation of his view. Even if he were alive, Foucault could not prohibit me from using his words to express my ideas. However, Foucault would be able to produce critical works that use *my* words, name, and ideas to express his idea that I am wrong.

Typically, under US Copyright law an author retains exclusive rights to the use of their work and/or likeness.[17] However, someone else can use copyrighted works without an author's permission if they do so for purposes including criticism, such as quoting text from others' articles as I have done throughout this chapter. In other words, Taylor Swift wouldn't have control over how her name "Taylor Swift" as well as the works that are authored by "Taylor Swift" were used or publicly displayed. In the United States the First Amendment to the Constitution guarantees the right to free speech, which includes using others' names or copyrighted material for purposes including criticism and commentary. The First Amendment is the basis for US parody law, which recognizes parody as a legitimate form of political and social criticism.[18] The US Supreme Court recognized parody as a form of criticism for, in both cases, the resulting work expresses a distinct (i.e., different) idea. According to parody law, it is permissible to use the work, image, or name of a public figure in the context of mockery, such as political cartoons or satirical advertisements (including religious or sacred figures).[19] Thus, I can use the name "Taylor Swift" or her image in the context of a satirical cartoon, comedy sketch, or critical article regardless of what Taylor Swift feels or thinks about it. I could even publish parody advertisements that use Taylor Swift's name and image in order to mock or insult her.[20] Parody has been recognized as a legitimate form of criticism because public figures have a greater degree of influence over others' beliefs and values. Basically, it is permissible to mock public figures because they have more power than the rest of us. The important point for present purposes is that parody law supports Barthes's and Foucault's shared view that authors do not have special authority over their works, names, *or* their likeness.

Copyright protects the economic interests of authors, ensuring that they receive profit from their work and prohibiting others from using their works in ways that diminish their economic success. On first pass, you might think that authorship just *is* ownership—if I am the author of a particular work, then I have a special relation to it, it is "mine" and so I am entitled to prohibit or allow others to treat it in certain ways.[21] In our current cultural and historical period, however, authorship is not merely exhausted by reference or description. While copyright protects an author's rights in virtue of creating a song as a vehicle to express an original idea (e.g., its lyrics), there are two different sets of legal protections: one for the song itself (specifically, for its lyrics and composition) and another for the recording of that song. The former is included in publishing rights and the latter is called the master rights. The entity or individual that pays for the recording typically retains the master rights.

As Darren Hudson Hick argues in Chapter 1 of this volume, Swift has effectively no control over her first six albums, with Sony enjoying 90 percent of the copyright entitlements to her songs, which renders her remaining control effectively "meaningless," and Big Machine Records (or its current owner) owning the master rights. Paradoxically, in the context of the music-industrial complex, one must sell their copyrights to enjoy the economic benefits of being a copyright holder. Artists typically fix the state of their publishing and master rights when they sign a recording contract with a record company, which stipulates how the works will be manufactured and distributed. As Theo Papadopoulos notes, "the role of the record company is to transform a musical work into a marketable commodity," a process which "can be an expensive and high-risk endeavor."[22] As such, record companies are more likely to shoulder the cost of recording and distributing an artist's music and thereby are granted the master rights to the recordings of the songs. While this might seem innocent, as a systematic historical phenomenon it entails that most artists do not enjoy the economic entitlements of the songs they otherwise composed and performed.

The Personal Is Political Is Economic: Taylor Swift's Self-appropriation

What does all this have to do with Taylor Swift? Well, Swift is a victim of institutional exploitation that treads on the distinction between master rights and publishing rights: while she maintains publishing rights over the songs she wrote or co-wrote for her first six studio albums (at least, all or part of the 10 percent that Sony doesn't own), she has zero controlling stake in the rights to the recordings. Through the "death of the author" a public figure becomes zombified, where their name operates in institutional and social contexts over which they have no special authority or control. However, Barthes's proclamation failed to anticipate how profit-driven institutions and industries would capitalize on the author's displacement. The institutional practices surrounding music copyright entail that being the author of a composition is not identical to being its owner or the owner of its recording, and each relationship is constituted by a set of legal, economic, and institutional permissions and entitlements. If one does not own the master rights, then their recordings are effectively zombified: the artist has no control over how a recording of their composition is used.

To own one's masters, then, allows one to license their recording to third parties or for commercial use, such as television, film, or streaming services. This means that if an artist does not own the master rights to a recording of a famous and profitable song, they will share little in the profits. So, while the song "Shake It Off" is attributed to the musician "Taylor Swift," Taylor Swift does not own the master rights and so is not entitled to dictate or control how the recording (or its album) is used. In general, Taylor Swift earns little from the first six albums composed and recorded by "Taylor Swift" in comparison to what the owners of their master rights earn. As Prince once warned, "If you don't own your masters, the master owns you."[23]

While it is possible for a songwriter to transfer their rights, they must do so in writing: by signing their name. This is perhaps most obvious in the case of "selling" one's catalog, which consists of transferring the publishing rights or the rights to one's lyrics and compositions. For example, Bob Dylan sold his musical catalog of over 600 songs to Universal Music, thereby forfeiting his right to determine how or when his songs are recorded by others and the economic benefits that follow.[24] If a film wanted to use a particular recording of a Dylan song, they would need permission from whomever owns the master rights. If someone wanted to record a cover of a given song for a film, they would need permission from the person or entity that owns the publishing rights. The fact that an artist can sell their catalog to a corporation or nonhuman entity is a reflection of our current social-historical situation, not a consequence of the nature of authorship itself. Even worse, the fact that there can be holding companies whose sole purpose is to purchase the rights to others' works is a symptom of the music-industrial complex, which both depends on and reinforces the unequal power relations between record labels (which are legally persons) and actual, concrete artists. When we combine zombification with the music-industrial complex, it becomes possible for an author's name to be associated with works over which they have no economic or institutional authority. This is where Swift's battle begins.

Further, record companies can use an artist's name and likeness for advertisement and promotion. However, "a lot of artists, especially in the early days of their career, don't realize that signing away your masters means selling the rights to their own work—sometimes for their entire career."[25] Swift, like so many other artists, was at an economic and thus institutional disadvantage when she signed her first record contract with Big Machine Records. As such, Swift signed away her master rights, giving the record company the authority over how her recordings would be used and the subsequent profit from their use. According to an interview with attorney Susan Hilderley, Swift's contract is what "you would expect for somebody who was an unknown artist when she signed," where artists typically do not own the masters for her own songs. Likewise, when record labels "make investments in unproven talent," the "trade is that, traditionally, the masters stay with the record company."[26]

I am placing Swift's predicament in tension with Barthes's and Foucault's insight, which reveals some nefarious consequences of the death of the author: the economic and thus political disempowerment of the author, such as the way that profit-driven institutions exploit legal and economic distinctions between publishing rights and master rights. The question then becomes: What recourse do artists such as Swift have to combat this form of institutional exploitation?

I believe Taylor Swift's act of re-recording is a way of engaging in an "institutional" battle with her zombie counterparts—her records and recordings for which she does not maintain the master rights. These are works that bear the name "Taylor Swift" but over which Taylor Swift has no control. While Swift has no special authority over her zombie counterparts, she is entitled to certain moves within the public institutions (because she co-owns the rights to the songs) that enable her to challenge, modify, or intervene in the relevant practices that determine facts about her zombie counterparts. Since Swift co-owns the rights to the compositions for her songs, she is entitled to record new versions of those songs in much the same way she could license another artist to record and publish a cover of them. For example, the re-appropriated "(Taylor's Version)" appended to the title of each re-recorded song and album actively impacts the economic success of the original "Taylor Swift" recordings. Per *The Week*, "re-recording the songs will make the original masters less valuable."[27] As such, I think Swift is engaging in an act of self-appropriation. As Sherri Irvin discusses in Chapter 3 of this volume, appropriation involves the use of preexisting works with little to no modification.[28]

Since Swift wrote her own songs she retains the production rights to her works, and so she can re-record the songs with minor modification—she can appropriate her own compositions to express a different idea.[29] However, she cannot use the original recordings. Crucially, appropriation art should not be mistaken for the original work, which in many cases requires that the audience have sufficient background knowledge and information. Swift clearly does not want audiences to mistake her re-recordings for the originals, which is why she adds "(Taylor's Version)" to every re-recorded song and album. Further, Swift can (and will) prohibit the licensing of the original recordings, only permitting the Taylor's Version of a song to be used in advertisements or other media.[30] Self-appropriation allows Swift to produce her *own* army of zombified versions of her *own* albums that compete with her original works, negatively impacting their economic success.

Swift is not the first artist to battle the music industry over zombification. Perhaps most famously, Prince changed his name to an undefined symbol as an act of resistance against and emancipation from his record label Warner Bros. In a press release, Prince noted that Warner Bros. "owns the name Prince and all related music marketed under Prince .... [T]he only acceptable replacement for my name, and my identity, was a symbol with no pronunciation .... It is my name."[31] According to the *Los Angeles Times*, "what Prince was fighting for, most crucially, was the right to own the mechanisms for how his music entered the world."[32] Prince did not object to being commodified per se, but to his lack of control over his own commodification. For Prince, the music industry exploited people of color because white music executives controlled and benefited from the work of Black artists.

Crucially, while performing under the symbol, (the Artist formerly Known as) Prince was negatively impacting the economic success of zombie "Prince's" works: the symbol was not pronounceable, and it required special software to duplicate in text. In other words, (the Artist Formally Known as) Prince created obstacles for media outlets to refer to "Prince" and his works, as well as causing issues for Warner Bros. in the attempt to promote and advertise "Prince's" music.[33] Consequently, Prince used his popularity and (limited) power to battle his zombie counterpart. Although (the Artist Formally Known as) Prince could not control how Warner Bros. used the name "Prince" and the recordings they owned, (the Artist Formally Known as) Prince could make certain moves, such as issuing a press release announcing a name change, that limited what Warner Bros. could do with "Prince's" music and name. Prince abandoned the symbol once he was free from the Warner Bros. recording contract.

Swift's act of self-appropriation is intended to expose the exploitative practices in the music industry more broadly. Swift has stated that she hopes to "change the awareness level for other artists and potentially help them avoid a similar fate" while also objecting to the misogynistic underpinnings of her work being owned by men and male-run companies: "the message being sent to me is very clear. Basically, be a good little girl and shut up. Or you'll be punished."[34] According to music scholar James Perone, "Swift has also exhibited a new type of feminism that is recognized as a message of empowerment by some women of her generation but is considerably more controversial among some feminists of the past."[35] Swift's ability to create her own zombie army reflects her extraordinary degree of institutional power, which is not typically enjoyed by other artists, especially artists of color. Further, as Irvin notes in this volume, Swift positioned herself as a victim (of Braun, of the music industry, and of Kanye West), a narrative that plays into long-standing racialized dynamics that position white women as victims.[36] In that sense, Swift is championing a form of "girlboss" feminism, which understands empowerment as women occupying positions of power that are typically reserved for (white) men. Further, Swift has wielded institutional power over other, younger and less-established artists, such as Olivia Rodrigo.[37] Swift's public proclamations as well as her sizeable fanbase have helped expose not only the difference between master rights and publishing rights, but the exploitative nature of the music-industrial complex more broadly—even if she sometimes benefits from it as well.[38]

Moreover, Swift's public battle with Big Machine Records is in line with her previous acts of advocacy—drawing attention to ways in which the music-industrial complex takes advantage of artists. Swift has offered a "very public defense of artists' rights, particularly as they intersect with new technologies," such as her objections to the royalty practices on streaming outlets such as Spotify and iTunes Radio.[39] In 2014 she removed her songs from Spotify in protest of its royalties policies, and in 2015 Swift published a letter criticizing Apple for failing to pay artists during a free trial of its service. According to *Billboard*, "when [Swift] signed a new global deal with Universal Music Group in 2018 … one of the conditions of her contract was that UMG share proceeds from any sale of its Spotify equity with its roster of artists— and make them nonrecoupable against those artists' earnings."[40] Swift's expressions of empowerment have not been limited to her songs.

Swift has used the various platforms with which she has been afforded through her success as a singer-songwriter to champion women's rights and artists' rights, such as in her 2016 Grammy speech when she "warned female artists to make sure that they allow no one to undercut them or to take credit for their work."[41]

Though Swift is not the first artist to re-record her compositions, her simultaneous advocacy for other artists makes her act markedly different than previous cases, such as Def Leppard and the Everly Brothers. While most instances of re-recording are done so for purely economic reasons, Swift is the first to also do so as a form of political advocacy.[42] In 2019 Swift observed that artists are "working off of an antiquated contractual system. We're galloping toward a new industry but not thinking about recalibrating financial structures and compensation rates, taking care of producers and writers."[43] Further, Swift understands that her status affords her protection that lesser-known artists lack: "new artists and producers and writers need work, and they need to be likable and get booked in sessions, and they can't make noise—but if I can, then I'm going to."[44] This is where being impossibly famous can be a very good thing: "I know that it seems like I'm very loud about this," she says, "but it's because someone has to be."[45] Swift's contributions to music and the seriousness with which she takes music and the recognition of songwriters were recognized by the performing rights licensing agency BMI, which established the Taylor Swift Award of which she was the first recipient in 2016.[46]

The fact that Swift hopes to create more and better opportunities for other, less famous artists is what distinguishes Swift's re-recordings from other cases. Swift explicitly notes that her plight will raise awareness and help other artists "learn about how to better protect themselves in a negotiation" because, "You deserve to own the art you make."[47] Swift is thus not *merely* doing it for monetary reasons, but she is also opening up new possibilities for other artists and raising awareness for how women are treated in the industry.

Conclusion: Zombification as Transformative Experience

I have argued that authors, as public figures, do not retain any special authority over their own works and likenesses. I call this process "zombification." Further, the music industry takes advantage of zombification by creating two distinct sets of rights: publishing rights, which govern the composition of a musical work, and master rights, which govern the recording of a composition. As a result, an artist's name can be associated with a recording or album but the artist themself has no authority over how the recording is used or entitlement to the economic benefits of its commercial use.

Although artists "choose" to participate in the institutional practices that give rise to zombification, the process itself is what L. A. Paul calls a "transformative experience," such that artists cannot know, beforehand, "what it's like" to become zombified—that is, to be a public figure and thereby to have their works governed and controlled by others. According to Paul, a transformative experience is one where an agent cannot predict beforehand what their expected utility will be once they have gone through the experience because the experience will radically and fundamentally change their preferences and values.[48] While Paul takes starting a family and becoming a vampire as instances of transformative experience, my analysis suggests that "zombification," or becoming a public figure, is likewise a transformative experience. Paul suggests that the concept of transformative experience has important implications for public policies and practices such as long-term prison sentences because such policies assume or take for granted that someone will be the same person throughout the experience. If becoming a successful public figure is a transformative experience, how, or when, should we reconsider the nature of ownership in the context of copyright? Hick, in Chapter 1 of this volume, for instance, suggests establishing a three-year "relicensing" period. Such a practice recognizes both the rights of the record companies, given their economic risks and investment, and the rights of the creator, given their zombified institutional status. This would also signal genuine change in the unjust institutional practices that affect Swift and countless other, less powerful, artists.

One of the ongoing themes in Swift's music is the notion of revenge: this is the guiding idea for her song "Look What You Made Me Do." While the lyrics she sings as a zombie happened before her masters were sold to a man who bullied and manipulated her, they now serve as a perfect illustration of her act of self-appropriation. Now, we can imagine that she is directing these lines not at a former friend, as on the original recording, but her former record company as well as the music industry itself. Look what you made her do, indeed.

Notes

1   In this way, a "zombie," as I'm using the term, is distinct from the notion of a "persona" that Ley David Elliette Cray analyzes in Chapter 8 of this volume. Whereas a zombie version of an artist (or other public figure) is created and controlled by individuals and entities other than the artist themself, they are largely responsible for their persona, that is, how they present themselves on stage, on their albums, at award ceremonies, etc.

2   Michel Foucault, "What Is an Author?," in *Aesthetics, Method, and Epistemology*, ed. James D. Faubion, trans. Robert Hurley and others (New York: New Press, 1998), 205–22; 206.

3   See, for example, Gottlob Frege, "On Sense and Reference," in *Translations from the Philosophical Writings of Gottlob Frege*, ed. and trans. Peter Geach and Max Black, 2nd edn (Oxford: Blackwell, 1960), 56–78; John Searle, "Proper Names," *Mind* 67, no. 266 (1958): 166–73; and Saul Kripke, *Naming and Necessity* (Cambridge, MA: Harvard University Press, 1980).

4   Frege, "On Sense and Reference."

5   William K. Wimsatt and Monroe C. Beardsley, "The Intentional Fallacy," *Sewanee Review* 54, no. 3 (1946): 468–88.

6   Roland Barthes, "The Death of the Author," in *Image—Music—Text*, trans. Stephen Heath (London: Fontana, 1977), 142–8.

7   Of course, Barthes is articulating a phenomenon that was already taking place, rather than introducing a wholly novel form of aesthetic interpretation.

8   Foucault suggests that "the work, which once had the duty of providing immortality, now possesses the right to kill, to be its author's murderer." ("What Is an Author?," 206).

9   Ibid., 221; my emphasis.

10 Further, a work is not merely a collection of items or pieces of paper, according to Foucault; it, too, becomes a function for discourse, for action: "even when an individual has been accepted as an author, we must still ask whether everything that he wrote, said, or left behind is part of his work" (ibid., 207).

11 Ibid., 211.

12 Ibid., 220.

13 Ibid., 222.

14 Ibid.

15 For example, when two individuals sign a marriage certificate their names function to establish a set of economic and legal entitlements and prohibitions. If "Charlie Smith" is married to "Avery Smith," then neither Charlie nor Avery is allowed to sign a marriage certificate with another individual. If Charlie is in the hospital, then Avery is entitled to visit as a next of kin. Consider this an "institutional" theory of marriage: marriage is a set of entitlements and prohibitions. In fact, arguments for the legalization of gay marriage turned on a model of marriage as not merely a special relationship between two people, but a set of economic and legal entitlements.

16 Even Kripke, in *Naming and Necessity*, acknowledges this point.

17 A copyright holder is the author of an idea, while the work is the vehicle through which the idea is expressed. Authorship entails copyright protections over the expression of an idea, which prohibit the unauthorized use of one's works or image unless doing so expresses a *different* idea. So, parody and criticism do not merely replicate copyrighted material, but use it as a vehicle to express an idea that is distinct from the original. For more, see Darren Hudson Hick, *Artistic License: The Philosophical Problems of Copyright and Appropriation* (Chicago: University of Chicago Press, 2017). Ironically, perhaps, the landmark decision in favor of parody involved musical parody.

18   A parody involves mimicking or mocking an existing work or figure. Crucially, parody requires mimicking or otherwise reproducing characteristic features of a work or individual to be recognized as such.

19   Copyright law and the First Amendment are components of communication and media law, in that they function to regulate communication and media technologies.

20   According to the fair use doctrine of US copyright law, I cannot use Swift's likeness or name to advertise my candle store. However, I could create parody ads for a made-up candle shop that mock or insult Swift.

21   This is similar to John Locke's theory of labor and ownership, in imbuing an item with my labor I retain a special (normative) relation to it—I have special rights (themselves understood as entitlements, permissions, and prohibitions). See Chapter 1 in this volume for a further discussion of Locke's view.

22   Theo Papadopoulos, "Are Music Recording Contracts Equitable? An Economic Analysis of the Practice of Recoupment," *MEIEA Journal* 4, no. 1 (2004): 83–104; 84.

23   DeCurtis, "O(+> Free at Last," 61–3.

24   In fact, Swift is an outlier in wanting to maintain her master rights. Many of her peers, including Katy Perry and Justin Bieber, have sold their master's rights for hundreds of millions of dollars. I have two points to make about this. First, many legacy artists such as Bob Dylan and Bruce Springsteen are selling their masters as a matter of estate planning— better to get their economic ducks in a row now than leave it to their heirs to fight over. Second, Swift's popularity is still rising, while others are waning. It makes more sense for an artist like Katy Perry to sell her masters now and coup nine figures than continue to earn dwindling royalties for "I Kissed a Girl" over the next twenty years.

25   Hannah Dudley, Head of Marketing & Promotion, Label at Amuse Records, quoted in "What Does It Mean to Own Your Masters?," *Amuse*, October 23, 2023, https://www.amuse.io/en/categories/industry/owning-your-masters/ (accessed January 18, 2024).

26   Brendan Morrow, "Why Taylor Swift Keeps Releasing All Those Re-recorded Albums," *The Week*, May 10, 2023, https://theweek.com/taylor-swift/1013413/why-taylor-swift-keeps-releasing-all-those-re-recorded-albums (accessed July 26, 2023).

27 Ibid. One of the parameters legal authorities consider when evaluating a copyright case (that is, one that involves unauthorized use of copyrighted material) is whether the replication negatively impacts the original work.

28 Swift refers to the re-recorded works as "copycat versions" in a 2019 Tumblr post. (Taylor Swift, "For Years I Asked, Pleaded for a Chance to Own My Work," *Tumblr*, June 30, 2019, https://taylorswift.tumblr.com/post/185958366550/for-years-i-asked-pleaded-for-a-chance-to-own-my [accessed July 26, 2023].)

29 When an artist signs a record contract, they also stipulate an amount of time before they can re-record the songs. I think it is interesting to consider how her re-recordings express a different idea than the originals, or at least, express *more* ideas than the original. For one, there is a difference in context when an artist sings a song that was written ten years ago, where the words can take on a different meaning in this new context. See Alex King's and Ley David Elliette Cray's chapters in this volume for further examinations of this issue.

30 As Swift claimed, "the reason I'm rerecording my music next year is because I do want my music to live on. I do want it to be in movies, I do want it to be in commercials. But I only want that if I own it." (Jason Lipshutz, "Billboard Woman of the Decade Taylor Swift: 'I Do Want My Music to Live On,'" *Billboard*, December 11, 2019, https://www.billboard.com/music/pop/taylor-swift-cover-story-interview-billboard-women-in-music-2019-8545822/ [accessed July 26, 2023].)

31 Quoted in Peter Szendy, *Hits: Philosophy in the Jukebox* (New York: Fordham University Press, 2012), 139.

32 August Brown, "What Today's Artists Learned from Prince's Approach to the Industry," *Los Angeles Times*, April 22, 2016, https://www.latimes.com/entertainment/music/posts/la-et-ms-prince-imaginative-legacy-music-business (accessed July 26, 2023).

33 Jem Aswad, "Why Prince Changed His Name to an Unpronounceable Symbol 30 Years Ago, and What Happened Next," *Variety*, June 7, 2023, https://variety.com/2023/music/news/prince-symbol-why-he-changed-his-name-1235635422/ (accessed July 26, 2023).

34 Taylor Swift, "Don't Know What Else to Do," *Tumblr*, November 14, 2019, https://taylorswift.tumblr.com/post/189068976205/dont-know-what-else-to-do (accessed July 26, 2023).

35   James Perone, *The Words and Music of Taylor Swift* (Santa Barbara, CA: Praeger, 2017), 78.

36   In her 2023 *Time* Person of the Year interview, Swift claimed that her 2016 feud with Kim Kardashian and Kanye West left her "cancelled within an inch of [her] life and sanity." However, it seems strange for a person to call a number one album that sold 1.2 million copies in its first week, as *Reputation* did a year later, a case of "cancelling." (Sam Lansky, "Person of the Year 2023: Taylor Swift," *Time*, December 6, 2023, https:// time.com/6342806/person-of-the-year-2023-taylor-swift/ [accessed January 18, 2024].)

37   When Rodrigo admitted that the bridge in her song "Déjà Vu" was inspired by Swift's bridge in "Cruel Summer," Swift and her co-writers earned co-writing credit for "Déjà Vu" and now enjoy millions in royalties. For more, see Gil Kaufman, "Taylor Swift, Jack Antonoff & St. Vincent Get Co-Writer Credits on Olivia Rodrigo's 'Deja Vu,'" *Billboard*, July 9, 2021, https://www.billboard.com/music/pop/taylor-swift-jack- antonoff-st-vincent-co-writer-credits-olivia-rodrigo-deja-vu-9598750/ (accessed July 26, 2023).

38   As of this writing, if you search "master vs publishing rights" on Google, most of the results will reference Swift.

39   Perone, *The Words and Music*, 83.

40   Lipshutz, "Billboard Woman of the Decade."

41   Perone, *The Words and Music*, 82.

42   For example, Def Leppard re-recorded their music in order to retain the rights and thus royalties, they were not attempting to advocate for artists' rights more generally.

43   Lipshutz, "Billboard Woman of the Decade."

44   Ibid.

45   Ibid.

46   Perone, *The Words and Music*, 84.

47   Taylor Swift, "For Years I Asked."

48   L. A. Paul, *Transformative Experience* (Oxford: Oxford University Press, 2014).

Bibliography

"4'33"." JohnCage.org. https://johncage.org/pp/John-Cage-Work-Detail. cfm?work_ID=17 (accessed August 8, 2023).

"Acquisition: James Luna." (2022). National Gallery of Art. January 28. https://www.nga.gov/press/acquisitions/2022/luna.html (accessed August 8, 2023).

"Adrian Piper, *My Calling (Card) #1*." Walker Art Center. https://walkerart.org/collections/artworks/my-calling-card-1 (accessed August 8, 2023).

"Adrian Piper. The Probable Trust Registry: The Rules of the Game #1–3." Staatliche Museen zu Berlin. https://www.smb.museum/en/exhibitions/detail/adrian-piper-the-probable-trust-registry-the-rules-of-the-game-1-3/ (accessed August 8, 2023).

Arning, Bill (1989). "Sturtevant." *Journal of Contemporary Art* 2 (2): 39–50.

Aswad, Jem (2023). "Why Prince Changed His Name to an Unpronounceable Symbol 30 Years Ago, and What Happened Next." *Variety*, June 7. Available online: https://variety.com/2023/music/news/prince-symbol-why-he-changed-his-name-1235635422/ (accessed July 26, 2023).

Bagley, Christopher (2014). "Sturtevant: Repeat Offender." *W*, May 8. Available online: https://www.wmagazine.com/story/sturtevant-moma-retrospective (accessed August 8, 2023).

Barthes, Roland ([1967] 1977). "The Death of the Author." In Stephen Heath (trans.), *Image—Music—Text*, 142–8. London: Fontana.

Beardsley, Monroe ([1958] 1981). *Aesthetics: Problems in the Philosophy of Criticism*. 2nd ed. Indianapolis, IN: Hackett.

Beaumont, Mark (2021). "Taylor Swift's New 'Fearless' Is a Success, But Beware the Dangers of the Re-record." *NME (New Musical Express)*, April 12. https://www.nme.com/blogs/nme-blogs/taylor-swifts-fearless-beware-of-the-rerecord-2918002 (accessed August 1, 2023).

Bell, Clive (1914). *Art*. London: Chatto and Windus.

Bennett, Tamera (2021). "Will Taylor Swift Change the Re-record Clause?" *Create Protect Blog*, December 22. https://www.tbennettlaw.com/blog/2021/12/22/will-taylor-swift-change-the-re-record-clause (accessed August 1, 2023).

Bicknell, Jeanette (2005). "Just a Song? Exploring the Aesthetics of Popular Song Performance." *Journal of Aesthetics and Art Criticism* 63 (3): 261–70.

Bicknell, Jeanette (2015). *A Philosophy of Song and Singing: An Introduction.* London: Routledge.

Blistein, Jon (2021). "Entertainment Giant HYBE, Home of BTS, Purchases Scooter Braun's Ithaca Holdings." *Rolling Stone*, April 2. Available online: https://www.rollingstone.com/pro/news/scooter-braun-ithaca-holdings-hybe-purchase-merger-1150462/ (accessed January 18, 2024).

Bräuer, Felix (2023). "Aesthetic Testimony and Aesthetic Authenticity." *British Journal of Aesthetics* 63 (3): 395–416.

Brown, August (2016). "What Today's Artists Learned from Prince's Approach to the Industry." *Los Angeles Times*, April 22. Available online: https://www.latimes.com/entertainment/music/posts/la-et-ms-prince-imaginative-legacy-music-business (accessed July 26, 2023).

Brown, Jeffrey H. (2019). "The Legal Take on the Taylor Swift Recording Dispute." *Best Lawyers*, December 5. https://www.bestlawyers.com/article/taylor-swift-recording-contract-controversy/2747 (accessed July 20, 2023).

Browne, David (2023). "Remaking Your Old Songs Used to Be Considered Lazy, Shady, and So Uncool. What Changed?" *Rolling Stone*, January 18. Available online: https://www.rollingstone.com/music/music-features/album-remakes-u2-taylor-swift-1234660335/ (accessed August 8, 2023).

Butler, Cornelia and Luis Pérez-Oramas (2014). *Lygia Clark: The Abandonment of Art, 1948–1988.* New York: Museum of Modern Art.

Byrne, David (2012). *How Music Works.* San Francisco, CA: McSweeney's.

Caramanica, Jon, Joe Coscarelli, Jon Pareles, Ben Sisario and Lindsay Zoladz (2021). "Taylor Swift Remade 'Fearless' as 'Taylor's Version.' Let's Discuss." *New York Times*, April 9. Available online: https://www.nytimes.com/2021/04/09/arts/music/taylor-swift-fearless-taylors-version.html (accessed August 8, 2023).

Carroll, Noël (1998). *A Philosophy of Mass Art.* Oxford: Oxford University Press.

Chittenden, Tara (2013). "In My Rearview Mirror: Female Teens' Prospective Remembering of Future Romantic Relationships through the Lyrics in Taylor Swift Songs." *Journal of Children and Media* 7 (2): 186–200.

Connolly, Michael Thomas (2021). "On the Record: An Audio Professional's Take on Vinyl." *Aesthetics for Birds*, April 7. https://aestheticsforbirds.com/2021/04/07/an-audio-professionals-take-on-vinyl/ (accessed January 10, 2024).

Coroneos, Kyle (2015). "Bullshit." *Saving Country Music*, September 21. https://www.savingcountrymusic.com/album-review-ryan-adams-1989/ (accessed June 1, 2023).

Coscarelli, Joe and Melena Ryzik (2019). "Ryan Adams Dangled Success. Women Say They Paid a Price." *New York Times*, February 13. Available online: https://www.nytimes.com/2019/02/13/arts/music/ryan-adams-women-sex.html (accessed December 18, 2023).

Cray, Wesley D. (2019). "Transparent and Opaque Performance Personas." *Journal of Aesthetics and Art Criticism* 77 (2): 181–91.

Cray, Wesley D. (2021). "Aesthetics from the Closet." *American Society for Aesthetics Newsletter* 4 (1): 1–3.

Cross, Anthony (2022). "Aesthetic Commitments and Aesthetic Obligations." *Ergo: An Open Access Journal of Philosophy* 8 (38): 402–22.

Crouch, Ian (2015). "Haters Gonna Hate: Listening to Ryan Adams's '1989'." *The New Yorker*, September 22. Available online: https://www.newyorker.com/culture/culture-desk/haters-gonna-hate-listening-to-ryan-adams-1989 (accessed June 1, 2023).

Danto, Arthur C. (1981). *The Transfiguration of the Commonplace: A Philosophy of Art*. Cambridge, MA: Harvard University Press.

Davies, Stephen (1991). "The Ontology of Musical Works and the Authenticity of Their Performances." *Noûs* 25 (1): 21–41.

Davies, Stephen (2003). "Ontology of Art." In Jerrold Levinson (ed.), *The Oxford Handbook of Aesthetics*, 155–80. Oxford: Oxford University Press.

Davies, Stephen (2004). *Musical Works and Performances: A Philosophical Exploration*. Oxford: Clarendon Press.

DeCurtis, Anthony (1996). "O(+> Free at Last." *Rolling Stone* (748), November 11: 61–3.

"Def Leppard Re-Recording 'Forgeries' of Old Hits." (2012). *Rolling Stone*, July 3. Available online: https://www.rollingstone.com/music/music-news/def-leppard-re-recording-forgeries-of-old-hits-247079/ (accessed August 8, 2023).

Dictionary.com, s.v. (2020). "caucacity." December 21. https://www.dictionary.com/e/slang/caucacity/ (accessed August 8, 2023).

Driessen, Simone (2020). "Taylor Swift, Political Power, and the Challenge of Affect in Popular Music Fandom." "Fandom and Culture." Ashley Hinck and Amber Davisson (eds.). Special issue, *Transformative Works and Cultures* 32: https://doi.org/10.3983/twc.2020.1843.

Driessen, Simone (2022). "Look What You Made Them Do: Understanding Fans' Affective Responses to Taylor Swift's Political Coming-Out." *Celebrity Studies* 13 (1): 93–6.

Duncan, Liam (2022). "How Much Do Songwriters Make Per Song, Per Stream and in Other Situations." *Music Industry How To*, December 29.

https://www.musicindustryhowto.com/how-much-do-songwriters-make-per-song-per-stream-in-other-situations/ (accessed July 20, 2023).

Dye, Eleanor (2024). "Paramore Are Set to 'Re-record Their Music after Row with Bosses at Atlantic' in a Move Inspired by 'Supportive' Pal Taylor Swift." *MailOnline*, January 7. https://www.dailymail.co.uk/tvshowbiz/article-12935887/Paramore-rerecord-music-inspired-taylor-swift.html (accessed January 15, 2024).

"Edible Estates." FritzHaeg.com. http://www.fritzhaeg.com/garden/initiatives/edibleestates/main.html (accessed August 8, 2023).

Finnis, John (2011). *Natural Law and Natural Rights*. Oxford: Oxford University Press.

Fitzjohn, Sean (2023). "Streaming Payouts Per Platform and Royalties Calculator." *Producer Hive*, June 21. https://producerhive.com/music-marketing-tips/streaming-royalties-breakdown/ (accessed July 20, 2023).

Flanagan, Andrew (2017). "Taylor Swift Returns to Spotify, Amends Her Relationship to Streaming." *NPR*, June 9. https://www.npr.org/sections/therecord/2017/06/09/532238490/taylor-swift-returns-to-spotify-amends-her-relationship-to-streaming (accessed July 20, 2023).

Fontinelle, Amy (2023). "Holding Company: What It Is, Advantages and Disadvantages." *Investopedia*, July 9. https://www.investopedia.com/terms/h/holdingcompany.asp (accessed January 18, 2024).

Forde, Eamonn (2024). "Taylor-made Deals: How Artists Are Following Swift's Rights Example." *The Guardian*, January 9. Available online: https://www.theguardian.com/music/2024/jan/09/taylor-swift-deals-how-artists-rights-example (accessed January 15, 2024).

Foucault, Michel ([1969] 1998). "What Is an Author?" In James D. Faubion (ed.), Robert Hurley and others (trans.), *Aesthetics, Method, and Epistemology*, 205–22. New York: New Press.

France, Lisa Respers (2023). "Taylor Swift Changes Controversial Lyrics for 'Better than Revenge.'" *CNN*, July. 7. https://www.cnn.com/2023/07/07/entertainment/taylor-swift-better-than-revenge-lyrics/index.html (accessed August 1, 2023).

Fraser, Bonnie and Miki Rich (2020). "Behind Stand Atlantic's Like a Version 'Righteous' (Interview)." Interview, *Triple J*, August 27. https://www.youtube.com/watch?v=6CrtLf-BC5k (accessed June 1, 2023).

Free Beer. "Free Beer—Performa Version." FreeBeer.org. https://freebeer.org/blog/ (accessed August 8, 2023).

Freeman, Abigail (2021). "Taylor Swift Is 'Free' Again, but Just How Much Is Her 'Fearless' Strategy Worth?" *Forbes*, April 9. Available online: https://www.forbes.com/sites/abigailfreeman/2021/04/09/taylor-swift-is-free-again-but-just-how-much-is-her-fearless-strategy-worth/ (accessed July 20, 2023).

Frege, Gottlob ([1892] 1960). "On Sense and Reference." In Peter Geach and Max Black (eds. and trans.), *Translations from the Philosophical Writings of Gottlob Frege*, 2nd ed., 56–78. Oxford: Blackwell.

Fried, Jeremy (2019). "Ally Aesthetics." *Journal of Aesthetics and Art Criticism* 77 (4): 447–59.

Goh, Katie (2021). "I Made My Peace: Fans Divided over Taylor Swift's Re-recording Project." *The Guardian*, April 15. Available online: https://www.theguardian.com/music/2021/apr/15/i-made-my-peace-fans-divided-over-taylor-swifts-re-recording-project (accessed November 29, 2023).

Goldie, Peter and Elisabeth Schellekens (2010). *Who's Afraid of Conceptual Art?* London: Routledge.

Gracyk, Theodore (1996). *Rhythm and Noise: An Aesthetics of Rock.* Durham, NC: Duke University Press.

Gracyk, Theodore (2017). "Performer, Persona, and the Evaluation of Musical Performance." *Contemporary Aesthetics* 15.

Grady, Constance (2019). "The Taylor Swift/Scooter Braun Controversy, Explained." *Vox*, July 1. https://www.vox.com/culture/2019/7/1/20677241/taylor-swift-scooter-braun-controversy-explained (accessed January 18, 2024).

graysonsix (2022). "What Songs Have the Possibility of Getting the Girl at Home Treatment?" *Reddit, r/TaylorSwift*, March 28. www.reddit.com/r/TaylorSwift/comments/tq441x/what_songs_have_the_possibility_of_getting_the/ (accessed August 1, 2023).

"Guaraná Power—Superflex." Superflex.net. https://superflex.net/works/guarana_power (accessed August 8, 2023).

"Haircuts by Children—Mammalian Diving Reflex." Mammalian.ca. https://mammalian.ca/projects/haircuts-by-children/ (accessed August 8, 2023).

Halperin, Shirley (2020). "Scooter Braun Sells Taylor Swift's Big Machine Masters for Big Payday." *Variety*, November 16. Available online: https://variety.com/2020/music/news/scooter-braun-sells-taylor-swift-big-machine-masters-1234832080/ (accessed January 18, 2024).

Halperin, Shirley and Eriq Gardner (2012). "Pour Some Sugar Again: Why Def Leppard Is Rerecording Hits." *The Hollywood Reporter*, August 2012.

Available online: https://www.hollywoodreporter.com/news/general-news/def-leppard-universal-recording-hits-356397/ (accessed August 1, 2023).

Haskitt, Scott (2012). "Rock of Ages 1983 vs 2012!! (Def Leppard A/B Comparison)." July 19, video, https://www.youtube.com/watch?v=I7QkpXNm76M (accessed January 18, 2024).

Hick, Darren Hudson (2008). "When Is a Work of Art Finished?" *Journal of Aesthetics and Art Criticism* 66 (1): 67–76.

Hick, Darren Hudson (2017). *Artistic License: The Philosophical Problems of Copyright and Appropriation*. Chicago: University of Chicago Press.

Hoby, Hermione (2014). "Taylor Swift: 'Sexy? Not on My Radar.'" *The Guardian*, August 23. Available online: https://www.theguardian.com/music/2014/aug/23/taylor-swift-shake-it-off (accessed August 1, 2023).

Horton, Donald and R. Richard Wohl (1956). "Mass Communication and Para-Social Interaction." *Psychiatry: Journal for the Study of Interpersonal Processes* 19 (3): 215–29.

Ingham, Tim (2019). "Taylor Swift Plans to Re-record Her Hits. Here's What She Might Be Facing." *Rolling Stone*, December 9. Available online: https://www.rollingstone.com/pro/features/taylor-swift-plans-to-re-record-her-hits-heres-what-she-might-be-facing-923019/ (accessed August 8, 2023).

Ingham, Tim (2020). "Taylor Swift: Scooter Braun Paying \$330M for Big Machine 'Wasn't Exactly a Wise Choice.'" *Music Business Worldwide*, April 23. https://www.musicbusinessworldwide.com/taylor-swift-scooter-braun-paying-330m-for-big-machine-wasnt-exactly-a-wise-choice/ (accessed July 20, 2023).

Irvin, Sherri (2005). "Appropriation and Authorship in Contemporary Art." *British Journal of Aesthetics* 45 (2): 123–37.

Irvin, Sherri (2012). "Artwork and Document in the Photography of Louise Lawler." *Journal of Aesthetics and Art Criticism* 70 (1): 79–90.

Irvin, Sherri (2022). *Immaterial: Rules in Contemporary Art*. Oxford: Oxford University Press.

Jagota, Vrinda (2023). Review of *Speak Now (Taylor's Version)*, by Taylor Swift. *Pitchfork*, July 12. https://pitchfork.com/reviews/albums/taylor-swift-speak-now-taylors-version (accessed November 29, 2023).

Kania, Andrew (2006). "Making Tracks: The Ontology of Rock Music." *Journal of Aesthetics and Art Criticism* 64 (4): 401–14.

Kaufman, Gil (2021). "Taylor Swift, Jack Antonoff & St. Vincent Get Co-Writer Credits on Olivia Rodrigo's 'Deja Vu.'" *Billboard*, July 9. Available online: https://www.billboard.com/music/pop/taylor-swift-jack-antonoff-st-vincent-co-writer-credits-olivia-rodrigo-deja-vu-9598750/ (accessed July 26, 2023).

Kawashima, Dale (2007). "Taylor Swift Interview." *SongwriterUniverse*, February 16. https://www.songwriteruniverse.com/taylorswift123.htm (accessed July 20, 2023).

Kawashima, Dale (2022). "The History of Music Publishing—An Overview." *SongwriterUniverse*, December 20. https://www.songwriteruniverse.com/historyofpublishing.htm (accessed July 20, 2023).

King, Alex (2023). "How Swiftomania Turns Fans into Professors." *Aesthetics for Birds*, October 26. https://aestheticsforbirds.com/2023/10/26/taylor-swift-easter-eggs/ (access January 10, 2024).

Kivy, Peter (1990). *Music Alone: Philosophical Reflections on the Purely Musical Experience*. Ithaca, NY: Cornell University Press.

Knopper, Steve (2023). "Labels Want to Prevent 'Taylor's Version'-Like Re-recordings from Ever Happening Again." *Billboard*, October 30. Available online: https://www.billboard.com/pro/taylor-swift-re-recordings-labels-change-contracts/ (accessed December 18, 2023).

Korn, Jennifer, Ramishah Maruf and Camila Bernal (2023). "Taylor Swift Fans Take Ticketmaster to Court over Eras Tour Ticketing Chaos." *CNN*, March 27. https://www.cnn.com/2023/03/27/media/taylor-swift-ticketmaster-court/index.html (accessed January 18, 2024).

Korsmeyer, Carolyn (2013). "Taste." In Berys Gaut and Dominic McIver Lopes (eds.), *The Routledge Companion to Aesthetics*, 3rd ed., 257–66. London: Routledge.

Kripke, Saul (1980). *Naming and Necessity*. Cambridge, MA: Harvard University Press.

Langston, Keith (2022). "2022 MTV VMAs Winners: See the Full List." *Entertainment Weekly*, August 29. https://ew.com/mtv-video-music-awards/mtv-vmas-2022-winners-list/ (accessed January 18, 2024).

Lansky, Sam (2023). "Person of the Year 2023: Taylor Swift." *Time*, December 6. Available online: https://time.com/6342806/person-of-the-year-2023-taylor-swift/ (accessed December 18, 2023).

Leonard, Will (1952). "Tower Tracker." *Chicago Daily Tribune*, April 16: A4.

Leopold, Todd (2016). "Taylor Swift Donates $250K to Kesha, Offers Support during 'Trying Time.'" *CNN*, February 23. https://www.cnn.com/2016/02/22/entertainment/taylor-swift-kesha-feat/index.html (accessed August 1, 2023).

Levinson, Jerrold (1979). "Defining Art Historically." *British Journal of Aesthetics* 19 (3): 232–50.

Levinson, Jerrold (2006). "Aesthetic Properties, Evaluative Force, and Differences of Sensibility." In *Contemplating Art*. Oxford: Oxford University Press.

Lipshutz, Jason (2019). "Billboard Woman of the Decade Taylor Swift: 'I Do Want My Music to Live On.'" *Billboard*, December 11. https://www.billboard.com/music/pop/taylor-swift-cover-story-interview-billboard-women-in-music-2019-8545822/ (accessed July 26, 2023).

Locke, John ([1689] 1988). *Two Treatises of Government*. Peter Laslett (ed.) Cambridge: Cambridge University Press.

Lowe, Tom (2023). "Better than Revenge, and the Original? Speak Now Taylor's Version Review." *The Boar*, July 23. https://theboar.org/2023/07/speak-now-taylors-version-review (accessed November 29, 2023).

Magnus, Cristyn, P. D. Magnus and Christy Mag Uidhir (2013). "Judging Covers." *Journal of Aesthetics and Art Criticism* 71 (4): 361–70.

Magnus, Cristyn, P. D. Magnus, Christy Mag Uidhir and Ron McClamrock (2022). "Appreciating Covers." *Nordic Journal of Aesthetics* 63: 106–25.

Magnus, P. D. (2022). *A Philosophy of Cover Songs*. Cambridge, UK: Open Book Publishers.

Mag Uidhir, Christy (2007). "Recordings as Performances." *British Journal of Aesthetics* 47 (3): 298–314.

"Marcel Duchamp. *In Advance of the Broken Arm*. August 1964 (fourth version, after the lost original of November 1915)." Museum of Modern Art. https://www.moma.org/learn/moma_learning/marcel-duchamp-in-advance-of-the-broken-arm-august-1964-fourth-version-after-lost-original-of-november-1915/ (accessed August 8, 2023).

Marder, Hannah (2021). "A Twitter User Showed How to Hide the Old Version of Taylor Swift's 'Fearless' and It's So Important to Do." *Buzzfeed*, April 9. https://www.buzzfeed.com/hannahmarder/how-to-hide-the-older-versions-of-taylor-swifts-fearless (accessed January 18, 2024).

"Marina Abramović: The Artist Is Present." Museum of Modern Art. https://www.moma.org/learn/moma_learning/marina-abramovic-marina-abramovic-the-artist-is-present-2010/ (accessed August 8, 2023).

Martínez Marín, Irene and Elisabeth Schellekens (2022). "Aesthetic Taste: Perceptual Discernment or Emotional Sensibility?" In Jeremy Wyatt, Julia Zakkou and Dan Zeman (eds.), *Perspectives on Taste: Aesthetics, Language, Metaphysics, and Experimental Philosophy*, 58–74. New York: Routledge.

Martín Martínez, Macarena (2020). "Corporeal Activism in Elizabeth Acevedo's *The Poet X*: Towards a Self-appropriation of US Afro-Latinas' Bodies." *Revista de Estudios Norteamericanos* 25: 1–23.

Marzorati, Gerald (1986). "Art in the (RE)Making." *Artnews* 85 (5) (May): 91–9.

McIntyre, Hugh (2023). "Taylor Swift Claims the Three Bestselling Albums in American in 2023." *Forbes*, November 5. Available online: https://www.forbes.com/sites/hughmcintyre/2023/11/05/taylor-swift-claims-the-three-bestselling-albums-in-america-in-2023/ (accessed January 18, 2024).

Melden, A. I. (1970). "Introduction." In A. I. Melden (ed.), *Human Rights*. Belmont, CA: Wadsworth.

Mercuri, Monica (2023). "Why Record Labels Are Upset with Taylor Swift's Success." *Forbes*, November 3. Available online: https://www.forbes.com/sites/monicamercuri/2023/11/03/why-record-labels-are-upset-with-taylor-swifts-success/ (accessed January 18, 2024).

"Mining the Museum: 'Metalwork, 1793–1880.'" Maryland Center for History and Culture. https://www.mdhistory.org/resources/mining-the-museum-metalwork-1793-1880/ (accessed August 8, 2023).

"Mining the Museum: Pedestals, Globe, and Busts." Maryland Center for History and Culture. https://www.mdhistory.org/resources/mining-the-museum-pedestals-globe-and-busts/ (accessed August 8, 2023).

Miss Americana (2020) [Documentary] Dir. Lana Wilson. Los Angeles, CA: Tremolo Productions. https://www.netflix.com/title/81028336.

Morrow, Brendan (2023). "Why Taylor Swift Keeps Releasing All Those Re-recorded Albums." *The Week*, May 10. Available online: https://theweek.com/taylor-swift/1013413/why-taylor-swift-keeps-releasing-all-those-re-recorded-albums (accessed July 26, 2023).

Murray, Connor (2023). "Every Major Event in Taylor Swift's Record-Breaking 2023—From the Eras Tour to Time Person of the Year." *Forbes*, December 6. Available online: https://www.forbes.com/sites/conormurray/2023/12/06/every-major-event-in-taylor-swifts-record-breaking-2023-from-the-eras-tour-to-time-person-of-the-year/ (accessed December 18, 2023).

Nicholson, Jessica (2022). "Taylor Swift Accepts Songwriter-Artist of the Decade Honor at Nashville Songwriter Awards: Read Her Full Speech." *Billboard*, September 21. Available online: https://www.billboard.com/music/country/taylor-swift-nashville-songwriter-awards-full-speech-1235142144/ (accessed June 1, 2023).

Nicolaides, Alexandra (2015). "Robert Barry: All the Things I Know … 1962 to Present." *The Brooklyn Rail*, https://brooklynrail.org/2015/03/artseen/ robert-barry-all-the-things-i-know-1962-to-present (accessed August 8, 2023).

Nisbett, Gwendelyn and Stephanie Schartel Dunn (2021). "Reputation Matters: Parasocial Attachment, Narrative Engagement, and the 2018 Taylor Swift Political Endorsement." *Atlantic Journal of Communication* 29 (1): 26–38.

Novato, Olivia (2023). "Here's What Changed in *Speak Now (Taylor's Version)*." *CR Fashion Book*, July 7. https://crfashionbook.com/heres-what-has-changed-in-speak-now-taylors-version/ (August 8, 2023).

Ochoa, Tyler T. (2001). "Patent and Copyright Term Extension and the Constitution: A Historical Perspective." *Journal of the Copyright Society of the USA* 49: 19–125.

"On Kawara: Date Paintings." Guggenheim Museums and Foundation. https:// www.guggenheim.org/video/on-kawara-date-paintings (accessed August 8, 2023).

Ordoña, Michael (2022). "Taylor Swift, in the Race for an Oscar, Brings 'All Too Well' to TIFF." *Los Angeles Times*, September 9. Available online: https:// www.latimes.com/entertainment-arts/music/story/2022-09-09/taylor-swift-tiff-oscar-all-too-well-toronto-2022 (accessed January 18, 2024).

Papadopoulos, Theo (2004). "Are Music Recording Contracts Equitable? An Economic Analysis of the Practice of Recoupment." *MEIEA Journal* 4 (1): 83–104.

Paul, L. A. (2014). *Transformative Experience*. Oxford: Oxford University Press.

Paul, Larisha (2023). "'Better than Revenge (Taylor's Version)': Why Taylor Swift Shouldn't Rewrite Her Own History." *Rolling Stone*, May 15. Available online: https://www.rollingstone.com/music/music-features/better-than-revenge-taylor-swift-speak-now-taylors-version-problematic-song-recording-1234732910/ (accessed August 8, 2023).

Pendleton, Devon, Claire Ballentine, Marie Patino, Chloe Whiteaker and Diana Li (2023). "Taylor Swift Hits Billionaire Status as Net Worth Surges with Eras Tour." *Bloomberg*, October 26. https://www.bloomberg.com/ graphics/2023-taylor-swift-net-worth-billionaire/ (accessed January 8, 2024).

Peoples, Glenn (2023). "Have Taylor's Version Re-recordings Crowded out the Originals?" *Billboard*, July 21. Available online: https://

www.billboard.com/pro/have-taylor-swift-re-recordings-hurt-originals-streaming-sales/ (accessed August 1, 2023).

Perone, James (2017). *The Words and Music of Taylor Swift*. Santa Barbara, CA: Praeger.

Polite, Brandon (2019). "Shared Musical Experiences." *British Journal of Aesthetics* 59 (4): 429–47.

Polite, Brandon (2023). "Taylor Swift, *Fearless (Taylor's Version)*." In Darren Hudson Hick (ed.), *Bloomsbury Contemporary Aesthetics*, London: Bloomsbury. http://dx.doi.org/10.5040/9781350895737.0014.

"Posters, Stickers, Billboards, Videos, Actions: 1985–2023." GuerrillaGirls. com. https://www.guerrillagirls.com/projects (accessed August 8, 2023).

"Post-Partum Document." MaryKellyArtist.com. https://www.marykellyartist. com/post-partum-document-1973-79 (accessed August 8, 2023).

"Robert Rauschenberg, *Erased de Kooning Drawing*, 1953" San Francisco Museum of Modern Art. https://www.sfmoma.org/artwork/98.298/ (accessed August 8, 2023).

Rohrbaugh, Guy (2003). "Artworks as Historical Individuals." *European Journal of Philosophy* 11 (2): 177–205.

Rohrbaugh, Guy (2017). "Psychologism and Completeness in the Arts." *Journal of Aesthetics and Art Criticism* 75 (2): 131–41.

Russell, Shania (2021). "Taylor Swift's All Too Well Short Film Has Higher Letterboxd Ratings than Parasite." *Slashfilm*, November 15. https://www. slashfilm.com/662048/taylor-swifts-all-too-well-short-film-has-higher-letterboxd-ratings-than-parasite/ (accessed January 18, 2024).

Sanchez, Chelsea (2023). "Taylor Swift Is Crowned as Spotify's Top Artist of the Year with 26 Billion Streams Worldwide." *Harper's Bazaar*, November 28. Available online: https://www.harpersbazaar.com/culture/art-books-music/a45975825/taylor-swift-most-streamed-spotify-artist-2023/ (accessed December 18, 2023).

sara (2021). "Taylor Swift Love Story 2008 vs 2021 Re-recording (Vocal Comparison)." February 12, video, https://www.youtube.com/ watch?v=osLG1XnYkbQ (accessed June 1, 2023).

Sarassa, Juan C. (2021). "How Spotify Royalties Actually Work." *Hypebot*, November 4. https://www.hypebot.com/hypebot/2021/11/how-spotify-royalties-actually-work.html (accessed July 20, 2023).

Savage, Mark (2019). "Taylor Swift Blasts 'Toxic Male Privilege' during Woman of the Decade Speech." *BBC News*, November 13. https://www. bbc.com/news/entertainment-arts-50763774 (accessed July 20, 2023).

Scruton, Roger (1997). *The Aesthetics of Music*. Oxford: Oxford University Press.

Searle, John (1958). "Proper Names." *Mind* 67 (266): 166–73.

Serrano Zamora, Justo (2017). "Overcoming Hermeneutical Injustice: Cultural Self-Appropriation and the Epistemic Practices of the Oppressed." *Journal of Speculative Philosophy* 31 (2): 299–310.

Sheffield, Rob (2022). "Taylor Swift, Film Nerd: 'All Too Well' Singer Gives Rare Solo Performance at Tribeca." *Rolling Stone*, June 11. Available online: https://www.rollingstone.com/music/music-news/taylor-swift-tribeca-film-festival-all-too-well-1366715/ (accessed January 18, 2024).

Simmons, A. John (1983). "Inalienable Rights and Locke's Treatises." *Philosophy & Public Affairs* 12 (3): 175–204.

Sisario, Ben, Joe Coscarelli and Kate Kelly (2020). "Taylor Swift Denounces Scooter Braun as Her Catalog Is Sold Again." *New York Times*, November 16. Available online: https://www.nytimes.com/2020/11/16/arts/music/taylor-swift-scooter-braun-masters.html (accessed July 20, 2023).

Snapes, Laura (2023). Review of *Speak Now (Taylor's Version)*, by Taylor Swift. *The Guardian*, July 7. Available online: https://www.theguardian.com/music/2023/jul/07/taylor-swift-speak-now-taylors-version-review (accessed November 29, 2023).

Spencer, Liv (2010). *Taylor Swift: Every Day Is a Fairytale—The Unofficial Story*. Toronto: ECW Press.

Steele, Anne (2021). "As Taylor Swift Rerecorded Her 'Red' Album, Universal Reworked Contracts." *Wall Street Journal*, November 12. Available online: https://www.wsj.com/articles/as-taylor-swift-rerecorded-her-red-album-universal-reworked-contracts-11636741201 (accessed January 18, 2024).

Suskind, Alex (2019). "New Reputation: Taylor Swift Shares Intel on TS7, Fan Theories, and Her Next Era." *Entertainment Weekly*, May 19. Available online: https://ew.com/music/2019/05/09/taylor-swift-cover-story/ (accessed August 1, 2023).

Swift, Taylor (2006). Liner notes for *Taylor Swift*. Big Machine Records, compact disc.

Swift, Taylor (2014). "For Taylor Swift, the Future of Music Is a Love Story." *Wall Street Journal*, July 7. Available online: https://www.wsj.com/articles/for-taylor-swift-the-future-of-music-is-a-love-story-1404763219 (accessed July 20, 2023).

Swift, Taylor (2019a). "For Years I Asked, Pleaded for a Chance to Own my Work." Tumblr, June 30. https://taylorswift.tumblr.com/

post/185958366550/for-years-i-asked-pleaded-for-a-chance-to-own-my (accessed January 18, 2024).

Swift, Taylor (2019b). "Taylor Swift on 'Lover' and Haters." Interview by Tracy Smith, *CBS News*, August 25. https://www.cbsnews.com/news/taylor-swift-on-lover-and-haters/ (accessed August 8, 2023).

Swift, Taylor (@taylorswift13) (2019c). "Don't Know What Else to Do." Twitter, November 15. https://twitter.com/taylorswift13/status/1195123215657508867 (accessed June 21, 2023).

Swift, Taylor (@taylorswift13) (2020). "After Stoking the Fires of White Supremacy and Racism your Entire Presidency." Twitter, May 29. https://twitter.com/taylorswift13/status/1266392274549776387?lang=en (accessed July 31, 2023).

Swift, Taylor (2021a). "Taylor Swift Says She Went 'Line By Line' on Every 'Fearless' Song | PEOPLE." Interview, *People*, April 9, https://www.youtube.com/watch?v=QAnbsUz1fOs (accessed June 1, 2023).

Swift, Taylor (2021b). "Taylor Swift's 10-Minute Version of All Too Well Almost Wasn't Recorded (Extended) | Tonight Show." Interview by Jimmy Fallon, *Tonight Show*, November 11. https://www.youtube.com/watch?v=0Kr4JO9591c (accessed June 1, 2023).

Swift, Taylor (2021c). "Taylor Swift Reacts to Princess Diana's Revenge Dress Fan Theory." Interview by Scott Evans, *Access Hollywood*, November 12. https://www.youtube.com/watch?v=XQEvgkfu5Dk (accessed June 1, 2023).

Swift, Taylor (2021d). Liner notes for Red (Taylor's Version). Republic Records, compact disc.

Swift, Taylor (2021e). "Taylor Swift Full Interview on Late Night with Seth Meyers." Interview by Seth Meyers, *Late Night with Seth Meyers*, November 14. https://www.youtube.com/watch?v=DYIOaifhjQU (accessed August 17, 2023).

Swift, Taylor (@taylorswift) (2023). *WELL. SO. I've been counting down for months and finally the "I Can See You" video is out. I wrote* [Photograph]. Instagram photo, July 8. https://www.instagram.com/p/CubIwi0ue3l/.

Swift Leaks 2.0 (2022). "Taylor Swift—'Red' Album Comparison (2012 vs Taylor's Version)." April 14, video, https://www.youtube.com/watch?v=geK8WKHNMXo (accessed June 1, 2023).

Szendy, Peter (2012). *Hits: Philosophy in the Jukebox*. New York: Fordham University Press.

Tavern, Mark (2020). "An Artist's Guide to Royalties, Recoupment & Cross-Collateralization." *DJ Booth*, July 30. https://djbooth.net/features/2020-07-

30-kreayshawn-contracts-recoupments-record-labels (accessed July 20, 2023).

"Taylor Swift." (2024). *Forbes*, updated February 13. Available online: https://www.forbes.com/profile/taylor-swift/ (accessed February 13, 2024).

"Taylor Swift: A Place in This World." (2006). [Documentary] Dir. Jim Rink, USA: Rink Entertainment. Available online: https://www.youtube.com/watch?v=4q2gNvaDtyA (accessed July 20, 2023).

Kworb. "Taylor Swift – Spotify Top Albums." (2024). Kworb.net, last updated February 12, 2024, https://kworb.net/spotify/artist/06HL4z0CvFAxyc27GXpf02_albums.html (accessed February 13, 2024).

Théberge, Paul (2021). "Love and Business: Taylor Swift as Celebrity, Businesswoman, and Advocate." *Contemporary Music Review* 40 (1): 41–59.

"'This is Propaganda,' Tino Sehgal, 2002." Tate. https://www.tate.org.uk/art/artworks/sehgal-this-is-propaganda-t12057 (accessed August 8, 2023).

Thomasson, Amie L. (2005). "The Ontology of Art and Knowledge in Aesthetics." *Journal of Aesthetics and Art Criticism* 63 (3): 221–29.

Thompson, Nato, ed. (2012). *Living as Form: Socially Engaged Art from 1991–2011*. New York: Creative Time.

Van Saaze, (2015). "In the Absence of Documentation. Remembering Tino Sehgal's Constructed Situations." *Revista de História da Arte* 4: 55–63.

Vats, Anjali (2023). "Owning Your Masters (Taylor's Version): Postfeminist Tactical Copyright and the Erasure of Black Intellectual Labor." In Jennifer C. Nash and Samantha Pinto (eds.), *The Routledge Companion to Intersectionalities*, 552–73. London: Routledge.

VocaDB. "Self-cover." Last modified February 7, 2024, https://vocadb.net/T/391/self-cover (accessed February 13, 2024).

Walton, Kendall L. (1970). "Categories of Art." *The Philosophical Review* 79 (3): 334–67.

Weatherby, Taylor (2023). "Taylor Swift Makes Grammy History (Again) with Best Music Video Win for 'All Too Well: The Short Film.'" *Grammy.com*, February 5. https://www.grammy.com/news/taylor-swift-all-too-well-the-short-film-best-music-video-winner-2023-grammys (accessed January 18, 2024).

"What Does It Mean to Own Your Masters?" (2023). Amuse, October 23. https://www.amuse.io/en/categories/industry/owning-your-masters/ (accessed January 18, 2024).

Willard, Mary Beth (2021). *Why It's OK to Enjoy the Work of Immoral Artists*. New York: Routledge.

Willman, Chris (2018). "Taylor Swift Stands to Make Music Business History as a Free Agent." *Variety*, August 27. Available online: https://variety.com/2018/music/news/taylor-swift-stands-to-make-music-business-history-as-a-free-agent-1202918336/ (accessed January 18, 2024).

Willman, Chris (2020). "Taylor Swift's 'Evermore' Sells a Million Worldwide in First Week." *Variety*, December 20. Available online: https://variety.com/2020/music/news/taylor-swift-evermore-sells-million-first-week-1234867490/ (accessed January 18, 2024).

Willman, Chris (2021). "iHeart Promises to Only Play Taylor Swift's New Versions of Her Songs, Once They're Out." *Yahoo!Entertainment*, November 17. https://www.yahoo.com/entertainment/iheart-promises-only-play-taylor-000228785.html (accessed June 1, 2023).

Wimsatt, William K. and Monroe C. Beardsley (1946). "The Intentional Fallacy." *Sewanee Review* 54 (3): 468–88.

Young, James O. (2016). "Appropriating Fictional Characters." In Darren Hudson Hick and Reinold Schmücker (eds.), *The Aesthetics and Ethics of Copying*, 153–72. London: Bloomsbury.